The NOLO *News*—
Our free magazine devoted to everyday legal & consumer issues

To thank you for sending in the postage-paid feedback card in the back of this book, you'll receive a free two-year subscription to the **NOLO** *News*—our quarterly magazine of legal, small business and consumer information. With each issue you get updates on important legal changes that affect you, helpful articles on everyday law, answers to your legal questions in Auntie Nolo's advice column, a complete Nolo catalog and, of course, our famous lawyer jokes.

Legal information online–24 hours a day

Get instant access to the legal information you need 24 hours a day.

Visit a Nolo online self-help law center and you'll find:

- hundreds of helpful articles on a wide variety of topics
- selected chapters from Nolo books
- online seminars with our lawyer authors and other experts
- downloadable demos of Nolo software
- frequently asked questons about key legal issues
- our complete catalog and online ordering info
- our ever popular lawyer jokes and more.

Here's how to find us:

America Online Just use the key word Nolo.

On the **Internet** our World Wide Web address (URL) is: http://www.nolo.com.

Prodigy/CompuServe Use the Web Browsers on CompuServe or Prodigy to access Nolo's Web site on the Internet.

A Legal
Guide for
LESBIAN
AND GAY
COUPLES

Ninth National Edition

by Attorneys Hayden Curry, Denis Clifford and Robin Leonard

Edited by Shae Irving

NOLO PRESS **BERKELEY**

YOUR RESPONSIBILITY WHEN USING A SELF-HELP LAW BOOK

We've done our best to give you useful and accurate information in this book. But laws and procedures change frequently and are subject to differing interpretations. If you want legal advice backed by a guarantee, see a lawyer. If you use this book, it's your responsibility to make sure that the facts and general advice contained in it are applicable to your situation.

KEEPING UP-TO-DATE

To keep its books up-to-date, Nolo Press issues new printings and new editions periodically. New printings reflect minor legal changes and technical corrections. New editions contain major legal changes, major text additions or major reorganizations. To find out if a later printing or edition of any Nolo book is available, call Nolo Press at (510) 549-1976 or check the catalog in the *Nolo News,* our quarterly newspaper.

To stay current, follow the "Update" service in the *Nolo News.* You can get the paper free by sending us the registration card in the back of the book. In another effort to help you use Nolo's latest materials, we offer a 25% discount off the purchase of any new Nolo book if you turn in any earlier printing or edition. (See the "Recycle Offer" in the back of the book.)

This book was last revised in: **August 1996**

NINTH EDITION	August 1996
Editor	Shae Irving
Illustrations	Linda Allison
Cover Design	Toni Ihara
Book Design	Nancy Erb
Proofreading	Lee Rappold
Index	Jane Meyerhofer
Printing	Consolidated Printers, Inc.

Curry, Hayden.
    A legal guide for lesbian and gay couples / by Hayden Curry, Denis Clifford & Robin Leonard. — 9th ed.
       p.   cm.
    Includes index.
    ISBN 0-87337-336-7
      1. Gay couples—Legal status, laws, etc.—United States.
    2. Lesbian couples—Legal status, laws, etc.—United States.
    I. Clifford,Denis.   II. Leonard, Robin.   III. Title.
    KF538.C87 1996
    346.7301'3—dc20
    [347.30613]   96-15945
                                CIP

Quantity sales: For information on bulk purchases or corporate premium sales, please contact the Special Sales department. For academic sales or textbook adoptions, ask for Academic Sales, 800-955-4775, Nolo Press, Inc., 950 Parker St., Berkeley, CA 94710.

ACKNOWLEDGEMENTS

We thank all those friends, new and old, who worked with us on this book; their assistance has been truly invaluable and working with them was fun. Special thanks to those people who read and critiqued the original manuscript back in 1980: Linda Gryczan; Gloria Bosque; Michael Fuchs; Linda Graham; Joseph Nieberding; Sue Saperstein; Kim Storch; Michael Thistel; Jim Duerr; Floyd S. Irvin; Patrick Ferruccio; Keith Kelgman; Donna J. Hitchens; Linda Guthrie; Zona Sage; Terri Lyons; Mary Morgan; Phyllis Lyon; Kay Clifford (Mom); Pamela Gray; and Roberta Achtenberg.

We also want to thank Ann Heron for her interest and contributions toward the reorganizion of the seventh edition. For keeping the book up-to-date in the mid-1990s, thanks go to Shae Irving for her tremendous editing and Stan Jacobson for his cite checking and other research.

Contents

Appendix

About the Authors

(A Little Bit of History)

First edition

A Legal Guide for Lesbian and Gay Couples was first published in 1980. At that time, Hayden Curry and Denis Clifford were partners in the Oakland, California, law firm of Clifford, Curry and Cherrin. They had met in 1967, in a special training program for recent law school graduates going into poverty law, and later worked together for several years in a neighborhood legal services office in East Oakland.

They proudly introduced themselves in the first edition of the book with the following personal statement:

"We've been close personal friends for almost two decades. Hayden is gay and has lived with his lover for many years. Denis is straight. We mention this because people are curious and we want to get it out and out of the way. For those of you who are interested, we speak a little more about who we are—and our friendship—in the About the Authors section at the beginning of this book.

"Because this book is designed for lesbians as well as gay men, we felt a special responsibility to seek out the advice, experience and resources of the lesbian community, especially the lesbian legal community. We didn't want to presume knowledge of their experiences. Obviously, there are many similar experiences in being a lesbian and being a gay man (calling a lesbian a "Dyke" and calling a gay man a "Faggot" hurt in much the same way). The law, too, treats the two communities as one. But aside from the anatomical, there are many differences between lesbians and gay men. One major difference is economic. As Phyllis Lyon, a lesbian activist in San Francisco, pointed out to us, gay men, on the average, make considerably more money than lesbians, who, as women, make between 65 and 70 cents (nationwide) for every $1.00 men make. Where appropriate, we discuss other important differences in the text. We want to thank the many lesbian women who helped us to assemble these materials. They provided information and encouragement, assisted with defining issues and problems, and helped scrutinize the manuscript from its initial draft to the finished product. And beyond all that, we made new friends."

In the About the Author section they referred to in their personal statement, Hayden and Denis described how they came to write this book:

"We feel this book has evolved from our earlier work with the civil rights movement and poverty law. One of the strongest conclusions we drew from our years of bringing 'test cases' for the rights of poor people was that the established (or establishment) legal system was cumbersome, and generally unsympathetic to minorities.

We came to believe that preventative law—people creating their own legal arrangements and avoiding courts and lawyers—was both eminently sensible and long overdue.

"It's ironic, but true, that while laboring in South Florida for the rights of the economically oppressed and racial minorities, Hayden was simultaneously suppressing his own awareness of himself as an oppressed minority—a gay man. It was necessary for him to reach the healthier and more supportive climate in Northern California before he could begin the process of publicly coming to terms with his identity, and be able to work overtly for his own minority group. Denis has been an observer and supporter of Hayden's coming-out process (and he hasn't exactly been standing still the last twenty-some years either).

"After leaving legal services, we set up our private law practice, which has served many lesbian and gay clients. Our belief that litigation and courts should be the last resort for problem-solving was reaffirmed by our clients' experiences; we began helping them devise ways to solve their problems outside traditional (and expensive) legal remedies.

"Writing this book has been a shared experience. We've both learned a lot. We don't believe people are confined to understanding only those who have the same sexual identity as they do. One of the beauties of being free is that people can learn, as we have, that our differences can bring us closer. We hope this book will do that for many lesbian/gay couples, and it was in this spirit of optimism that we worked and wrote together."

Fifth edition

As Hayden and Denis revised and updated this book for the fifth edition in early 1989, they contemplated the changes in the lesbian and gay community over the previous nine years. In describing themselves, they wrote: "Hayden has a great many more wrinkles than he had nine years ago; he got them the old-fashioned way, he earned them. And Denis has worry lines too. Although, we must say, growing older seems like a rather fine alternative these days."

Hayden, unaware that the AIDS virus lived inside him, wrote about the disease's effect on the lesbian and gay community in the special introduction to the fifth edition.

"The tragedy of AIDS continues. In February, we buried our good friend Dan Bradley. Dan's story is similar to many of ours. When we worked with him in legal services in the late 60s and early 70s we didn't know the torments he was going through discovering his homosexuality. By the late 70s, when the cultural and political climate had become positive, Dan, in true Bradley fashion, burst out of his closet with an announcement in the New York Times—'High Government Official Announces He Is Gay.' In the early and hopeful 80s, Dan became a national gay rights leader. But his true heroism came after he was diagnosed with AIDS. Rather than retreat into his illness, he used the small energy he had to fight for the rights of people with AIDS and ARC. Now Hayden has made Dan's quilt for the Names Project; Hayden's mother did the needlepointing.

"We've lost many wonderful friends and many more are ill. The political right has used AIDS to fan hatred and discrimination against us. Much of our time is spent caring for our brothers, and our political energies are sapped by health care and survival issues.

"There's another side to this tragedy. We've matured as a group. We've coalesced as a community. We're vastly proud of the compassion we, men and women, have shown each other, and the organizations we've built.

"We've set up programs to care for our community: volunteers become buddies to care for people with AIDS, whether to clean their apartments or take them to the hospital; friends and groups organize meal rotations or give out free food; volunteers care for pets and eventually find new homes for the dogs and cats of those who die; visiting parents and families are given housing when they come to visit; many parents of someone who has died are adopted by lovers and friends of that person. And we've created our own memorial: the Names Project encourages the friends of someone who died due to the virus to stitch a 3' x 6' quilt for that person. The individual quilts are woven together; as anyone who's seen it knows, each patch is a beautiful and powerful expression of love and grief. Quilts contain favorite teddy bears, black chiffon dresses or jogging t-shirts, with sentiments ranging from 'Dear brother, our parents wouldn't let me put your name on this, but I love you' to 'Thank you for sharing your time here with me.'

"The lesbian community has shown deep concern, caring and commitment. They've taught gay men a lot about taking care of themselves. And the lesbian community has emerged powerfully: lesbians are running for political office and having babies. One synagogue in San Francisco with a special outreach to the gay and lesbian community boasts nearly 40 children members. A glorious generation is on its way, children that are exceptionally wanted and loved. We know of at least one memorial scholarship set up for the children of lesbian and gay parents. And we pray to whatever gods we believe in that this scourge of a virus will pass and that these children will grow up in healthy environments. We already know they're growing up in loving ones.

"We've proven ourselves a proud, caring and dedicated clan. We're exhausted. We're sad. We'll do what's needed of us."

Sixth edition

Hayden Curry died on September 30, 1991, from AIDS. Denis Clifford wrote the following memorial to Hayden, which first appeared in the sixth edition of *A Legal Guide for Lesbian and Gay Couples:*

"I first met Hayden in 1967, when we were both in a special training program for poverty lawyers. Right away, I was taken with his flair and zest for life. After two years working with migrant workers in rural Florida, Hayden moved to California in 1969. For five years we worked together in a legal services office in East Oakland, California. We were both East Coast refugees—he'd gone to Yale, then University of Virginia law school. We became best friends. After we left legal services, we were law partners for several years. We remained very close until his death.

"Hayden and I shared many wonderful adventures. He was a seeker, adventurer, philosopher and bon-vivant. He was a good friend of many in the Nolo Press family, in whose hearts he will always be smiling.

"The following is from Hayden's obituary:

'Hayden was a proud participant in gay life in the Bay Area. Living in what he termed the "supportive climate" of Northern California, he publicly presented himself as gay in the early 1970s. Fully accepting himself, he opened his loving heart and flamboyant spirit to his many, many friends…. Hayden became seriously ill in March of 1991. He bore his afflictions with such grace and courage that he truly transcended his disease, becoming increasingly luminous in spirit until his death.'

"His premature death is a tragedy. He will be missed."

Seventh edition

With the publication of the seventh edition of *A Legal Guide for Lesbian and Gay Couples* in 1993 Robin Leonard was added as an author. Robin has been an active member of whatever lesbian and gay community she's lived in since the late 1970s. She came to Nolo Press in 1985 after practicing law in San Francisco, and was the editor of the fifth and sixth editions of this book.

Robin and Denis worked together updating the material to reflect the new direction in which the lesbian and gay community was (and is still) going. Although AIDS continued and continues to take its tragic toll, the 1990s began the era in which lesbians and gay men got married (even though the law didn't recognize it), registered as domestic partners and challenged traditional limits on the definition of family. And the community continued to have a lot of kids. The San Francisco synagogue Hayden wrote about in 1989 as having nearly 40 children members had 75 kids and three grades in its religious school in 1993 (135 children in 1996).

Robin and Denis made a commitment to making Hayden's voice and spirit come through in their words. And, beginning with the seventh edition, they dedicated *A Legal Guide for Lesbian and Gay Couples* to Hayden's memory.

Introduction

This book is designed to help lesbian and gay couples understand the laws that affect them and to take charge of the legal aspects of their lives. Much of the material covered can also be very useful for lesbians and gays who aren't in a couple.

Many of the legal consequences of "coupling" are immediately apparent, but many others don't surface until times of stress—misunderstandings, separation or death. Married couples' relationships are defined by law; lesbian and gay couples, as of January 1996, can't legally marry. This discrimination can mean, among other things, higher estate tax rates and insurance payments, the unavailability of marriage discount prices or memberships, and significant obstacles in adopting, but it also allows lesbian and gay couples the freedom to create their own legal relationships.

This is an optimistic book. Our purpose is to explain your legal alternatives and show you how to use them to contribute to a harmonious and productive life together. We feel strongly that discussing and planning the financial, practical and legal aspects of a relationship leads to greater understanding and trust. It's possible to use the law in a positive, conflict-avoiding way. Unfortunately, however, there's also a less

happy theme to this book—failure to work out your legal relationship with each other can lead to surprising, and dire, consequences. We've heard too many horror stories not to warn you.

This is also a practical book. We supply sample form legal documents such as living together agreements, durable powers of attorney, wills, parenting agreements and the like so you can design and prepare your own documents. We focus on the nitty-gritty of daily life; we spend little time discussing broader political concerns, such as the essential struggle of lesbians and gays to remove prejudice from the laws and culture of America. One of the happiest results of this struggle is that it is now matter-of-fact that many thousands of lesbians and gay men live together as couples in pursuit of life, liberty and happiness.

This doesn't mean that the political work is over—it obviously isn't—but that our focus is on the personal and not the political. Certainly you'll find evidence of our anger toward, and frustration with, a society that has made being lesbian or gay so difficult. The AIDS crisis has led to increased oppression and the increased need for prudence. And the information we provide is especially essential if you haven't told your family, friends or the world about your relationship and sexual orientation.

Lesbians, Gay Men and "The Law"

Most lesbian and gay people we know are wary of "the law," even if they're lawyers themselves, and for good reason. For eons, the law has been a force for oppression. The litany of codified homophobia includes sodomy laws, loitering laws, exclusion from the military, prohibitions against child custody—the list goes on and on. In addition, the law has permitted—and in some cases even encouraged—many other types of oppression, such as job and housing discrimination, and police entrapment. Obviously, a legal system that makes people criminals because of sexual orientation doesn't engender trust.

In 1986, the U.S. Supreme Court upheld the constitutionality of enforcing Georgia's sodomy statute against gay men.[1] But states are free to offer their citizens more protection than is given by the federal Constitution. Thus, whether or not it's legal for you to have sex with your lover depends on where you live. Twenty states still have laws against private, consensual sodomy—sometimes heterosexual and homosexual, sometimes just homosexual. If you feel like an outlaw, it may very well be because you are.

Below is a summary of state sodomy laws—to find out about any changes, contact the National Gay and Lesbian Task Force, at 1734 14th St., NW, Washington, DC 20009, (202) 332-6483, and ask for the "Privacy Project Fact Sheet" (also known as the "Sodomy Map").

State	Status of sodomy law	Maximum sentence
Alabama	Heterosexual and homosexual sodomy illegal	20 years
Alaska	No sodomy law	
Arizona	Heterosexual and homosexual sodomy illegal	30 days
Arkansas	Homosexual sodomy illegal	1 year
California	No sodomy law	
Colorado	No sodomy law	
Connecticut	No sodomy law	
Delaware	No sodomy law	
District of Columbia	No sodomy law	
Florida	No sodomy law	
Georgia	Heterosexual and homosexual sodomy illegal	20 years
Hawaii	No sodomy law	
Idaho [2]	Heterosexual and homosexual sodomy illegal	Life
Illinois	No sodomy law	
Indiana	No sodomy law	
Iowa	No sodomy law	
Kansas	Homosexual sodomy illegal	6 months
Kentucky	No sodomy law	
Louisiana[3]	Heterosexual and homosexual sodomy illegal	5 years
Maine	No sodomy law	
Maryland [4]	Homosexual sodomy illegal	10 years
Massachusetts [5]	No sodomy law	
Michigan [6]	No sodomy law	

State	Status of sodomy law	Maximum sentence
Minnesota	Heterosexual and homosexual sodomy illegal	1 year
Mississippi	Heterosexual and homosexual sodomy illegal	10 years
Missouri	Homosexual sodomy illegal	15 years
Montana[7]	No sodomy law	
Nebraska	No sodomy law	
Nevada	No sodomy law	
New Hampshire	No sodomy law	
New Jersey	No sodomy law	
New Mexico	No sodomy law	
New York	No sodomy law	
North Carolina	Heterosexual and homosexual sodomy illegal	10 years
North Dakota	No sodomy law	
Ohio	No sodomy law	
Oklahoma	Heterosexual and homosexual sodomy illegal	10 years
Oregon	No sodomy law	
Pennsylvania	No sodomy law	
Rhode Island	Heterosexual and homosexual sodomy illegal	20 years
South Carolina	Heterosexual and homosexual sodomy illegal	5 years
South Dakota	No sodomy law	
Tennessee[8]	No sodomy law	
Texas[9]	Homosexual sodomy illegal	$500 fine
Utah	Heterosexual and homosexual sodomy illegal	6 months
Vermont	No sodomy law	
Virginia	Heterosexual and homosexual sodomy illegal	5 years
Washington	No sodomy law	
West Virginia	No sodomy law	
Wisconsin	No sodomy law	
Wyoming	No sodomy law	

Sodomy laws aren't the only manifestation in a legal system that continues to discriminate against lesbians and gay men. Although our legal system generally does a good job of protecting certain freedoms, like freedom of speech, even here the rights of lesbian and gay men have taken a back seat to judicial homophobia. In 1987, the U.S. Supreme Court ruled that Congress and the U.S. Olympic Committee can control the use of the word "Olympics" by denying San Francisco Arts and Athletics, Inc. the use of the phrase "Gay Olympics" to describe their every-four-years international athletic competition.[10]

As we head toward the 21st century, we are struck by the recent gains, losses and near misses celebrated and suffered in the lesbian and gay community. President Clinton's ambiguous support for lesbians, gay men and people with HIV is sometimes welcome (such as the appointment of lesbian Roberta Achtenberg to the Department of Housing and Urban Development), and other times painful to accept. We can only hope that someday the U.S. Supreme Court favorably resolves the issue of gays and lesbians in the military—we know that the White House and Congress won't.

We can celebrate the U.S. Supreme Court's decision upholding our victory in Colorado, which overturned Amendment 2 and allows basic civil rights protections for lesbians and gay men in Aspen, Boulder and Denver to be enforced once again. Although lesbians and gay men narrowly won in Oregon in 1992, convincing voters to reject a law that would have defined homosexuality as "unnatural, perverse and abnormal"—the lesbian and gay community cannot afford, in time, resources and self-esteem, to continue to fight such battles. Yet sadly, this drain continues to be necessary as legislation similar to that which passed in Colorado is being proposed in states and municipalities throughout the country.

One of the consequences of our homophobic laws is that as of January 1996, lesbian and gay couples in America cannot legally marry, no matter how deep their love and how firm their commitment. (A case working its way through Hawaii's courts could change this. See Chapter 1. And gay and lesbian couples can legally marry in Denmark, Greenland, Norway or Sweden, but at least one partner must be a citizen of one of those countries and the couple must reside in the country for at least two years before marrying.) By not being allowed to marry, lesbian and gay couples are denied the many legal rights that come with marriage. These rights include the rights to:

- file joint income tax returns

- create a marital life estate trust

- claim estate tax marital deduction

- claim family partnership tax income

- recover damages based on injury to your lover

- receive survivor's benefits

- enter hospitals, jails and other places restricted to "immediate family"

- live in neighborhoods zoned "family only"

- obtain health insurance, dental insurance, bereavement leave and other employment benefits

- collect unemployment benefits if you quit your job to move with your lover to a new location because he or she has obtained a new job

- get residency status for a noncitizen spouse to avoid deportation

- automatically make medical decisions in the event your lover is injured or incapacitated (otherwise, parents, adult children or siblings are given the right), and

- automatically inherit your lover's property in the event he or she dies without a will (otherwise, it goes to parents, children and siblings).

We are mistrustful of our legal system for another reason. The law tends to be cumbersome, time-consuming, expensive and incredibly picky. As you'll see throughout this book, we urge you to avoid courts and litigation if at all possible. But avoiding lawsuits doesn't mean you can avoid the legal system altogether. The fact that lesbian and gay couples are no longer in the closet and live together openly necessarily brings them into contact with the meshes of the law. This is especially true if the couple, or one or both individually, have children or significant amounts of money or property. We're often asked such questions as, "Is it possible for a court to remove my child from my home because I live with my lover?" "If I die, can my lover inherit my car and my house?" "Can a hospital legally prevent me from visiting my lover in intensive care?"

We answer these specific questions later in the book. What we can tell you generally, however, is that the opportunities for legal hassles to intrude into a couple's life are endless, and the best way to avoid entanglements with the law is to take matters into your own hands. In this book, we give you the information necessary to create legal documents to give yourselves many of the rights which accompany marriage. Although we can't show you a document that will let you file a joint income tax return (it doesn't exist), we can show you how one partner who supports the other can claim the supported person as a dependent on his income tax return.

Some Words About Words

Wouldn't it be simple if there were a genie who created words for such realities as "a man who loves men" or "a woman who loves women" or "comrades through life who share sexual intimacies" that meant exactly what we wished them to mean, neither more nor less? These words would be free of latent sexual prejudice and orientation, and their meaning and political acceptability wouldn't erode over time. Unfortunately, the opposite has been more the case, as words have been part of the perpetuation of homophobia. "Faggot," for instance, is derived from the French word for the bundles of sticks used to burn homosexuals at the stake, and its use should serve as a reminder of that oppression. As Truman Capote said, "A fag is a homosexual gentleman who has left the room."

Words free of ugly overtones, which accurately (to say nothing of poetically) describe the realities we discuss in this book aren't easy to find. What do you call the person you live with? "Co-vivant" does have a delightful French ring to it, but seems more than slightly pretentious. "Living in bedlock without benefit of wedlock" is silly, but at least it rhymes. How about "consort" or "URAW," a welfare department term for a person living with an "unrelated adult woman" (URAM, for men).

"Lover" and "partner" are the words we use. They are accurate and succinct. We also use the words "lesbian" and "gay" because those are the words used most often in our own particular culture (San Francisco Bay Area) by women and men to identify themselves. As for general pronouns, sometimes we use "she," sometimes "he," and sometimes the awkward "he or she."

We know that creating and using words untainted by the prejudices of the past and reflective of pride and self-worth is important, so we've tried to be sensitive to the power and implication of words. But finally, words are just that—words; they won't break our bones, and we're all free to use the ones we like best. When Christopher Isherwood was asked what he liked to be called, he answered, "I don't really like the word 'gay' for it makes us seem like silly ninnies. I rather like the karate chop sound of 'faggot.' The word 'homosexual' is too much of mouthful. Frankly, when alone and with friends, I say 'queer.'" [11]

Endnotes

[1]*Bowers v. Hardwick*, 478 U.S. 186 (1986).

[2]The Idaho Supreme Court has ruled that because no maximum penalty is stated in the statute, life imprisonment is permissible. *State v. Hayes*, 824 P.2d 163 (1992).

[3]In 1995, the Louisiana Supreme Court upheld the constitutionality of the state's sodomy law. *Louisiana v. Baxley*, 656 So.2d 973 (1995).

[4]The Maryland Supreme Court struck the ban on heterosexual sodomy, but declared homosexual sodomy to still be an "unnatural and perverted sexual practice." *Schochet v. State*, 580 A.2d 176 (1990).

[5]Although the sodomy statute is still on the books, the Massachusetts Supreme Judicial Court has ruled it unconstitutional except in cases involving violence, public sex or minors. *Commonwealth v. Ferguson*, 422 N.E.2d 1365 (1981).

[6]A Michigan trial court declared unconstitutional the sodomy law prohibiting heterosexual and homosexual sodomy and carrying a 15-year maximum prison sentence. The Michigan attorney general chose not to appeal. *Michigan Organization for Human Rights v. Kelley*, Wayne County Circuit Court, #88-815820CZ (July 9, 1990).

[7]Although the sodomy statute is still on the books, a district court has declared it unconstitutional as applied to adults who engage in consensual, private homosexual sex. An appeal to the Montana Supreme Court is expected. *Gryczan v. State of Montana*, Montana First Judicial District Court #BVD-93-1869 (February 16, 1996).

[8]Although the sodomy law is still on the books, the Court of Appeals of Tennessee has ruled it unconstitutional as applied to adults who engage in consensual private homosexual sex. Another appeal is expected. *Campbell v. Sundquist*, C.A. #01A01-9507-CV-00321.

[9]In January of 1994, the Texas Supreme Court refused to rule on a challenge to the Texas sodomy statute. The court side-stepped the issue of whether or not the law was unconstitutional under the Texas constitution, instead ruling that the lawsuit was premature because no one was currently being prosecuted under it.

[10]*San Francisco Arts & Athletics, Inc. v. United States Olympic Committee*, 483 U.S. 522 (1987).

[11]Despite its growing use in our community, we don't use "queer," simply because many gay and lesbian people find it offensive or simply don't like it. ■

CHAPTER 1

Creating Family: Marriage, Domestic Partners and More

In this chapter, we discuss:

• gay and lesbian marriages

• domestic partnerships

• states granting benefits (such as unemployment insurance) to partners in lesbian and gay couples where previously only married spouses were given those benefits

• case law expanding the definition of "family," and

• adult adoptions.

According to *Webster's New Collegiate Dictionary*, a family is "the basic unit in society having as its nucleus two or more adults living together and cooperating in the care and rearing of their own or adopted children." Despite this all-inclusive definition, a lesbian or gay couple—with or without children—is hardly the image conjured up when most people create a picture of a family.

Nevertheless, lesbian and gay couples consider themselves to be families. And over the past 20 years, same-sex couples have sought societal recognition of their families. It began in the early 1970s, when lesbian and gay couples applied for marriage licenses, asked courts to allow one partner to adopt the other, and took other steps to legally cement their relationship. Most of these efforts failed.

By the mid-1980s, the emphasis changed to seeking "domestic partnership" recognition for same-sex couples from both municipalities and private companies. This effort continues, with increasing strength, in the 1990s. And the desire to marry has again emerged. Some couples are applying to the state for marriage licenses and suing their states when their requests are denied. Others (*many* others) are participating in their own ceremonies, sanctioned by their friends, families and spiritual communities.[1]

Before getting into gay and lesbian marriages, we cannot ignore the debate that exists in the lesbian and gay community on the subject. For many, the right to marry is a basic civil right—as long as lesbians and gay men are denied the right to marry their lovers, they will be considered second-class citizens. And as long as society offers benefits based on the status of marriage, then lesbian and gay couples want their fair share.

To others—especially many lesbian feminists—marriage is a sexist and patriarchal institution that lesbians and gay men should not seek to be a part of. As one writer stated:

First, marriage will not liberate us as lesbians and gay men. In fact, it will constrain us, make us more invisible, force our assimilation into the mainstream, and undermine the goals of gay liberation. Second, attaining the right to marry will not transform our society from one that makes narrow, but dramatic, distinctions between those who are married and those who are not married to one that respects and encourages choice of relationships and family diversity. Marriage runs contrary to two of the primary goals of the lesbian and gay movement: the affirmation of gay identity and culture, and the validation of many forms of relationships.2

We find this debate to be intellectually and politically fascinating (and we certainly have our opinions about lesbians and gay men seeking the right to marry), but we have decided to keep our own opinions out of print. We include information on lesbian and gay marriages because any "Legal Guide for Lesbian and Gay Couples" should include it, and because many readers have asked for it.

A. Lesbian and Gay Marriage

In 1978, the United States Supreme Court declared marriage to be "of fundamental importance to all individuals."[3] In that case, the court described marriage as "one of the 'basic civil rights of man'" and "the most important relation in life." The court also noted that "the right to marry is part of the fundamental 'right to privacy'" in the U.S. Constitution. The court wrote:

We deal with a right of privacy older than the Bill of Rights—older than our political parties, older than our school system. Marriage is a coming together for better or worse, hopefully enduring, and intimate to the degree of being sacred. It is an association that promotes a way of life, not causes; a harmony in living, not political faiths; a bilateral loyalty, not commercial or social projects.

Although marriage has been declared a fundamental right, as of January 1996, no state recognizes same-sex marriages. (As mentioned earlier, a Hawaii case could change this. Also, Denmark, Greenland, Norway and Sweden permit same-sex marriages, but only if at least one partner is

a citizen of one of those countries And Hungary now permits same-sex couples to qualify for common-law marriage.) Only a handful of states bar same-sex marriages or require that partners be a man and a woman or of the opposite sex, though numbers are increasing as conservative legislatures react to the potential for legal same-sex marriages in Hawaii. Examples include Texas ("a license may not be issued for the marriage of persons of the same sex"), Florida ("no county clerk ... shall issue a license for ... marriage unless one party is male and the other party is female") and California ("marriage is a personal relation arising out of a civil contract between a man and a woman").[4] Georgia, Utah and South Dakota have also joined these ranks, passing anti-same-sex marriage laws in response to the Hawaii case. Despite this trend, most state laws neither prohibit same-sex marriages, nor include the kind of restrictions Florida and California have.

Bear with us as we give you a little bit of history of gay and lesbian marriages. It's interesting reading, shows the depth of desire of many lesbians and gay men in wanting a state-recognized relationship with their lovers, and is relevant to the discussion and debate of the 1990s.

Baker v. Nelson (Minnesota, 1971). A gay male couple argued that the absence of sex-specific language in the Minnesota statute was evidence of the legislature's intent to authorize same-sex marriages. The court relied on dictionary definitions of marriage to reject their argument. The couple also claimed that prohibiting them from marrying was a denial of their due process and equal protection rights under the Constitution. The court simply stated "we do not find support for [these arguments] in any decision of the United States Supreme Court."[5]

Jones v. Hallahan (Kentucky, 1973). A lesbian couple argued that denying them a marriage license deprived them of three basic constitutional rights—the right to marry, the right to associate and the right to freely exercise their religion. The court relied on dictionary definitions of marriage to conclude that marriage means the union of one woman and one man. The court refused to address the constitutional issues, holding that "the relationship proposed does not authorize the issuance of a marriage license because what they propose is not a marriage."[6]

Singer v. Hara (Washington, 1974). A gay male couple argued that denying them the right to marry violated the state's Equal Rights Amendment (ERA). The court disagreed, holding that the purpose of the statute was to overcome discriminatory legal treatment as between men and women "on account of sex." To hold that the voters intended to permit same-sex marriages with the adoption of the ERA would be "to subvert the purpose for which the ERA was enacted by expanding its scope beyond that which was undoubtedly intended by the majority of the citizens of this state who voted for the Amendment."[7] (Remember this case when you reach the discussion, just below, on the Hawaii case.)

Adams v. Howerton (Colorado, 1975). The couple, a male American citizen and a male Australian citizen, challenged the Board of Immigration Appeals refusal to recognize their marriage for the purpose of the Australian obtaining U.S. resi-

dency as the spouse of an American. (The couple participated in a marriage ceremony with a Colorado minister and had been granted a marriage license by the Boulder, Colorado, county clerk. The county clerk's action did not go unnoticed; at least five other same-sex couples were granted licenses.)

The court first asked whether the marriage was valid under Colorado law and concluded it was unclear. The court then asked if the marriage met the requirements of the Immigration Act. First, the court ruled that the word "spouse" ordinarily means someone not of the same sex. Then the court looked at the 1965 amendments to the Act which expressly barred persons "afflicted with sexual deviations" (homosexuals) from entry into this country. The court concluded that it was unlikely that Congress intended to permit homosexual marriages for purposes of qualifying as a spouse of a citizen, when amendments to that section explicitly bar homosexuals from entering into the U.S.[8]

Thorton v. Timmers (Ohio, 1975). A lesbian couple sought a marriage license. In denying their request that the court order the clerk to issue them a license, the court concluded that "it is the express legislative intent that those persons who may be joined in marriage must be of different sexes."[9]

Gay and lesbian couples stopped going to court to seek marriage licenses in the mid-1970s. In the mid-1980s and the 1990s, however, the fight resumed.

De Santo v. Barnsley (Pennsylvania, 1984). Here's a twist. When this couple split up,

John De Santo sued William Barnsley for divorce, claiming that the couple had a common-law marriage. A common-law marriage is one where the partners live together for a long period of time, intend to be married and hold themselves out as married, without going through a formal marriage ceremony. Only a handful of states recognize common-law marriages—Pennsylvania is one of those states. The court threw the case out, stating that if the Pennsylvania common-law statute is to be expanded to include same-sex couples, the legislature will have to make that change.[10]

Matter of Estate of Cooper (**New York, 1990**). Cooper died, leaving the bulk of his property to his ex-lover. His current lover sued to inherit as a "surviving spouse" under New York's inheritance laws. The court concluded that only a lawfully recognized husband or wife qualifies as a "surviving spouse" and that "persons of the same sex have no constitutional rights to enter into a marriage with each other."[11]

Dean v. District of Columbia (**Washington, DC, 1995**). Two men sued the District of Columbia for the right to get married. They lost their case at the lower level and appealed. They lost again at the appellate level when the court decided, under current D.C. laws, that the district can refuse to grant marriage licenses to same-sex couples.[12]

Baehr v. Mike (**formerly Baehr v. Lewin**) (**Hawaii, ongoing**). On May 5, 1993, the Hawaii Supreme Court ruled that denying same-sex couples the right to get married may violate the state constitution.[13] The court did not say that gay men and lesbians have the right to marry—in fact, discrimination based on sexual orientation was not even discussed in the opinion. Instead, the court said that denying a person the right to marry because his or her partner was of the same sex—not of the opposite sex—raised gender-discrimination concerns under the "equal protection" clause of the state's constitution. (Importantly, Hawaii has an Equal Rights Amendment that requires the highest level of scrutiny in a gender-discrimination case.) The court fell short of calling the denial of the right to marry a violation of the constitution. Rather, the court sent the case back to a lower court for a trial, at which the state will have the chance to prove that it has a "compelling interest" in denying same-sex marriages.

The trial is scheduled for August 1, 1996. When the trial judge issues a decision, the losing side will no doubt appeal and the Hawaii Supreme Court will again rule on the matter, probably not until 1997 or 1998. Unless the make-up of the Hawaii Supreme Court radically changes, most legal experts predict that the court will rule in favor of same-sex marriages, given the very favorable language used by the court the first time.

And so, it is quite possible that lesbian and gay couples will be able to enter into legally recognized marriages by the end of 1996 in Hawaii. Whether or not other states would uphold those marriages is another question altogether. The federal Constitution requires that each state give "full faith and credit" to the laws and legal actions of other states. Therefore, if same-sex marriage becomes legal in Hawaii, couples from the other 49 states and the District of Columbia should be able to vacation in Hawaii, visit the justice of the peace and go back home legally married.

But as we warned in the Introduction, the American judicial system has a significant homophobic edge to it. No doubt, a state bureaucrat in at least one of the other 49 states would refuse to accept the same-sex Hawaii marriage and the dispute would go the U.S. Supreme Court. The U.S. Supreme Court would have to decide which takes precedent: the full faith and credit clause of the U.S. Constitution or a state's assertion that same-sex marriages violate the public policy of that state. Virtually all constitutional scholars agree that in any other kind of case the U.S. Supreme Court—especially the conservative justices who like to be consistent in constitutional

interpretations—would rule that full faith and credit takes precedent. But can you imagine Justices Rehnquist, Scalia and Thomas voting in *favor* of same-sex marriages?

So don't order those tuxedos and satin dresses yet, boys and girls.

The *Baehr* (Hawaii) case is not the only same-sex marriage case currently pending. As of January 1996, lawyers working on behalf of gay and lesbian couples are pursuing challenges in Alaska and Florida, and are assessing possible cases in other states.

If you are considering filing a lawsuit to try and secure the right to marry in your state, please, please, please contact one of the gay and lesbian legal organizations listed in Chapter 10, Section E2. The lawyers in

these organizations have studied the issue exhaustively. Before filing a marriage case or encouraging you to do so, they will weigh the pros and cons for your specific state. They may encourage litigation if your state has no sodomy law, a gender-neutral marriage law, a statewide gay rights law and a liberal-leaning high court. They can also tell you what efforts are taking place in your state and can offer assistance if you do pursue the case. Because these cases have national ramifications, pursuing a case without first weighing the likelihood of victory could lead to a very bad precedent.

If you are interested in working towards the legalization of same-sex marriage, you can contact the Forum on the Right to Marriage (FORM). FORM was established in 1995 and is in the process of setting up chapters throughout the country. For more information, call Form at 617-868-3676. You may also want to contact the Marriage Project of the Lambda Legal Defense & Education Fund. The Marriage Project acts as the clearinghouse for the National Freedom to Marry Coalition; it can provide you with information about working, nationally or locally, for same-sex marriage. Call Lambda at 212-995-8585.

B. Domestic Partnerships

Despite the fact that an estimated mere 10% of American families are made up of a working husband, a stay-at-home wife and children, our legal and social systems still provide benefits and protections based on that model. Having been left out, lesbian and gay activists in the early 1980s sought recognition of their relationships and new definitions of family. And so, domestic partnerships were born. Domestic partners

are unmarried couples—same sex or opposite sex—who live together and seek economic and noneconomic benefits granted their married counterparts. These benefits include:

- health, dental and vision insurance
- sick and bereavement leave
- accident and life insurance
- death benefits
- parental leave (for a child you co-parent)
- housing rights and tuition reduction (at universities), and
- use of recreational facilities.

When a state, municipality, county, organization, private company, or university or college considers providing domestic partnership benefits, it must address several important issues: Who qualifies as a domestic partner—should heterosexual couples be covered as well as gay and lesbian couples? How will an employer identify the employee's domestic partner—by registration? Must the couple be together a minimum number of years? Must the couple live together? Must they share expenses? How does a couple terminate their domestic partnership?

If you are interested in working with your employer or city government toward obtaining domestic partnership benefits, we recommend that you get a copy of *Recognizing Lesbian and Gay Families: Strategies for Obtaining Domestic Partners Benefits*, published by the National Center for Lesbian Rights. (See Chapter 10, Section E, for NCLR's address and phone number.) That book describes most of the domestic partnership programs that exist, including how the various entities answered the above questions. It also suggests various strategies gays and lesbians can use in trying to secure domestic partnership benefits. Another helpful publication is the *Domestic Partner Health Care Benefits Sourcebook,* published by and available from A. Foster Higgins and Company in San Francisco. Call (415) 981-5009. You also may want to look at a law review article, *Extending Family Benefits to Gay Men and Lesbian Women,* 68 Chicago-Kent Law Review 447 (1992).

In 1982, the *Village Voice* newspaper became the first private company to offer its employees domestic partnership benefits. The City of Berkeley was the first municipality to do so in 1984. And in 1995, the State of Vermont became the first state to extend domestic partnership benefits to its public employees. Below we provide partial lists of municipalities and counties, private companies and organizations, and colleges and universities that offer domestic partnership benefits—we also describe some of the challenges faced by institutions wanting to offer coverage. The complete list of institutions is extensive; the benefits offered by each is not. In some cases, all that may be offered is bereavement or sick leave. But as lesbians and gay men seek recognition of their families, even small gains must be considered victories.

1. Municipalities and Counties

As many as 30 municipalities and counties offer some domestic partnership benefits for its employees. A few also allow any city residents to register as domestic partners, even though they obtain no tangible benefits by doing so. Domestic partnerships vary a lot from city to city, but essentially the partners must live together in an exclusive relationship and share the basic necessities of life.

Among the municipalities and counties that have domestic partnerships are:

- Alameda County, California
- Berkeley, California
- Laguna Beach, California (includes registration for all residents)
- Los Angeles, California
- Marin County, California (includes registration for all residents)
- San Diego, California
- San Francisco, California (includes registration for all residents)
- San Mateo County, California
- Santa Cruz, California
- West Hollywood, California (includes registration for all residents)
- Hartford, Connecticut (includes registration for all residents)
- Chicago, Illinois
- Oak Park, Illinois
- Tacoma Park, Maryland
- Boston, Massachusetts (includes registration for all residents)
- Cambridge, Massachusetts
- Ann Arbor, Michigan
- East Lansing, Michigan
- Minneapolis, Minnesota (includes registration for all residents)
- Chapel Hill, North Carolina (includes registration for all residents)
- Ithaca, New York
- New York, New York (includes registration for all residents)
- Portland, Oregon
- Travis County, Texas
- Burlington, Vermont

- Seattle, Washington (includes registration for all residents)
- Madison, Wisconsin.

Cities and counties offering sick leave, bereavement leave and parental leave have had few problems implementing their programs. After all, by offering these domestic partner benefits, the institution has made the commitment to absorb these costs.

Providing health, dental or vision insurance, however, has not been as easy. A commitment on paper does not translate into a tangible benefit if the city or county's insurance carrier refuses to extend coverage to the domestic partner of a city employee. In Ann Arbor, for example, the city has been unable to find an insurance carrier willing to cover the domestic partners of its non-unionized employees; the union that represents 80% of the city's employees won't support domestic partner benefits out of fear of losing other benefits in exchange. And in Minneapolis, a Court of Appeals has held that the city charter does not permit the extension of health insurance benefits to the same-sex partners of city employees.

The City of Berkeley allows its employees to choose among several different health insurance companies. When the city began offering coverage to domestic partners, only one company Berkeley did business with refused to participate; the city dropped the carrier. One of the other companies originally required a 2% fee to cover unexpected costs incurred because of the domestic partners. That company removed the fee after a few years.

2. Private Companies and Organizations

As we've mentioned, the *Village Voice* newspaper was the first, and for a long time appeared to be the last, private employer or membership organization to offer domestic partner benefits. In the late 1980s and early 1990s, however, many other companies joined in—there are now over 100 private sector employers who provide domestic partner benefits to their employees. Included are:

- Advanced Micro Devices
- American Friends Committee (National Quaker Organization)
- American Psychological Association
- Apple Computer
- Barnes & Noble Booksellers
- Ben & Jerry's Homemade
- Blue Cross-Blue Shield
- Coors Brewing Co.
- Episcopal Diocese of Newark, New Jersey
- Home Box Office
- Levi Strauss & Co.
- Lotus Development Corporation
- MCA (owner of Universal Studios)
- Microsoft Corporation
- Seattle Times
- Sony Entertainment
- Viacom
- Xerox Corporation.

Many other private employers and organizations are exploring the possibility of extending domestic partnership benefits. And a few—including AT&T—are exploring it in court, against their will. When AT&T employee Marjorie Forlini died, her surviving lover, Sandra Rovira, sought payment for herself and her children under the "sickness-death benefits" Marjorie was given as a part of her employment. Despite AT&T's personnel policies which claim not to discriminate based on sexual orientation, AT&T has continued to deny the request. (A court ruled in favor of AT&T in 1993; Sandra has appealed.)

Even if your employer isn't willing to grant you domestic partner benefits, you may be able to obtain some from private businesses. For examples, airlines which used to let frequent flyer members use their accumulated miles only for their spouses, now usually let you bring anyone. Several other institutions, such as museums, health clubs and public television stations, which used to offer membership discounts to married couples, now offer them to "any two people" or "a household," regardless of marital status or sexuality.

3. Colleges and Universities

Nearly 50 colleges and universities offer some type of domestic partnership benefits to students or staff, or both. To obtain an updated list, contact the National Gay and Lesbian Task Force—the address and phone number is in Chapter 10, Section E.

Some of the major campuses to extend such coverage include:
• Brown University
• Columbia University
• Georgia State University
• Harvard University
• New York University
• North Dakota University
• Northeastern University

• Princeton University
• Smith College
• Stanford University
• State University of New York at Stony Brook
• University of Colorado
• University of Michigan
• University of Minnesota
• University of New Mexico
• University of Oregon
• University of Pennsylvania
• University of Pittsburgh
• University of Wisconsin.

In addition, a discrimination claim against the University of Chicago for refusing to provide domestic partners benefits was filed with the Chicago Commission on Human Relations. The claim charges that the university is violating Chicago's human rights law banning discrimination based on sexual orientation and marital status.

C. New Definitions of Spouse and Immediate Family

One tragedy of society's failure to recognize lesbian and gay relationships is that government benefits traditionally awarded to married spouses—such as unemployment insurance and workers' compensation—are denied to same-sex partners. Similarly, lovers of lesbians and gay men have been denied the right to sue for emotional distress or to stay in an apartment after their lover dies when their name isn't on the lease because they were not considered "immediate family." Slowly, however, things are changing.

Although we report on the victories achieved by lesbian and gay couples, these cases are still not the norm. Most lesbian and gay partners are denied unemployment, workers' compensation and emotional distress recoveries on the grounds that they are not spouses or members of each other's immediate family.

1.   Government Benefits

Several years ago, a gay man in California was awarded unemployment insurance from the state when he left his job to care for his lover who had AIDS. Married partners have for years received benefits if they quit their jobs to care for terminally ill spouses. In extending the benefits to gay couples, the Unemployment Appeals Board declared that gay relationships are often as serious, loving and committed as marriages.

More recently, a lesbian (Susan) who quit her job in California to accompany her lover to Pennsylvania to begin a medical residency was awarded unemployment insurance. Initially denied benefits on the ground that she quit her job to move "with an individual with whom she's in an nonmarital relationship," Susan appealed. The Unemployment Appeals Board judge who decided the case simply stated that benefits are available when a person leaves his or her employment to accompany a spouse to a place from which it is impractical to commute and that the applicant's "spouse was accepted into residency and this certainly provided good cause for the couple to move." The judge knew the couple was lesbian, but clearly chose to

refer to them as spouses, without regard to their sex or sexual orientation.[14]

In another California case (yes, there are reasons gay men and lesbians flock to the Golden State), a gay man was awarded workers' compensation death benefits when his lover, a county district attorney, committed suicide because of job-related stress. The Workers' Compensation Appeals Board found that the lover was dependent on the employee for support, and said that the homosexual relationship of the two men shouldn't preclude the lover's rights to benefits.

2.   Defining "Family"

New York City has a rental vacancy rate of approximately 0%; this means that affordable and decent housing is virtually impossible to find for those without it. When a lover dies and the survivor's name was not on the lease or named as the successor in interest to a co-op or condominium, lesbians and gay men, dealing with the death of their mate, have suffered the added injustice of losing their homes. In addition, when a tenant's lover moves into an apartment, the tenant risks violating the standard lease clause limiting occupancy to the named tenant and the tenant's "immediate family."

Between 1979 and 1983, several cases were litigated in New York addressing these problems. The essential issue in each case was the definition of "immediate family." The cases seesawed back and forth. In the first case, the court denied the surviving lover a place to live, stating "[no] authority ... holds [that] homosexuals living together constitute a family unit." Two years later, the same court upheld the eviction of a lesbian whose lover had moved in with her, stating that "[two] lesbians living together do not constitute a ... family."[15]

But less than a year later, another court refused to let a landlord evict a man and his female lover simply because her name was not on the lease.[16] The court held that the eviction violated New York City's Human Rights Law barring discrimination on the basis of marital status. The court chastised the landlord, stating:

In this day and age, [landlords cannot] continue to ignore and to refuse to accord legitimacy to couples living together without the officialization of marriage. Couples, both heterosexual and homosexual, are increasingly turning to "nonmarital" living arrangements, for a variety of reasons. These relationships are frequently no more temporal than marital relationships, and many may last longer than their marital counterparts.

In the same year, another court refused to allow the eviction of a gay male couple, holding that the traditional nuclear family is no longer the reality for many people, and that the tenant did not breach the "immediate family" clause in his lease.[17] But just a year later, a court upheld the eviction a different gay man for violating the "immediate family" clause.[18]

In 1983, New York's highest court gave the final word—at least for a few years.[19] It upheld an eviction of a woman for breaching the "immediate family" clause of her lease when her male lover moved in. The court asserted that:

Whether or not he [her lover] could by marriage or otherwise become part of her immediate family is not an issue ... Were the

additional tenant a female unrelated to the tenant, the lease would still be violated without reference to marriage.

This decision lasted only six years. In 1989, New York's highest court reversed itself.[20] After Leslie Blanchard died, his lover, Miguel Braschi, sought to stay in the rent-stabilized apartment the two men shared for over 11 years, despite the fact that only Leslie's name was on the lease. The landlord instituted eviction proceedings against Miguel, who fought back. The court ruled:

We conclude that the term family should not be rigidly restricted to those people who have formalized their relationship by obtaining, for instance, a marriage certificate or an adoption order. The intended protection against sudden eviction should not rest on fictitious legal distinctions or genetic history, but instead should find its foundation in the reality of family life. In the context of eviction, a more realistic, and certainly equally valid view of a family includes two adult lifetime partners whose relationship is long-term and characterized by an emotional and financial commitment and interdependence.

Courts have been called upon to define "family" in other contexts. In Denver, for example, a city worker who took three days off to care for her seriously injured lover was granted sick leave by a hearing officer who declared the sick leave policy to care for family members applicable to all city employees, regardless of sexual orientation.[21] In Washington, D.C., a woman was allowed to file a claim under the District's Wrongful Death Act after her lover died from injuries sustained when a tree branch broke through the windshield of the car she was driving. A court found that the surviving partner qualified as her deceased lover's "next of kin."[22] And in California, a surviving lover of a man who died from AIDS was awarded $175,000 by a court for emotional distress experienced after a funeral company mishandled the deceased man's ashes in breach of the contract the deceased man signed with the company. This expanded the definition of family, as previously such recoveries were limited to spouses.[23]

LEGALLY DEAR, YOU AND MISS FRIM ARE STRANGERS. YES, I KNOW YOU LIVED TOGETHER 26 YEARS...

D. Adult Adoption—One Way to Cement a Relationship

One of the legally recognized relationships that a handful of couples unable to marry have entered into is that of adoptive relatives. The first known same-sex adult adoption took place in 1971. While his appeal for a marriage license was pending before the Minnesota Supreme Court, Jack Baker was adopted by his lover, James McConnell. (See Section A, above, for information about their marriage.) The men emphasized that they were trying to legitimize their relationship, as well as qualify for automatic inheritance. And Baker wanted to become eligible for the in-state tuition rate at the University of Minnesota because McConnell was a resident of that state.

Three New York City men have sought to adopt their lovers. In *In re Adoption of Adult Anonymous*, the judge allowed the adoption because:

- sodomy is not illegal in New York
- New York's incest law only prohibits sexual relations between *blood* relatives, and
- the men claimed legitimate economic reasons—facilitating inheritance, handling insurance policies and pension plans, and acquiring suitable housing.[24]

A similar adoption was permitted in *In re Adult Anonymous II* (great names, these cases have) one year later.[25] In *In re Adoption of Robert Paul P.*, however, the court denied a same-sex adult adoption application holding that "the evasion of existing inheritance laws [was] a main purpose of [the] adoption."[26]

More recently, the Delaware Supreme Court approved a same-sex adult adoption. The court specifically stated that the couple's desire to formalize their close emotional relationship and facilitate estate planning were permissible reasons to allow the adoption.[27]

These cases aptly demonstrate the reasons lesbian and gay couples want their relationships legally recognized—to benefit from housing, inheritance, investment and other laws. But there are barriers you will likely face if you try to adopt your lover. First, a court may prove reluctant to grant a same-sex adult adoption when it is clear that the relationship is a sexual one. Adoption connotes parent and child; to allow lovers to use it to confer legal status upon themselves is repugnant to many people.

Same-sex lovers planning to adopt face four other potential barriers:
- state laws barring adult adoptions—Alabama, Arizona, Hawaii, Michigan, Nebraska and Ohio all have such laws
- sodomy statutes
- incest statutes, and
- laws specifying a minimum age difference between the adoptive parent and child.

Only a handful of states prohibit adult adoptions. Sodomy, however, is still illegal in nearly half of the states. And in most states, incest laws prohibit sexual relations between an adoptive parent and child.

These are the outside forces that keep lesbians and gay men from adopting their lovers. But many other factors give lesbians and gay men reason to pause. First, as lesbians and gay men seek the right to raise children, adopting a lover seems inappropriate. Second, adoption is permanent—most same-sex lovers want the option of ending their relationship. Finally, adoption necessarily means that the court must terminate the parent-child relationship between the person to be adopted and his legal parents. For a lesbian or gay man with a positive relationship with her or his parents, this could be both destructive and insulting.

Other Ways to Create a Family

Marriage, domestic partnerships and adoption aren't the only ways to cement a relationship with your lover. You can also write a living together contract. We cover general living together agreements in Chapter 6, and agreements for buying a house together in Chapter 7. And of course, you should "plan your estate"—that is, draft a will or living trust—leaving your property to your lover. We cover estate planning in Chapter 5.

E. The Sad Side of "Marriage"

Wouldn't it be wonderful if lesbians and gay men fell in love, moved in together and lived happily (or mostly happily) ever after? It does happen, on occasion. But, human beings and human nature being what they are, relationships can turn sour.

1. Breaking Up

Ending a relationship can be harder than starting one. If you have kids, we suggest you read Chapter 3. For help on dividing your property, take a look at Chapter 9. Here, we just want to talk about ending your "family" status.

If you went through some kind of union, commitment or marriage ceremony, you are not required to take any steps to end the relationship—remember, you are not legally married. Many people go back to whomever officiated at their ceremony and seek help in splitting up. Sometimes, a couple will stand before friends and community to assert their new status as single people and to commit to working toward a healthy end of the relationship. Of course, if this "touchy feely" stuff seems strange to you, you can simply pack your bags and move out. (As Paul Simon said, there are "50 ways to leave your lover.")

If you registered as domestic partners, be sure to de-register. If one of you adopted the other, you may want to have a lawyer look at your state's adoption statute to see if there are grounds to rescind the adoption decree.

2.   When Relationships Turn Violent

We'd like it if there were no need for this section. But violence and abuse are a very real part of the gay and lesbian community—an estimated 10%-33% of all lesbian and gay relationships involve some abuse—but only recently have lesbians and gay men been willing to talk about it.

If you are the victim of domestic violence, your number one concern is your own safety. You may be ashamed, embarrassed or feeling guilty, and all of those feelings are understandable. But it's most important that you get out of your living arrangement and into a safe environment. If you are a lesbian, contact a battered women's shelter. If you're concerned about the homophobia you may encounter—or if you're a gay man with no shelter to turn to—then go to a friend or supportive relative.

You may feel very alone, and unwilling to report the abuse, for any of the following reasons:

- few others report gay/lesbian incidents of violence

- authorities may not understand the nature of your relationship

- the abuser may have threatened to "out" you if you report the abuse

- the lesbian and gay community rarely reprimands abusers

- there are no shelters for gay men; lesbians often meet with homophobia, non-acceptance or inadequate counseling at shelters for women

- the secrecy of a closeted relationship can lead to the escalation of abuse

- because of society's lack of support for gay and lesbian relationships, there's very little counseling available for abusers and victims, and

- because of insensitivity, police, when called, may arrest both abuser and victim.

A few states, including California, Massachusetts and Ohio, cover same-sex relationships in their domestic violence statutes. This means that you can get a restraining order to keep the abuser away from you. You will probably need the help of a lawyer or women's clinic.

For more information on gay and lesbian domestic violence, look at any of the following:

- *Violent Betrayal: Partner Abuse in Lesbian Relationships*, by Claire Renzetti (St. Josephs University Press 1992)

- *Men Who Beat the Men Who Love Them*, by David Island & Patrick Letellier (Haworth Press 1992)

- *Fatal Defense: An Analysis of Battered Woman's Syndrome Expert Testimony for Gay Men and Lesbians Who Kill Abusive Partners,* by Denise Bricker, 58 Brooklyn Law Review 1379 (Winter 1993).

Endnotes

[1]Two books that explore same-sex union ceremonies are *Ceremonies of the Heart: Celebrating Lesbian Unions*, ed. by Becky Butler (Seal Press), and *Lesbian and Gay Marriage: Private Commitments, Public Ceremonies*, ed. by Suzanne Sherman (Temple University Press). In addition, the film *Chicks in White Satin* documents the wedding of a San Diego lesbian couple. The film received a Best Short Documentary Academy Award nomination in 1994.

[2]Paula L. Ettelbrick, "Since When Is Marriage a Path to Liberation," originally appeared in *OUT/LOOK National Gay and Lesbian Quarterly*, No. 6 (Fall 1989) and was reprinted with minor changes in *Lesbian and Gay Marriage: Private Commitments, Public Ceremonies*. The other side of the debate has been expressed by Thomas B. Stoddard, "Why Gay People Should Seek the Right to Marry," in *OUT/LOOK* and *Lesbian and Gay Marriage*, alongside the Ettlebrick article. Other thought-provoking articles on the gay and lesbian marriage debate are in Volume 1 (Summer 1991) of *Law and Sexuality*, a journal published by students at Tulane University School of Law.

[3]*Zablocki v. Redhail*, 434 U.S. 374 (1978).

[4]Texas Family Code §1.01; Florida Statute §741.04; and California Family Code §300.

[5]291 Minn. 310. A few year's later, Baker's lover, McConnell, applied for increased veterans' benefits, claiming that Baker was his dependent spouse. Although they had participated in a marriage ceremony with a minister, the court held that *Baker v. Nelson* closed the issue and that McConnell was not entitled to increased benefits. *McConnell v. Nooner*, 547 F.2d 54 (1976).

[6]501 S.W.2d 588.

[7]11 Wash. App. 247.

[8]673 F.2d 1036 (9th Cir. 1982). (The Immigration Act no longer bars lesbians and gay men from coming to the U.S. See Chapter 2, Section F.)

[9]No. 74-2623 (Court of Common Pleas, Montgomery County).

[10]476 A.2d 952 (1984).

[11]564 N.Y.S.2d 684 (1990). The highest court in New York refused to hear an appeal of this case in 1993.

[12]653 A.24 307 (D.C. 1995).

[13]852 P.2d 44 (Hawaii 1993).

[14]California Unemployment Insurance Appeals Board, Case No. OAK—45316-0001 (February 21, 1992).

[15]*Avest Seventh Corp. v. R.*, 109 Misc. 2d 248 (1981).

[16]*Yorkshire House Associates v. Lulkin*, 114 Misc. 2d 40 (1982).

[17]*420 East 80th Co. v. Chin*, 115 Misc. 2d 195 (1982).

[18]*Evangelists Associations v. Bland*, 117 Misc. 2d 558 (1983).

[19]*Hudson View Properties v. Weiss*, 59 N.Y.2d 733 (1983).

[20]*Braschi v. Stahl Associates Co.*, 74 N.Y.2d 201 (1989).

[21]The case was reported in the December 21, 1992 issue of the *National Law Journal*.

[22]*Solomon v. District of Columbia*, Family Law Reporter 21 1316 (1995).

[23] The case was reported in the Jue 26,1992 issue of the *San Francisco Recorder*.

[24]106 Misc. 2d 792 (1981).

[25]452 N.Y.S.2d 198 (1982).

[26]63 N.Y. 2d 233 (1984).

[27]*In re Adoption of Swanson*, 623 A.2d 1095 (1993). ∎

Living Together and the Real World

When you and your lover decide to live together, you are probably (or hopefully) acting on romantic impulses. Unfortunately, practical problems inevitably tag along in the wake of romance. Most of these problems aren't legal and don't involve lawyers. All the barristers in the world can't help you when you and your lover discuss where to vacation, what to play on the stereo and what to hang on the living room wall.

Many day-to-day hassles, however, are connected with law. Some, such as employment discrimination, aren't addressed because they aren't specifically related to living together as a lesbian or gay couple. In this chapter, we focus on the legal situations lesbian and gay couples face, living in the world. Our goal is to be specific enough to be helpful without being overly technical. If you need more information on a subject, see Chapter 10, *Help Beyond the Book*.

Although lesbian and gay couples lose the practical benefits and protections of marriage, there are some advantages to being a same-sex couple and not married. For example, gay and lesbian couples in which both earn an income pay far less in income taxes than do married couples in which both earn money. This is because the tax code was written several generations ago to favor working men with stay-at-home wives.

In addition, reasonably discrete gay couples sometimes find it easier than unmarried straight couples to rent a home in many parts of the country. Few landlords worry about two people of the same sex sharing a place to live. Instead, they usually see "two nice young men" or "two lovely young ladies" rooming together to save expenses until one of them gets married. For similar reasons, lesbian and gay couples traveling often face less trouble than do unmarried straight couples. Of course, there are disadvantages. For one, family plans offered by the travel industry aren't normally available to lesbian and gay couples.[1]

Tragically, lesbian and gay couples have few legal protections. No federal law prohibits discrimination against lesbian and gay people or couples in areas such as employment, housing, public accommodations or credit. Protections exist in a number of states and many municipalities (see accompanying chart), but often places that pass antidiscrimination ordinances are places that largely accepted lesbian and gay people before the laws were passed.

We mean no criticism of antidiscrimination ordinances when we say that in cities such as Madison and San Francisco these laws are more symbolic of lesbian and gay political acceptance than they are the wedges to bring about change. We support and applaud lesbian and gay political activists while, at the same time, we've written a book about living, not fighting political struggles. It is important to remember, however, that because of many pioneering political battles, lesbian and gay couples can live openly in several parts of the world.

Selected states and municipalities with gay rights protections[2]	public employment	private employment	public accommodations	housing	credit
Anchorage, Alaska	•				
Tucson, Arizona	•				
California	•	•	•		
Aspen, Colorado	•	•	•	•	
Connecticut	•	•	•	•	•
District of Columbia	•	•	•	•	•
Key West, Florida	•	•	•	•	•
Miami, Florida	•	•	•	•	
Atlanta, Georgia	•				
Hawaii	•	•			
Chicago, Illinois	•	•	•		•
Ames, Iowa	•	•	•	•	•
Iowa City	•	•	•		•
New Orleans, Louisiana	•	•	•	•	
Portland, Maine	•	•	•		•
Baltimore, Maryland	•	•	•	•	
Massachusetts	•	•	•		•
Ann Arbor, Michigan	•	•	•	•	•
Detroit, Michigan	•	•	•	•	•
Minnesota	•	•	•		
St. Louis, Missouri	•	•	•		•
New Jersey	•	•	•	•	•
Albuquerque, New Mexico	•				
Albany, New York	•	•	•	•	•
Buffalo, New York	•				
Ithaca, New York	•	•	•	•	•
New York, New York	•	•	•	•	
Raleigh, North Carolina	•				
Syracuse, New York	•	•	•	•	
Columbus, Ohio	•	•	•	•	•
Portland, Oregon	•	•	•	•	
Harrisburg, Pennsylvania	•	•	•		•
Philadelphia, Pennsylvania	•	•	•		•
Pittsburgh, Pennsylvania	•	•	•		•
Rhode Island	•	•	•		•
Austin, Texas	•	•	•		•
Vermont	•	•	•	•	•
Alexandria, Virginia	•	•	•	•	•
Pullman, Washington	•			•	•
Seattle, Washington	•	•		•	•
Wisconsin	•	•	•	•	•

California's Public Accommodations Law

California Civil Code Section 51 bars discrimination by business establishments on account of sex, race, color, religion, ancestry, national origin, or blindness or other physical disability. California appellate courts have ruled that this list is illustrative, not restrictive, and that all forms of arbitrary discrimination—including sexual orientation discrimination—by a business establishment are prohibited.

In the fall of 1993, an appellate court ruled that a business violated this law when it refused to include a photo of a gay male couple in the high school reunion memory book it was printing for the reunion celebration of one of the men. Interestingly, the court ruled that the business engaged in unlawful sex discrimination—refusing to print the photo because his partner was a man, not a woman—not sexual orientation discrimination.

In early 1994, the very conservative California Supreme Court ordered that this case be "depublished"—meaning it must be removed from books that publish case opinions and cannot be cited or relied upon as authority.[3] (California does recognize some exceptions to this rule, however, and a creative lawyer could probably cite an unpublished opinion.)

A. Can I Take My Lover's Last Name?

When Reverend Jim Dykes and his lover affirmed their commitment, they decided to symbolize that commitment by sharing the same last name. They agreed that hyphenated names were ungainly; Jim chose to take his lover's last name. "We decided I would change my name to Dykes," he told us, "because my lover comes from a wonderful Southern family with a proud and historic name."

Lots of lesbian and gay men change their names. Some women who changed their name in a heterosexual marriage want to return to their premarital name. Gay and lesbian partners in a couple sometimes hyphenate their names or choose a name that's the combination of the two. (Audrey Berman and Sheila Gander become Audrey and Sheila Bergan.) And then there are people like Jim Dykes, who simply take their lover's last name.

Changing your name is perfectly legal and usually easy. Bear in mind, however, that you cannot change your name to defraud creditors, for any illegal purpose or to benefit economically by the use of another person's name—that is, you probably can't become Bette Midler or Gore Vidal. Otherwise, you can change your name for any reason and assume any name you wish.

You can change your name in one of two ways—usage or court order.

1. Change of Name by Usage

One way to change your name is simply to use a new one. Last week you were Steve Nurd; this week you're Steve Savage. If you use Savage consistently and insist it's your name, it is. The obvious example of usage name change is marriage. There's no legal proceeding (aside from the marriage itself) when one spouse changes her name to the other's. She simply does it—and it's perfectly legal. Any adult can accomplish a similar name change, although you must obtain a court order to change a child's name.

The keys to changing your name by usage are consistency and stubbornness. You must use your new name in all aspects of your life—socially, professionally and on identity cards and personal documents such as credit cards, driver's license and your Social Security card. Getting most documents with your new name shouldn't be a hassle. Clerks are familiar with changing forms for women after marriage and quite agreeably change a woman's name on request. More men are changing their name after marriage—often by hyphenating their name with their wive's—so few clerks will hassle a man requesting a new document to reflect a name change. Many organizations and agencies have a specific form to request a name change. Others will accept an official-looking form declaring your name change.

2. Change of Name by Court Order

The second way to change your name is by court order. Getting a court order is usually pretty simple: You fill out and file at the courthouse a short petition, publish legal notice of your intention to change your name in a local legal newspaper (which no one reads) and attend a routine court hearing.

Unfortunately, we do know of one court—in Delaware—which refused to grant a name change after the petitioner stated that she is a lesbian who wants to take her partner's last name. This seems to be an unusual case and it is presently on appeal. You may, however, choose to be cautious with what you tell a court about your name change.

If you live in a state where you must give a reason for the change and you'd rather not tell the judge that you're changing your name to your partner's, you don't have to. You can state that your new name will make it more convenient for business or simply state that you like the new name better.

 Each state has its own laws governing the court order method. While the procedures are similar, if you're serious about changing your name by court order, check your state laws, available at any law library or major public library. In California, *How to Change Your Name*, by Loeb & Brown (Nolo Press), will help you do the job quickly and efficiently.

Once you obtain the court order changing your name, you must still change your records, identity cards and documents. All you need to do is show the various bureaucrats the judge's order.

B. Renting a Home Together

One first and favorite act of togetherness for many couples is living together. It is often easiest psychologically for the two people moving in together to obtain a new place. It's common, however, for one partner to move in with the other. These living arrangements, as well as sexual orientation discrimination in housing, are covered in this section.

For information on buying a home together or moving into your lover's purchased home, see Chapter 7.

1. Sexual Orientation Discrimination

If you live in a state or municipality with a law prohibiting sexual orientation discrimination in housing and you believe you're being discriminated against because you are gay or lesbian, call the local city attorney's office and find out what agency is responsible for enforcing the gay rights ordinance. Remember that the list of gay and lesbian civil rights, above, is not complete. Even if a state or municipality is on the list and "housing" is not checked, you may still have protection. For example, California's legislature passed a law granting protection to gay and lesbian civil rights in employment. But over a decade ago, a California court ruled that housing discrimination against gays and lesbians violated the state civil rights law.[4]

Even if you're protected by a non-discrimination ordinance and have filed a complaint under the law, some landlords may go out on a limb to try to prove that they don't have to rent to you. One possible landlords' argument is that being forced to rent to a certain type of person—gay men or lesbians or unmarried heterosexual couples—violates their protected religious beliefs. The good news is that such an argument failed before the California Supreme Court in 1996 and would likely fail in other locations where lesbian, gay or unmarried renters are protected by law.[5]

If you live in a place with no anti-discrimination ordinance and a landlord discriminates against you, there's usually not much you can do. So the question is whether or not to inform a prospective landlord that you're gay. It's far from automatic that a landlord will discriminate against you because of your sexual orienta-tion. There are all sorts of landlords. Some "love their gay boys because they do know how to keep an apartment." Most are concerned with money and responsible tenants, not your private life. But it's not the landlord's business, and nothing legally requires you to volunteer the information. This is a tactical, not a legal, decision. If the landlord lives downstairs and is almost sure to figure it out, it may make sense to be candid. If the landlord lives halfway across the country, why bother?

Once you're living in your new place, you might be concerned about being evicted if the landlord discovers your relationship. If you rent under a month-to-month tenancy, not in a rent control area, your landlord can simply give you a 30-day notice to get out. It can be for any reason or no reason at all, and you have no protection.

If you have a lease or live in a "just cause" rent control area, the landlord must show that you broke a term of the lease or rental agreement, such as you failed to pay the rent, made too much noise (disturbing the "quiet enjoyment" of your neighbors), damaged the apartment and refused to pay for repairs, got a pet in violation of a "no pets" clause or something else. Being gay or lesbian is not a "just cause."

But most leases prohibit illegal activity on the premises, and a landlord might threaten to evict you in a state where sodomy is illegal. (See Introduction.) And a conservative judge (who decides if the landlord can evict you) or a conservative sheriff (who does the physical evicting) may require the landlord to present little proof that you're gay. But if the landlord encounters an open-minded judge, this sort of eviction will be extremely difficult. To prove that illegal activities transpired on the property, the landlord would have to present evidence, not just vague suspicions. If you keep your mouth shut, such proof would be difficult, if not impossible, to get.

Read your lease or rental agreement carefully. Some leases and rental agreements contain illegal provisions, such as one giving the landlord the right to evict you with no court action if you're late with the rent. Before signing a lease or rental agreement, ask the landlord to cross off any clause that rubs you the wrong way. Watch especially for clauses prohibiting "immoral behavior" or "association with undesirable people." In the states with sodomy laws, an "immoral behavior" clause can be a problem if the landlord wants to evict you. If your landlord agrees, cross out the offending language and have your landlord add his or her initials.

A friend experienced the following nasty situation many years ago:

One night, my landlady, who lived downstairs, telephoned and shouted, "It's illegal, you two living together. Get out or I will call the cops." To be honest, even though I was a lawyer, the call was so incredibly jarring and frightening that my first response was to do just that—to get out. But after talking it over with my lover, we decided that we had to stay and fight. And then, after staying long enough to establish the fact that we weren't being driven out, we realized that we wanted to move. Right or wrong, legal or illegal, wasn't the question. We simply didn't want to live above someone who was so hostile. We learned one valuable lesson from the experience though: never rent from someone who lives in the same building, unless you know she's okay.

If your landlord evicts or otherwise harasses you because you're gay, and you want to fight it, you'll have to file a written response to the eviction papers and raise the defense that you're being illegally discriminated against. Keep in mind, however, that even if an ordinance prohibits sexual orientation discrimination in housing, you could have a problem. A smart landlord will give a nondiscriminatory (phony) reason for evicting you.[6]

2.   Renting a Home Together

It's wonderful for a couple to move into new quarters together. The new apartment or house represents a fresh start, with no ghosts of past relationships or already-established territorial rights. There's no need to say, "Well, I guess I can move my clothes out of *my* hall closet to give you more room" or "I painted the bathroom red, white and blue stripes, and I'm not about to repaint it soft yellow." Whatever relationship you establish with your landlord, the crux of living together will be the understandings you two work out. Don't underestimate the need to be clear. Renting a place to live isn't only a monetary investment; it also provides you with a special haven of relaxation and refuge. Obviously, it's worth a little effort to ensure that you both will feel secure and protected.

Below is an agreement covering moving into a newly (jointly) rented living space.

RENTING TOGETHER CONTRACT

Audrey Rabinowitz and Candice Dunk just rented Apartment 6B at 1500 Avenue B, New York, New York, and agree as follows:

1. We will each pay one-half of the rent and one-half of the gas, electricity, water and fixed telephone charge. Each person will pay for her long-distance calls. Our rent will be paid on time and the electricity, gas, water and telephone bills will be paid within ten days of receipt.

2. If either wants to leave, she will give the other and the landlord at least 30 days' written notice. The person moving agrees to pay her rent (before she moves) for the entire 30-day period, even if she leaves sooner.

3. We intend to live as a couple and neither of us wants a large number of house guests. Therefore, no third person will be invited to stay overnight without the permission of both of us.

4. If we want to stop living together but both want to remain at this address, a third party will flip a coin to decide who stays. The loser of the coin flip will move out within 30 days and will pay all her obligations for rent, utilities and any damage to the apartment.

Dated: _____   Signature: _____
                                           Audrey Rabinowitz

Dated: _____   Signature: _____
                                           Candice Dunk

Some people adopt an approach more rational than flipping a coin to decide who gets to stay in the event there is a conflict. They have an "objective" third person decide, who will base her decision on proximity to work, needs of any children, relative financial status and other relevant facts. This approach can work well, but don't pick a close friend. If she's ever called upon to make a decision, she's likely to end up a friend of only one of you.

3. Moving Into Your Lover's Rented Home

What happens when one of you moves into a house or apartment rented by the other? Is the move legal? Is the original tenant required to tell the landlord that someone has moved in?

Legally, you must notify your landlord that you are living with someone only if your lease or rental agreement specifically requires you to or limits the number of people who can occupy your unit. But even without a requirement, it's normally wise to notify your landlord. He will almost surely figure it out, and it's especially important to avoid looking sneaky if you have a month-to-month tenancy in a non-rent control area where the landlord can evict for any reason. Whether you tell the landlord that you're lovers or merely roommates is entirely up to you.

Usually, the landlord will want more rent for the additional person. Unless the amount is exorbitant, you're probably wise to accept the increase. Even if your lease or rental agreement requires notice to the landlord of a new tenant, all that usually results is an increase in rent.

If your lease doesn't cover someone else moving in, you can probably bargain with your landlord. For your landlord to get you out before the lease expires, he would have to establish that you have violated one or more lease terms.

Even if your lease prohibits someone else from moving in, once your landlord accepts rent knowing that you live with someone, many courts will refuse to let him enforce the lease prohibition. If your lease states that the premises shall not be used for "immoral or illegal purpose," it is highly unlikely your landlord can terminate the lease simply because you live with someone, unless your state has a sodomy law. Even then, the landlord's case would be difficult to prove.

a. Is There a Legal Relationship Between the New Tenant and the Landlord?

If Renee moves into Jane's apartment does Renee have a legal relationship with Jane's landlord? More specifically, does Renee have a legal duty to pay rent if Jane fails to? If Jane moves out, does Renee have the right to stay? If Jane damages the formica or lets her dog scratch the wall, does Renee have a legal obligation to pay the landlord for the damages?

There are no simple answers to these questions. If Renee just spends a few nights, she'd have no rights as a tenant and no obligation to pay rent. The same would be true during the first weeks of her tenancy, if she moves in. Jane, not Renee, entered into a contract with the landlord. But just as Renee has no legal obligations at this early stage, she has no rights either. If Jane moves out, Renee can't stay unless the landlord consents.

Renee can easily turn into a tenant with all the legal rights and responsibilities that go with tenant status by doing any of the following:

- Having the landlord prepare a new lease that includes both Jane and Renee as tenants.
- Talking to the landlord and agreeing orally to a tenant-landlord relationship. Renee must be careful of two things, however. First, an oral agreement is difficult to prove—if the landlord reneges, Renee may have a hard time proving she made an agreement. Second, an oral agreement can be easily implied from a casual conversation. Suppose Renee meets the landlord in the laundry room, introduces herself, explains that she's moved into Jane's apartment and agrees to pay rent. The landlord says "okay." A valid agreement has been formed. Renee can be evicted only in a formal court action, but is liable for all rent and damage to the apartment. If you're not sure you want to become a tenant, be careful of casual conversations with the landlord.
- Paying rent directly to the landlord or property manager. If Renee does this, especially repeatedly, an "implied contract," as it is known in legalese, is formed. Nothing formal has been said or written down, but the conduct of both Renee and the landlord clearly creates a landlord-tenant relationship.

b. ***Putting Your Agreement in Writing***

When one lover moves into an apartment or house already rented by the other, turning it into a shared home requires a great deal of sensitivity and openness, especially by the person who was there first. Sometimes, a party to rechristen the home your shared home provides a valuable symbolic "rite of passage."

However you manage the exciting emotional change, it's a good idea to write down your economic and legal understanding. If you fall into tough times, a question like, "whose apartment is this?" can come up and cause pain, even paranoia. If you write down your understanding when you begin living together, you are forced to clarify the issues while you're both loving, not combative. Below is a sample that may help.

MOVING-IN CONTRACT

Roger Rappan and Peter Majors agree as follows:

1.   Roger will move into the apartment that Peter has been renting at 111 Prairie Street, Chicago, Illinois, on August 1, 19__ and will pay Peter one-half of the $900 monthly rent on the first of each month. Because Peter has been renting under a lease, he will continue to pay the landlord on the first of each month for the remainder of the lease term (six months).

2.   Roger and Peter will each pay one-half of the electric, gas, water, garbage and monthly telephone service charge. Peter will collect the payments, because the accounts are in his name.

3.   For the first six months, Peter retains the first right to stay in the apartment should he and Roger decide to separate. If either person decides that Roger should move out during this period, he shall give (or be given) 30 days' written notice and shall be responsible for his share of the rent and utilities during the 30 days.

4.   After the initial six-month period, if Peter and Roger decide to continue living together, they shall jointly lease the apartment and change half of the utilities into Roger's name. From this point forward, they have equal rights to stay in the apartment, should they break up. If both want to retain the apartment, but either or both wants to end the relationship, a third party will flip a coin to determine who gets to stay.

Dated: _____   Signature: _____
                                                 Roger Rappan

Dated: _____   Signature: _____
                                                 Peter Majors

4.   Legal Relationship of Tenants to Each Other

Although many tenants have problems with their landlords, the truth is that people sharing a home get into more hassles with one another than they do with their landlord. One reason is that we deal with landlords at arm's length and take steps to protect ourselves. We aren't usually businesslike with those we love. But whatever the reason, we've learned that paying reasonable attention to business details helps to preserve romance.

Let's assume you find that wonderful little affordable house next to the park and you and your lover happily sign a lease, or reach a rental agreement with your landlord. Are you each obligated to pay one-half of the rent? No. You've each made a contract obligating you to pay all the rent and be financially responsible for all damage done.

Example: John and Alfonso agree to verbal month-to-month tenancy in a brown-shingle bungalow. After three months, John becomes unhappy with the relationship. One day, he refuses to pay his share of the rent and attacks the house. The result is two broken windows, a badly dented radiator and a refrigerator without a door. Not surprisingly, Alfonso asks John to move out, which he does. Alfonso also asks John to pay for the damage and for his half of the rent. John laughs. Alfonso is legally responsible for all the rent and damage, and the landlord can sue him if he doesn't pay. Alfonso can sue John for reimbursement, but good luck collecting.

Example: Louise and Arlene sign a one-year lease. After six months of amicably living together, Arlene quits her job and leaves. The parting isn't so amicable after Arlene informs Louise that she knows Louise is responsible and will take care of the rent. Louise is liable for it all for the remaining six months. Louise, however, does have a partial out. If she doesn't want to stay, she can try to find someone to take over the remainder of the lease. Even if the lease prohibits subletting and the landlord insists on enforcing it, Louise can legally move out with no financial obligation as long as she finds a suitable new tenant who will pay at least the same rent. This is because the law requires the landlord to do whatever possible to re-rent the apartment ("mitigate damages," in legalese), and not just sit back and insist on the lease payments.

Even though you have a particular legal relationship with the landlord, you will be best off if you come to a complete understanding between yourselves—who pays what portion of the rent, who gets the place if you split up and the like—and write it down. (Use the examples from above.) This isn't binding on your landlord; the main purpose is to record your understandings in the event a dispute later arises.

5. Moving On

What do you do if you decide to go separate ways, but never made a written living together agreement specifying who gets the place? All you can do is make the best effort to compromise, remembering that, in most good compromises, each person believes he gave at least 60%.

Here are a few suggestions when both people want to stay, but not with each other, and haven't written anything down.

- If one person occupied first, pays the rent *and* is the only one who signed the lease or rental agreement, she has a superior claim to the apartment. But she must give the other person (with whom she has a sort of tenant-subtenant relationship) reasonable time (at least 30 days) to find another place.

- If the partners have an equal relationship with the landlord (both pay rent or both signed a lease or rental agreement), they probably have equal rights to stay. This is true even if one occupied first. Flip a coin or have a third person mediate or arbitrate to settle the dispute. Avoid court action if you can. (See Chapter 9, Section B, on gay and lesbian dispute resolution services.)

C. Will I Lose My Public Benefits If My Lover Moves in With Me?

Lesbians and gay men who receive public benefits sometimes worry that they will lose the benefits if their lover moves in. The rules vary from state to state, but in many places, having a lover move in can cause problems, especially if you receive general welfare or Aid to Families with Dependent Children (AFDC). If you receive benefits based on your financial condition and a physical or mental condition—aid to the aged, blind or disabled, for example—you don't risk any loss. These programs function like Social Security—once you qualify, you're left alone.

General welfare, AFDC and food stamp programs, however, are based on your financial condition only. They are large and expensive programs, often the subject of political attack. As a result you may be scrutinized in an effort to weed out "welfare cheats."

An AFDC or general welfare recipient is legally required to tell the welfare department of all changes in her circumstances that could affect her grant. This includes living with a lover (in welfare department terms an "URAW"—unrelated, adult woman) who may be paying some bills. If the recipient doesn't report her lover's presence and the department discovers it, the recipient can be penalized, or even have her grant terminated, on ground of "noncooperation" with the department. If the recipient reports that she's living with her lover, she'll face other problems.

If the welfare department determines that the lover is contributing money to the recipient, her grant will be reduced, normally by the amount contributed. A person is considered to be "contributing" whether she gives $20 a month cash, pays $20 of the rent, pays for food or buys the kids $20 worth of clothing. Moreover, some state regulations presume that a live-in lover contributes a set amount per month to the recipient's family, whether or not she does. And if the lover moves in with a recipient and doesn't contribute toward rent and utilities (or claims she doesn't), she's committing a crime of living off a welfare grant she doesn't qualify for.

The best advice is to treat your lover as a roommate. Under welfare rules, a roommate is not presumed to contribute anything to a welfare recipient. In some counties, welfare officials may require a sworn statement by the "roommate" that she does not contribute to the recipient's support. And if your total rent exceeds the maximum amount allowed by welfare officials, be sure to tell the welfare officials that your "roommate" pays more. (Make sure the bigger room is "hers.")

Also, keep all finances separate. Avoid letting the recipient have any access or control over any of her lover's money or the welfare department will conclude the lover is "contributing" to the family. Avoid letting the lover have access to the recipient's money or the welfare department will conclude the lover is living off the recipient's grant.

Keep food separate, at least in theory; be able to show the welfare department that you buy and store food separately. Keep cupboards marked with each woman's name in case of a home visit by the social worker. Tell the social worker that you prepare and eat all meals separately. Keep a receipt book or ledger showing that your lover pays her share, and only her share, of household expenses, such as rent and utilities. These shares are calculated on a welfare department schedule. Your lover should keep the car registered in her name only, and state that you don't have permission to use it. Yes, all this is quite a hassle, but welfare crackdowns come unpredictably and can lead to jail sentences, not just the termination of benefits.

Having a Child by Artificial Insemination

If you have a child by artificial insemination and apply for AFDC, be aware of the following: If your state doesn't automatically terminate the donor's parental rights and obligations, the welfare department might look for the donor, bring a paternity action to have him declared the father and request that he support the child. Before applying for AFDC, consult a legal aid attorney who can help you keep the donor's identity private.

All of this sounds technical as well as burdensome, we know. But technical or not, we want to stress that it is very important. If possible, try to discuss your situation with a sympathetic case worker before you set up housekeeping or apply for benefits. Most welfare departments can be a bit easier to deal with if you use a little advance planning.

D. Cash and Credit

As most of us eventually learn, often to our chagrin or regret, money is funny stuff

and can do strange things to people. While most of us aspire to rise above crass money concerns, it doesn't require a big dose of realism to see that any couple must clearly agree who pays for the rent, car installments or groceries. If one partner feels she is being monetarily exploited, she is almost guaranteed to be resentful, and perhaps even enraged. A written agreement is essential—though it's surely no substitute for trust and communication. Contracts won't enable two people to continue loving one another or prevent them from splitting up, but if times get hard, a written agreement can do wonders to reduce paranoia and confusion, and help people deal with one another fairly.

1.   Joint Accounts—Dos and Don'ts

As soon as a couple moves in together, questions come up about pooling money (and the property obtained with that money) or keeping it all separate. Because you live with someone doesn't mean your financial lives need become one. If you want to combine finances, be sure you really know and trust your partner. Don't feel pressured to combine everything when you're just starting out simply because the lesbian couple upstairs—who have been together 32 years—have only one bank account.

If you combine bank or credit accounts (meaning both names are on the accounts), both partners are responsible for all activity that takes place with the account. You're equally liable for bounced checks, overdrafts, charges over the limit and all the rest. If, on the other hand, you keep your property and debts separate, you'll have no financial obligation if your lover lives beyond his financial means. This means your paycheck cannot be garnished and your property cannot be taken to satisfy your lover's overdue bills. If your lover declares bankruptcy, your property cannot be taken, as long as you have kept it separate.

Most lesbian and gay couples choose to pool or not pool their resources under one of the following models.

Marriage Model. Property owned prior to the relationship remains the owner's separate property. Property acquired during the relationship is jointly owned, no matter who earns the money to pay for it or who actually acquires it. You put most or all accounts—bank, credit and the like—in both names. If you split up, the property acquired during the relationship is divided fairly or equally.

Socialist Model. You open joint accounts and pay the joint bills out of joint accounts to which you have contributed according to your abilities (such as three-fourths and one-fourth).

Business Partnership Model. You open joint accounts for limited purposes, such as paying household expenses (including the rent) or to fund a distinct project—for example, renovating a house together, saving for a vacation or making a joint investment. If you open a joint account for a specific purpose (such as a vacation), identify it as such. Ask the bank if you can name the account—"The Anderson-Henry Vacation Account." You can supplement your accounts with a living together contract specifying the percentage ownership in all property accumulated together. We use partner-ship-style agreements in many of the sample contracts in this book. (See Chapters 6 and 7.)

Splitsies Model. Here each partner agrees to be absolutely responsible for his or her own support. Like college roommates, each buys separate food, clothes, entertainment and everything else. This couple has no joint accounts. This arrangement can be taken to extremes or can be worked out in a fairly easy-going, common sense, "I-paid-for-breakfast, you-pay-for-lunch" way.

a. Joint Bank Accounts

In general, joint bank accounts are sensible if you limit their purpose and keep adequate records. That said, let us add that we know many lesbian and gay couples who have peacefully maintained joint bank accounts for years. But still, a joint account is a risk; each person has the right to spend all the money, unless you require both signatures on checks and withdrawals—and that can be cumbersome. Another problem is recordkeeping. It's hard to know how much money is in an account if you both write checks and make withdrawals. How many of us dutifully write down withdraw-als every time we visit the ATM? Can (should) we expect our lovers to do any better?

Obtaining a joint account isn't a problem. Financial institutions are happy to have your money under any name or names. You'll have to decide how many signatures will be necessary to write a check or make a withdrawal. It's easier to require only one signature, but it's riskier, too.

b.   Joint Credit Accounts

Joint credit card accounts are even riskier than joint bank accounts—if your lover goes nuts, the most damage he can do with a joint bank account is for the amount you have deposited (or up to your overdraft protection). With a joint credit card, he can charge to the credit limit and potentially do damage to your credit rating. If you want to be generous, you are better off being generous with cash, not credit. Nevertheless, many lesbian and gay couples open joint credit card accounts—again, some for broad purposes and some for limited purposes.

It's fairly easy to put two names on a credit card. You fill out a joint credit card application. Many companies have changed the blanks formerly labeled "spouse" to "co-applicant" or "co-applicant/spouse." If the application form hasn't, cross off the word "spouse" and write in "co-applicant." Don't present yourself as spouses—those terms have specific legal meanings (having to do with liability and responsibility) and lying on the application is fraud.

As long as one of you has sufficient income or savings to be considered a good credit risk (that is, you'll pay the bills), you'll probably get the credit card. Creditors will generally open joint credit accounts—and why shouldn't they? A joint account means more people are responsible for a debt. Thus, if Roger and James have a joint credit card, and Roger lets his sister Fiona charge $2,500 on it, Roger and James are both legally obligated to pay the bill, even if James didn't know about it, or knew about it and opposed it. Similarly, if James retaliates by leaving Roger and going on a

buying binge, Roger is legally responsible for all the charges James makes.

If one of you has a poor credit history, you may be denied a joint card, even if the other's credit is A1. Creditors have tightened their requirements, in light of the relatively high number of defaults and bankruptcies happening in the early '90s. The partner with better credit may have to reapply in his name only. (See Section D1d, below.)

 Just as it doesn't make sense to crawl into bed with someone who has the flu, it isn't wise to open a joint credit account with someone who has a bad case of spendthriftitis. If your lover owes money, her creditors can cause you difficulties if you've mixed your money and property. Indeed, when living with someone with debt problems, sign a contract keeping everything separate to avoid possible confusion.

If you break up, immediately close all joint accounts. All too often, one person feels depressed during the break-up and tries to pamper himself or herself with "retail therapy." Don't just allot the accounts so that each of you keeps some of them. You're both still liable for all accounts—and you could get stuck paying his or her "therapy" bill.

c.   Credit Discrimination

Discrimination against lesbians and gays in credit is no longer common. At least in major urban areas, ability to pay seems to be the criterion used—not sexual identity.

If you believe you were discriminated against when requesting credit, check to see if your state or local municipality has a law barring sexual orientation discrimination. Then see if it covers credit transactions. If it does, report the creditor to the agency that oversees the law.

Beyond this, there is probably little you can do. A federal law bars creditors from discriminating on account of race, color, religion, national origin, sex, marital status or age, or because all or part of a person's income derives from public assistance.[7] It is unlikely that courts will interpret this law to include sexual orientation. In fact, in 1995 a federal court decided the first case we know of that involved such a claim. The court held that a creditor's denial of a low-interest home loan to a gay man and his partner because they were neither "married nor immediate family members" did not violate the Act.[8]

d. Checking Your Credit

If you've lived together for a long period of time, or have had joint credit cards or bank accounts, it's possible that your credit histories have become intertwined, or even erroneously attributed to each other. This is usually not to your advantage, especially if one of you has bad credit. What can you do, aside from getting angry when your credit application is denied? Simple. Check your credit rating.

Credit bureaus are companies that specialize in keeping credit histories on almost everyone. When a bank, department store, landlord or collection agency wants information about a person, they can get it by paying a small fee to a credit bureau. The

federal Fair Credit Reporting Act gives you the right to examine your credit file. If the file contains false or outdated information, the credit bureau is required to correct it, or, if it disputes your claim that it's false or outdated, to include your version of the dispute in your file.[9]

2. Buying and Investing Together

Many couples make purchases and investments together, such as houses and cars. Joint home ownership is covered in Chapter 7. Here we cover joint ownership of and investment in other assets.

It's not difficult to make any joint purchase or investment. Salespeople are used to seeing all combinations of people buying and investing together. In major urban areas, you may be able to find gay or lesbian investment brokers, car brokers, loan brokers and the like. Take a look at the classified section of your local gay or feminist newspaper.

If you make a joint purchase or investment, you should prepare an agreement reflecting your joint ownership or investment percentages. Samples are in Chapter 6. If your purchase or investment comes with an ownership document (car title slip, for example), be sure to complete the document thoroughly. Even if only one of you takes out a loan to finance the purchase or uses separate money to invest or buy, you can both be legal owners, if that's what you want.

Certain property items come with title documents—common examples are motor vehicles and stock certificates. Stock certificates and other documents showing how investments are held are prepared by investment brokers or the company in which you invest. Title documents for motor vehicles are prepared by your state motor vehicle department.

The purpose of a title document is to show the type of ownership you have. In most states, there are three possible ways to jointly own and register property with title certificates. (This information is general. Different states have different procedures. For motor vehicle purchases, check with the local department of motor vehicles for details.)

- *Or,* as in "Renee Parker or Jane Axelrod." If one owner dies, ownership and registration may be transferred to the survivor without going through a court probate proceeding. The "or" form, however, normally permits either owner to sell the car without the permission, or even knowledge, of the other. Also, in many states, the "or" form by itself does not clearly determine whether or not the survivor legally receives the deceased's half.

- *And,* as in "Renee Parker and Jane Axelrod." If one owner dies, her one-half usually passes by her will or living trust, or if she didn't prepare anything, to her "next of kin" (children, parents or siblings). If she wants her lover to inherit her share, she must have a will or living trust so stating. (See Chapter 5.) The "and" form requires both owners' signatures to sell or give away the property.

- *Joint tenants,* as in "Renee Parker and Jane Axelrod as joint tenants" (or JTWROS or "joint tenants with right of survivorship"). If one person dies, ownership passes automatically to the survivor. In many states, creditors won't let the buyers put title in joint tenancy until the loan for the purchase is completely paid off. Joint tenancy requires both signatures to sell or give the property away.

3. Can We File Joint Income Tax Returns?

Only legally married couples who are married on December 31 of the tax year can file joint income tax returns. As of January 1996, nowhere in the United States can lesbian and gay couples legally marry. Lesbian and gay couples can legally marry in Denmark, Greenland, Norway or Sweden if one partner is a citizen of one of those countries. It is doubtful that the marriage would be recognized in this country, however, so even gay and lesbian couples married in other countries probably can't file joint tax returns here. (See Chapter 1 for more information on lesbian and gay marriage.)

If one partner supports the other, however, the supporter can file a tax return as a single person and claim the other as a dependent. This is possible if you meet the five following tests:

Unmarried person. If the supported person is married and files a joint tax return with his spouse (this will be unusual in your situation), the supporting partner in this relationship cannot claim him as a dependent. There's one exception—if the married couple did not earn enough to have to file a tax return, and did so only to get a refund, the supporting partner can claim the dependent.

Citizen or resident. The supported person must be either a U.S. citizen or resident alien, or a citizen of Canada or Mexico.

Income. The supported person's gross income cannot exceed $2,300. Nontaxable money, such as gifts, welfare benefits and nontaxable Social Security benefits don't count toward gross income.

Support. The supporting partner must provide at least 50% of the other partner's total support for the year. Support includes food, shelter, clothing, medical and dental care and education.

Relationship. Normally, dependents must be related by blood, marriage or adoption. But IRS rules also state that "a person who lived in your home as a family member for the entire year can also be considered a dependent. But the relationship must not violate local law." Three calls to the IRS asking what that

sentence meant lead to "it says what it says." (And that was the clearest and most intelligent response.) Our advice: If you meet the other four tests and live in a state where sodomy is against the law, go ahead and claim your lover as a dependent. The worst that can happen is that the IRS won't allow your deduction and your tax bill will be recomputed without the deduction. If you want to fight it, we recommend that you get a copy of *Stand Up to the IRS*, by Frederick W. Daily (Nolo Press).

E. Insurance

Ambrose Bierce observed that insurance is "an ingenious modern game of chance in which the player is permitted to enjoy the comfortable conviction that he is beating the man who keeps the table." Like Bierce, we're no great fans of insurance. Sure, insurance can be necessary or prudent, but it often seems that a giant corporation makes a lot of money by pandering to people's fears or taking advantage of their most basic needs and desires, like making sure their children will be provided for if they die.

Aside from our mistrust of large organizations—not to mention the TV ads full of cavalry charges, folksy neighbors and MTV-style camera work—we're frankly bothered by that contemporary killjoy, the idea that you shouldn't breathe unless you're insured against all possible disasters. Every time a fence closes off a field or an owner blocks off a swimming hole or some other accommodation closes down because people can't afford insurance and won't proceed without it, we all lose. You've heard it at least a dozen times. "Our insurance company says we won't be covered if we let you ..." Or "We're very sorry, but our lawyer won't let us take the risk." It seems like every week an ice-skating rink or child care center closes because it couldn't get or afford insurance.

But sure, there are times when you do need insurance—your home burns down, a child runs in front of your car, someone steals your color TV and VCR or you suffer an injury. Certainly, those so inclined can have lots of fun imagining possible needs for insurance. We do believe that everyone should have automobile (liability) insurance and health insurance. And sadly, people with HIV or another life-threatening illness probably should have disability insurance to prepare for the time they are unable to work.

Beyond that, it is our opinion that most Americans are overinsured much of the time. But rather than whine about insurance, our concern is with the problems lesbian and gay couples face in getting insurance—any kind of insurance. We will let you decide whether or not you need it. If you have a problem obtaining the kind of insurance you want, try to find a gay or lesbian insurance agent. Ask your friends or check the ads in your local gay paper.

1. Health Insurance

It's a great mistake not to have health insurance—assuming you qualify for it and can afford it. Of course, you will want to get insurance before any illness or injury occurs. Some insurance companies will cover you after you suffer an ailment—such as a back injury—but won't pay any coverage for your back. As they put it, they exclude "pre-existing conditions."

Many people obtain health insurance through employment; far more do not, and either have no insurance or purchase it on their own. Group health plans (usually available only through employment) are frequently less expensive and/or provide better coverage than individual plans. In addition, group plans rarely require medical examinations or questionnaires before covering employees. For information on obtaining insurance coverage for your lover or your lover's child through domestic partner benefits, see Chapter 1, Section B.

Affordable health care and health care in general for people with HIV and other life-threatening illnesses continue to be highly charged political issues. We don't have the space to write about them here. Suffice it to say, however, that the lesbian and gay community has gained "health care savvy" over the past decade or so. We support all efforts to make affordable health care a right, not a privilege, in this country.

2. Disability Insurance

Disability insurance pays you a certain sum of money (depending on how much insurance you have) each month while you are unable to work. You may have a state disability plan through your job. Don't assume your employer contributes to the state program—if your employer is self-insured, your coverage will be very different. If you do have state disability insurance, be aware that some states pay out only for a year or two, which is little help if your disability is chronic or long-lasting. In addition, anyone who has had Social Security deducted from his or her pay may qualify for Social Security Disability Insurance (SSI). AIDS qualifies for SSI; cancer may not.

Even if you're covered by state or federal disability plans, the maximum benefits payable in the event of disability may be inadequate. To determine if you need private disability insurance, find out if you're covered by other plans and, if so, how much you'll receive if you're disabled. Also check how many days must lapse between the disability and the coverage—some plans don't take effect for six months. Private disability insurance can help and can literally be a life-prolonger for people with AIDS or cancer. Most insurance agents will be delighted to tell you more about disability insurance than you ever thought you'd want to know.

3. Life Insurance

Most lesbian and gay people we know don't have life insurance, and, with a few exceptions, we don't see any reason for them to get it. Of course, many people get life insurance as a benefit of employment, but otherwise, life insurance makes sense only if:

- you have minor children and there would be insufficient money for their support (remember to consider any Social Security they'll receive) if you die without insurance, or

- you include life insurance in your overall "estate plan"; this especially makes sense if your lover is dependent on you or you rely heavily on each other's incomes—for example, you need both paychecks to make your mortgage payments (see Chapter 5).

If you have a life insurance policy, you can name your lover as the beneficiary. When asked the nature of the relationship, you may have to state "business partners," which is true if you own any property—even a set of dishes—together. You cannot, however, buy a policy on your lover's life and name yourself as the beneficiary. Insurance companies don't believe that non-married partners have an "insurable interest" in each other, and limit buying insurance on another person to married spouses or business partners.

4. Homeowner's or Renter's Insurance

Homeowner's (or hazard) insurance is sold to homeowners when they buy a house. It insures the house against fire, flood and other acts of destruction. Any lesbian or gay couple that buys a house together will be required to have homeowner's insurance. You shouldn't have any trouble getting a joint policy. (See Chapter 7 for more information on buying a house together.)

Renter's insurance protects tenants against the loss of their property due to theft or some act of destruction. (A landlord's homeowner's policy covers only the building structure, not your possessions.) Although we know one gay couple that was refused a joint renters' policy, most lesbian and gay couples have no trouble getting joint renters' insurance. The couple denied the insurance was told by the company that it didn't insure gay couples because if the couple broke up and one person moved out, taking the other's possessions, the remaining person could claim "theft" of the missing property. (That is indeed what the insurance agent said—we checked.) Of course, this characterization of gay relationships is nonsense, but so is all discrimination that lesbian and gay couples face in their lives.

Our friends wound up with two policies (one each), but most people we know get one policy. Insurance companies, for the most part, insure property—not people—and are willing to issue one policy for a given address. They don't care who lives in the place or what the relationship is. If you do have to buy two policies, it's usually more expensive than covering everything with one policy. (But on the whole, renter's insurance is pretty cheap.) In addition, we've been told by a gay insurance agent that if you buy two policies, use the same insurance company. Two giant companies asked to settle a claim may try to shift

responsibility to the other, rather than write you a check and let you replace the lost, stolen or damaged property.

5. Automobile Insurance

Being the registered owner of a car carries with it possible liability. In most states, a registered owner is financially responsible for any accident caused by his car, even if someone else is driving. The owner (or his insurance company) can pursue the driver for the money paid to the injured person, but the owner is liable even if the driver takes the first boat to Tahiti. The reason for this is simple and sound: It encourages car owners to carry insurance, and to carefully select who can drive their cars. As a practical matter, it means that you don't let just anyone (even your lover) drive your car unless you have ample insurance.

We strongly urge car owners to carry auto insurance—and in many states it is legally required. The automobile is the only lethal weapon most people use regularly. The statistical risk of an accident is all too high, and, if an accident occurs, there's a good chance that the damage will be serious. If you don't carry insurance, you may be wiped out economically, and even worse, an injured person may go without compensation because of your irresponsibility.

If you and your lover each own a car separately, you will have trouble getting one insurance policy. Insurers won't insure you and your cars as if you were married, but rather, will write you each a separate policy, and name the other as secondary driver. Of course, this costs more, which is probably one reason companies do it. If you really want one policy, change your title slips (you have to call the motor vehicles department), putting both cars in one person's name. The insurance will list the owner as the primary driver, and the other as a secondary driver. Of course, you'll need a separate written agreement stating clearly who really owns which car.

Even if you and your lover jointly own a car, you may have some trouble securing the policy you want. You shouldn't have too much trouble getting a joint policy, as long as your household looks stable and your driving records are good. But you may run into some other snags.

Some insurance companies refuse any secondary coverage to unrelated people who co-own a car. This means that you and your lover would be insured for accidents that occur when you're driving or riding in the car you own, but not while driving or riding in other cars (such as a rental car) or while you are a pedestrian. And other companies require that you designate just one person the "primary owner"—the company then provides secondary insurance for that person only. You may have to talk with a number of insurance agents before you find a policy that will provide complete coverage for both you and your lover.

F. Can My Foreign Lover Come Visit or Live With Me?

Suppose a fantasy comes true: You take a trip abroad and meet the person of your dreams, who just happens to be a citizen of that distant land. You come home and go back to work to earn money to take your next vacation. In the mean time, your new lover wants to know if any laws will stop him from visiting you in America. More optimistically, he wants to know that if he arrives here and you find that the sparks still fly, he can stay here with you.

1. Visiting the United States

Until 1990, lesbians and gay men coming to the United States for any reason at all could be denied entry if immigration authorities learned of their sexual orientation. This is because the former immigration law barred the admission of "sexual deviants" to the U.S. Although a 1983 court decision made it difficult for the Immigration and Naturalization Service (INS) to enforce the law, that case was limited to California, Nevada, Arizona, Idaho, Montana, Washington, Oregon, Alaska and Hawaii.[10] In other parts of the country, INS officers routinely told lesbians and gay men to go home when their sexual orientation became known. Now, however, no law restricts gay men and lesbians from entering the U.S. for a visit.

HIV, however, is still on the list of contagious diseases that denies entry to this country. This means that any person known to have HIV cannot come to the U.S., even for a short visit, unless the Justice Department issues a waiver. Although President Clinton had expressed interest in removing HIV from the list, Congress overrode him and enacted it into law.

2. Moving to the United States

Our friend Jane was traveling in Venice, and sent the following letter:

I met a woman named Sophie near the Bridge of Sighs whose hair smells of apples. She dresses in feathers and taffeta; her eyes are filled with magic and her heart with tenderness. She knows strange songs. I think I'm in love.

Jane was determined that theirs was a travel romance that wouldn't die after a few letters. Several months after Jane returned from her trip, Sophie came to the U.S. on a six-month tourist visa. As the six-month period was coming to an end, Jane and Sophie struggled to figure out a way for Sophie to stay.

There are thousands of Sophies in the world—lesbians or gay men who are not U.S. citizens or permanent residents who want to move to the U.S. Most Sophies want to move here for one of the following reasons:

• Like our Sophie, she or he gets involved with a U.S. citizen or permanent resident, and the couple wants to live together in the U.S. A heterosexual U.S. citizen/ resident can simply marry the non-citizen/resident and petition the government for residency rights for his or her spouse. Similarly, a U.S. citizen/resident can petition the government for residency rights for a parent, child over age 21 or sibling. Jane and Sophie considered adoption—that is, Jane would adopt Sophie—but the adopted child must be under age 14 to qualify for U.S. residency following a foreign adoption.

• Some Sophies aren't involved with Americans, but with a person from his or her own country who gets a temporary visa to work, study or do business in the U.S. The heterosexual spouse of Sophie is entitled to bring Sophie to the U.S. for the duration of the visa. A gay or lesbian Sophie must stay home.

• Sophie resides in a country that persecutes lesbians and/or gay men, and seeks refugee asylum in the U.S. (Our Sophie, who is from Italy, would not qualify for refugee status.) To qualify, the person must convince the INS that he or she has a well-founded fear of persecution based on his or her sexual orientation. (Until mid-1994, the person had to argue that persecution based on sexual orientation could even qualify someone for asylum; then the person had to show the actual fear of persecution. In June of 1994, however, the Justice Department expressly ruled that sexual orientation persecution would qualify.) Several cases have been filed in the U.S., but only a handful have succeeded—blocking the deportation of a gay Cuban, a gay Nicaraguan, a gay Brazilian and a gay Mexican.

At least two dozen other cases are pending involving gays and lesbians from Colombia, Turkey, Russia, Iran and Hong Kong.

Anyone seriously considering applying for refugee status in the U.S. should contact a gay-sensitive immigration attorney, one of the gay legal organizations listed in Chapter 10, Section E, and the International Gay and Lesbian Human Rights Commission, 1360 Mission Street, Suite 200, San Francisco, CA 94103, (415) 255-8680 (phone), (415) 255-8662 (fax). An attorney will want to gather evidence such as the text of anti-gay laws from the country of origination and documented persecutions of other homosexuals. (IGLHRC may have this information.)

Countries With Residency Rights for Lovers of Gay Men and Lesbians

In the following countries, gay men and lesbians are permitted to stay based on their involvement with a citizen or permanent resident of the country:

- **Australia.** Must be together two years before non-citizen/resident can apply for permanent residency.

- **Denmark.** Must be together two years before non-citizen/resident can apply for permanent residency. The couple may also register as domestic partners. (See Chapter 1.)

- **Netherlands.** Must be together three years before non-citizen/resident can apply for permanent residency.

- **New Zealand.** Must be together four years before non-citizen/resident can apply for permanent residency.

- **Norway.** Must be together two years before non-citizen/resident can apply for permanent residency.

- **Sweden.** Must be together two years before non-citizen/resident can apply for permanent residency.

- **Canada.** The Lesbian and Gay Immigration Task Force is lobbying the Canadian Parliament and has filed two cases in an effort to allow partners of Canadians to remain in the country. In both cases, the lovers were allowed to stay, although not because of the relationships. Gay and lesbian activists in Canada do expect the law to be changed to allow gay and lesbian lovers of Canadians to obtain residency.

When Jane and Sophie talked to us, we told them that legally, their future together in the U.S. looked bleak. We suggested that if Sophie had worked in a senior level position with a multinational corporation or had any special skills and had worked for at least two years in that field using her skills, she might qualify for an immigrant visa as a special worker or skilled worker. Sophie looked distraught, however, knowing she didn't possess any special skills. That was the last we saw of them for over a year. When we met again, they were arm-in-arm, and all smiles. Jane told us that they proceeded on a course that would have been illegal for us, as attorneys, to suggest, but which worked.

She and Sophie met Jacob, a gay American man who needed to marry for professional reasons. They arranged a marriage, along with a tidy prenuptial agreement keeping all their property separate. Sophie moved some clothing and a toothbrush to Jacob's apartment and even lived with him until they passed the grueling INS post-marriage interview, where the INS tries to weed out "fraudulent" marriages. After the interview, she moved in with Jane. We mentioned that we knew other couples forced to adopt the same subterfuge, but that we also knew the INS's high priority on discovering these "fraudulent" marriages. Jane responded that they were familiar with the INS practices and in consequence had been scrupulously discreet, telling absolutely no one about the arrangement who didn't need to know. We wished them good luck.

Support for Lesbian and Gay Inter-National Couples

The Inter-National Spouses Network is an organization that provides mutual support, public education and lobbying efforts for inter-national lesbian and gay couples seeking immigration rights for the non-U.S. partners. The organization appealed to the Attorney General (the Justice Department has jurisdiction over the Immigration and Naturalization Service) to prepare an administrative order recognizing lesbian and gay relationships for immigration purposes on humanitarian and compassionate grounds. The INS's response was that it couldn't issue an order because the INS can grant visas only to legally recognized married partners of U.S. citizens or permanent residents. (Kind of circular, don't you think?) You can contact the Inter-National Spouses Network at 1010 University Ave., #171, San Diego, CA 92103, (619) 688-0094.

Endnotes

[1] This is changing, however. A wonderful book for lesbian and gay couples planning a trip across the Atlantic is *Are You Two...Together? A Gay and Lesbian Travel Guide to Europe*, by Lindsy Van Gelder and Pamela Robin Brandt (Random House). Also, many large cities have lesbian or gay operated travel agencies. Several gay and lesbian resorts, hotels, cruise lines and the like have opened over the past few years. And in 1992, mi casa; su casa (my house is your house), an international home exchange for gay and lesbian travelers, began in Oakland, California.

[2] For a complete list, contact the National Gay and Lesbian Task Force, 1734 14th St., N.W., Washington, DC 20009; (202) 332-6483.

[3] *Engel v. Worthington*, 19 Cal.App.4th 43 (original cite); 94 Daily Journal D.A.R. 1467 (depublication cite).

[4] See *Hubert v. Williams*, 133 Cal.App.3d 1 (1982).

[5] *Smith v. Fair Employment and Housing*, 12 Cal. 4th 1143 (1996).

[6] There are many books on landlord-tenant law, including Nolo's *Tenants' Rights*, by Myron Moskovitz and Ralph Warner (California Edition). Also, tenants' advocacy groups exist in many cities. If you have a serious problem and you can't get help or information any other way, consider a one-time consultation with a lawyer. (See Chapter 10.)

[7] Equal Credit Opportunity Act (ECOA) 15 U.S.C. § 1691.

[8] *Bagley v. California Federal Bank*, CV 93-7027 (C.D. Cal., 1995).

[9] For more information on credit bureaus and paying debts, see *Money Troubles: Legal Strategies to Cope With Your Debts*, by Robin Leonard (Nolo Press).

[10] *Hill v. INS*, 714 F.2d 1470 (9th Cir. 1983). ∎

CHAPTER 3

I'm Mom, She's Mommy (Or I'm Dad, He's Papa)

The desire to be a parent and raise a child is perhaps as prevalent among lesbians and gay men as it is among non-gays, and the reasons are just as complex. Many feel the basic human desire to parent and nurture. Some believe that having a child ensures their immortality; still others wish to meet their parents' insistence on grandchildren. Indeed, for many lesbians and gay men, the only undesired consequence of their sexual orientation is the inability to have a child with the person they love.

Lesbians and gay men who wish to raise a child often face social and legal obstacles. But those barriers were much greater ten years ago than they are today. Laws relating to lesbian and gay couples having and raising children are changing with fascinating rapidity. (By the time you read this, the law will have no doubt changed in some states.) After centuries in which it was impossible for a person to be openly gay and raise a child, a growing number of segments of American society have begun to understand that a person's (or couple's) sexual orientation has no bearing on the ability to love and parent.

There are many excellent materials on the emotional and financial realities of raising a child.[1] Although we provide the most up-to-date information we have, let us again emphasize that this area of law changes so quickly there may be new legal developments by the time you read these words. Don't rely on our information as being definitive, but treat it as a place to start your own exploration of the process of bringing a child into your home.

Besides the obvious opportunities to become a "Big Brother" or the loving "aunt" to the little girl down the street, there are ways to legally cement your relationship with a child. Women, obviously, can bear children, and men may be able to arrange to have a child with a surrogate mother. Both men and women can become adoptive parents, foster parents or guardians.

Before we get further into this chapter, let us remind you of something you probably already know. Don't underestimate the power of a child. The entry of a small being into your lives will change you drastically—and permanently. The mother of one of the authors, who raised seven children, wrote:

Most people take on the job, whether it's their own biological child or an adopted one, with unreasonable expectations as to the amount of pleasure versus the amount of frustration and resentment. Maybe children should come labeled "Warning, the Surgeon General advises that child raising may be dangerous to your health, way of life, and peace of mind."

Still, children offer fulfillment and fun, and most parents we know (including the author's mom) are pretty pleased with their lot, all things considered. A lesbian or gay

couple must decide up front the practical issues in raising a child:

- Who will make day-to-day decisions?
- How open will you be with neighbors, school officials and doctors?
- Will one of you stay home with the baby?
- If not, how will you handle child care— and illnesses, emergency calls from schools and the like once your child starts school?

These are only some of the issues. We aren't authorities on child raising. We know many, many gay men and lesbians who are raising children, and are cheered by what we see. Love, commitment and understanding are clearly what matter most. The best creative expression of this that we know of is the film *Choosing Children,* about lesbian mothers who chose to become parents *after* coming out.[2]

Doctors Who Reach Out to Children of Gay and Lesbian Parents

In San Francisco, a clinic affiliated with the University of California has opened to treat the children of lesbian and gay parents. The doctors who opened the Rainbow Clinic feel that pediatric care will improve when a family knows it can be open about who they are without feeling stigmatized or ostracized. The clinic provides routine and emergency pediatric services, and as it grows, intends to offer discussion groups for gay and lesbian parents, a resource library and services for gay and lesbian adolescents.

A. Who Is a Legal Parent?

There are all kinds of parents in this world—loving, compassionate, youthful, open-minded, distant, stern—the adjectives go on and on. But when we describe parents—ours or any others we know—the last term we'd use is "legal." Yet for gay and lesbian couples wanting to raise a child, the question of legal parent is of utmost importance. (Before we get into how it applies to lesbian and gay parents, bear with us as we explain a little about heterosexual parents.)

A legal parent is a parent who has the right to be with a child and make decisions about the child's health, education and well-being. A legal parent is also obligated to support that child. When a married couple has or adopts a child, both partners are automatically considered legal parents. Even if they split up and the court awards custody to one parent and orders the other to pay child support, they both remain legal parents unless a court terminates either mom's or dad's parental rights. This rarely happens, unless the parent abandons a child or consents to the adoption of the child by the other parent's new spouse.

If the parent does not consent to adoption by the other parent's new spouse, also know as the stepparent, then the stepparent is not a legal parent. As much as he may be involved in raising and supporting the child, if the couple splits up, he won't be entitled to custody or obligated to pay child support. (In a few states, he may be granted visitation with the child if he has formed a psychological bond with the child and it would be in the child's best interest to continue the contact.)

So now let us tell you what this has to do with you. You see, the great gay and lesbian baby boom of the 1980s and 1990s (an estimated 10,000 lesbians and gay men have had or adopted children during the past 10-15 years) has had only one major downside: Until recently, in most families, only one partner was recognized as the legal parent. Only one of you can be a biological parent. And we all assumed that state laws were written in a way to make adoption and foster parenting available only to married couples or single people. And if a "single" person (such as the partner of the biological parent) sought to adopt, the biological parent's rights would first have to be terminated—hardly a result a lesbian or gay couple wanted.

But then gay and lesbian lawyers got smart. They began reading the text of state adoption statutes. Most laws, they realized, authorized adoptions by married couples and single people, but didn't expressly exclude unmarried couples. Similarly, they read stepparent adoption statutes. While all these statutes expressly authorized adoptions by the new spouse of a legal parent if the other legal parent was dead, had his parental rights terminated, abandoned the child or consented to the adoption, the statutes did not forbid an unmarried partner from becoming a stepparent.

And now the good news: As of January 1996, joint adoptions by lesbian and gay couples or second-parent (the equivalent of stepparent) adoptions have been granted in many states. Alaska was the first state to grant a joint adoption—it did so in 1985. Since then, joint adoptions have been granted in California, Colorado, the District of Columbia, Illinois, Indiana, Massachusetts, Michigan, Minnesota, New Jersey, New York, Oregon, Pennsylvania, Texas, Vermont and Washington.

Of course, some courts and legislatures are attempting to block joint adoptions by lesbian and gay couples. In New York, courts have denied second-parent adoptions in the past, but this is likely to change—a 1995 ruling from the New York Supreme Court has cleared the way for joint adoptions throughout the state. Similar rulings in favor of joint adoptions have been issued by the highest courts in the District of Columbia, Massachusetts and Vermont.

Unfortunately, the Wisconsin Supreme Court denied a second-parent adoption in 1994. And as we go to print, the high court ruling allowing joint adoptions in the District of Columbia is under threat from Congress. The House Appropriations Committee, while giving final approval to the District of Columbia budget, approved an amendment that bans all adoptions by unmarried couples. If this measure passes, it won't bar lesbians or gay men from adopting children, but it will end the legal recognition of same-sex families bestowed by the court decision.

In California, joint adoptions became almost routine in recent years, especially in San Francisco, Los Angeles, Alameda and other liberal counties. In 1995, however, California Governor Pete Wilson overturned a Department of Social Services policy that allowed adoptions by qualified unmarried couples, whether gay or straight. Now, lesbian and gay couples will be automatically rejected by state social workers in their bids to adopt children—they will have to fight their cases in court. But the good news is that in most cases, they'll win.

Joint adoption procedures vary widely from state to state. In Minnesota, for example, the court typically terminates the parental rights of the biological parent and then grants a joint adoption. In Washington, on the other hand, joint adoptions are handled like stepparent adoptions, which are simplified and don't require a social worker.

Most of these cases are done as quietly as possible, with little press and hoopla. Lawyers who represent gay and lesbian parents have developed excellent relationships with county social workers and judges who grant adoptions. Most cases end at the trial court level—this means no one appeals. And it's not a surprise, given that no one usually opposes an adoption. The judge doesn't have to make a decision about placing a child in a gay household—the child will be raised there no matter what the judge decides. And judges love to grant adoptions—an adoption gives a judge a chance to put a family together, rather than to watch one fall apart.

If you want to petition a court for a joint or second-parent adoption—whether or not your state is listed above—you will need the help of a lawyer. If you know people who have been granted a joint or second-parent adoption, call them and find out who they used. If you don't know anyone to call, contact the National Center for Lesbian Rights, Lambda Legal Defense and Education Fund or Gay and Lesbian Advocates and Defenders—the three national lesbian and gay legal organizations. Their addresses and phone numbers are in Chapter 10, Section E. They should be able to help you find a lawyer nearby.

And if your lawyer needs assistance in preparing materials for court, let him or her know that the National Center for Lesbian Rights has available a trial brief (the argument your lawyer must submit to the court) about why a joint and second-parent adoption is not about gay rights, but is simply in your child's best interest.

Can Your Child Have More Than Two Legal Parents?

The gay and lesbian community has created all kinds of families over the past 10-15 years. As gay men and lesbians gain the rights to jointly parent, they must ask another logical question: Can a child have *more* than two legal parents?

We know of lesbians and gay men who marry and have children—what legal role with the children, if any, do the lovers of the parents have? Or what about lesbian and gay couples who raise a child together—that is, four parents to one child (perhaps a ratio more families ought to try)?

And even more common is for a lesbian couple to have a child using the semen of a gay male friend. Often, the man is merely a donor—neither he nor the moms want him involved with raising the child. But sometimes, the man is actively involved in raising the child. Can the child have three legal parents? The answer is "possibly." In Alaska and Oregon, courts have declared both partners in a lesbian couple and the gay man who fathered the child all to be the legal parents of the child. A similar case is pending in California.

B. Protections for "Unrecognized" Co-Parents

If only one of you is (or will be) the legal parent of your child, you will need to outline, in writing, your understanding. The purpose is to give the nonlegal parent as much protection as possible vis-a-vis the child in the event the legal parent is absent or the couple splits up.

Quite frankly, the enforcement of this kind of an agreement is shaky, at best. In general, when parents split up and fight over custody or child support, they can get before a judge in one of two ways: as part of a divorce or as part of a paternity (proof of fatherhood) case. Clearly, the legal system will have to come up with a third method for gay and lesbian legal co-parents.

Until recently, when a legal parent and her partner split up, there has been virtually no way for the nonlegal parent to assert her rights in court. Lesbian co-parents in California, Florida and New York, for example, while receiving sympathy from the judge, didn't get visitation rights with the child they raised with the legal parent. But things seem to be slowly changing. Since the end of 1994, court-ordered visitation has been granted to lesbian co-parents in Michigan, New Hampshire, Utah and Wisconsin. The Wisconsin Supreme Court is the first state high court to hold that a lesbian co-parent can seek visitation after the breakup of her partnership with a child's biological mother.

No matter what the state of the law, we recommend that you take two steps if only one of you is the legal parent of your child: First, write up your agreement specifying that although only one of you is the legal parent, you both consider both of you parents, with all the rights and responsibilities that come with parenting. Include a mandatory mediation (non-adversarial dispute resolution) and arbitration clause in your agreement in the event you do break up. Second, if you should split up, **honor the agreement.** It will only hurt your child if you don't.

AGREEMENT TO JOINTLY RAISE OUR CHILD

We, Erica Lang and Maria Ramos, make this agreement to set out our rights and obligations regarding our child who'll be born to us by Erica. We realize that our power to contract, as far as a child is concerned, is limited by state law. We also understand that the law will recognize Erica as the only mother of the child. With this knowledge, and in a spirit of cooperation and mutual respect, we state the following as our agreement:

1. It's our intention to jointly and equally parent, including providing support and guidance. We will do our best to jointly share the responsibilities involved in feeding, clothing, loving, raising and disciplining our child.

2. Erica will sign a consent for medical authorization giving Maria equal power to make medical decisions she thinks are necessary for the child.

3. We both agree to be responsible for our child's support until she or he reaches the age of majority (or finishes college). We each agree to contribute to our child's support equally. This agreement to provide support is binding, whether or not we live together.

4. Our child will be given the last name "Ramos-Lang."

5. Erica agrees to designate Maria as guardian of Erica's estate, and of the child, in her will. We understand that naming Maria legal guardian of the child in Erica's will isn't legally binding, but believe it should be persuasive in court.

6. Because of the possible trauma our separation might cause our child, we agree to participate in a jointly agreed-upon program of counseling if either considers separating.

7. If we separate, we will both do our best to see that our child grows up in a good and healthy environment. Specifically, we agree that:

a. We will do our best to see that our child maintains a close and loving relationship with each of us.

b. We will share in our child's upbringing, and will share in our child's support, depending on our needs, our child's needs and on our respective abilities to pay.

c. We will make a good-faith effort to jointly make all major decisions affecting our child's health and welfare.

d. We will base all decisions upon the best interests of our child.

e. Should our child spend a greater portion of the year living with one of us, the person who has actual physical custody will take all steps necessary to maximize the other's visitation, and help make visitation as easy as possible.

f. If either of us die, our child will be cared for and raised by the other, whether or not we are living together. We will each state this in our wills.

8. Should any dispute arise between us regarding this agreement, we agree to submit the dispute first to mediation. If mediation is not successful, we agree to submit to binding arbitration, sharing the cost equally. In the event of such dispute, the arbitrator will be _____. **[See Chapter 9, Section B, for more detailed information on arbitration and mediation.]**

9. We agree that if any court finds any portion of this contract illegal or otherwise unenforceable, the rest of the contract is still valid and in full force.

Executed at: _____

Dated: _____   Signature: _____
                                        Erica Lang

Dated: _____   Signature: _____
                                        Maria Ramos

C. Having Your Own Child

The birds and the bees are doing it,

Lesbians, even Lebanese are doing it,

Guys in heels and silk chamois are doing it.[3]

They are having babies. With great planning and consideration, lesbians and gay men are bringing much wanted and well-loved children into the world. Some lesbians and gay men have married just to have children. We won't discuss this here; there's ample literature—both fiction and nonfiction—about the consequences of such arrangements. Aside from marriage, there are other ways to have your own child. Lesbians can get pregnant. Gay men don't have the same biological opportunity, but can try to find women willing to bear their children.

If you are like most lesbians and gay men who consider having a child, you may be asking any of the following questions:

• Is it possible for my lover and me to raise a child without interference from the sperm donor?

• If the sperm donor now agrees to let me bring up the child myself, how can I be sure he'll never seek custody?

• If I agree to be a sperm donor, can I later be held liable for support?

• Is it really possible—and legal—for me to pay a woman to give birth to my child?

The answers are complex. A man and a woman can write an agreement concerning their rights and obligations to each other and the child, but neither the child nor the state is bound by the agreement. A child has the right to receive support from both legal parents (unless a parent's rights have been terminated or that parent is not *legally* considered to be a parent) until she becomes a legal adult. Agreements regarding custody and visitation are recognized by courts, but a court can decide that an agreement isn't in "the best interests of the child" and ignore it.

A lesbian who doesn't want to share parenting with her child's father has several choices. The most obvious is to not let him know he's parenting. While this approach can sometimes work, it often presents problems. For one, having casual sex with someone can be dangerous. Second, it often takes more than one or two leaps in the hay to get pregnant. And third, there are moral questions—should a woman feign a relationship with a man just to get pregnant? Should the mother conceal the identity of the father from the child when the mother knows it?

1. When a Lesbian and a Gay Man Parent Together

One arrangement is for a lesbian and gay man to have and raise a child together. They don't have to get married, and often they don't. They won't have an intimate relationship, other than being good friends and the parents of the same child.

Example: Julie wanted a child. She also wanted one of her male friends to be the father so that the child would have the emotional and financial support of a father. She ruled out her straight friends, fearing that they'd be preferred if any custody dispute developed. On the other hand, she was concerned about the HIV status of her gay male friends.

Her friend Victor also wanted to be a parent. He agreed to be tested for HIV every month for six months. If the results were negative, he would parent with Julie—she would have custody and he would have visitation. They knew they were each obligating themselves for support until the child reached legal adulthood.

Julie and Victor arranged for counseling, to get support for their arrangement and to test the sincerity of their commitment. They realized that their agreement would probably not be legally binding if challenged in court, but they knew it was important to write down their understanding, both for clarity and to refresh their memories in the future.

Here's the agreement they made regarding their daughter, Leslie.

CONTRACT REGARDING CHILD SUPPORT AND CUSTODY

This agreement is made between Julie Shatz and Victor Lawrence to express our understanding as to our rights and responsibilities to our child. We fully realize that our power to make this contract is limited by state law. With this knowledge, and in a spirit of cooperation and mutual respect, we wish to state the following to be our agreement:

1. Within ten days after the birth, Victor will sign a statement acknowledging that he's the father; his name will be on the birth certificate.

2. Our child will be given the last name Shatz.

3. Julie will have physical custody; Victor will have reasonable rights of visitation. Julie will be sensitive to Victor's needs and will cooperate in all practical ways to make visitation as easy as possible.

4. Both of us will do our best to see that our child has a close and loving relationship with each parent.

5. Victor will provide support in the amount of $200 a month for the first year after our child is born. Thereafter, we will arrive at a mutual agreement each year for the amount Victor will pay, taking into account:

    a. The needs of our child

    b. Increases in the cost of living

    c. Changes in Victor's salary and income

    d. Changes in Julie's salary and income.

6. We will make a good-faith effort to jointly make all major decisions affecting our child's health and welfare.

7. If either Julie or Victor dies, our child will be cared for and raised by the other.

8. If any dispute or problem arises between us regarding our child, we agree to seek counseling and professional help to try to resolve those problems.

Dated: _____ Signature: _____
                                              Julie Shatz

Dated: _____ Signature: _____
                                              Victor Lawrence

Signing a parenthood statement. If the biological father will be involved with raising the child and he isn't married to the mother, he should sign a written statement acknowledging paternity as soon as possible after the child's birth. In addition, the mother should sign a statement acknowledging his parenthood. Whether or not he signs a statement, the father is legally responsible for support. Signing a statement is the simplest way to avoid the brambles of the law concerning legitimacy, inheritance, father's rights and the like. Signing just after the baby is born (before any disputes arise) is the best protection for the mother, the baby and especially a father who wants rights of visitation as well as duties of parenthood.

Below is a parenthood statement. You will want to prepare three copies—and date, sign and notarize all three. The mother and father should each keep a copy, and the third copy should be kept safe for the child. While legal distinctions between "legitimate" and "illegitimate" children are fast disappearing, they still come up. Having the father sign this statement makes a child legitimate in almost all states, as if the parents had been married.

ACKNOWLEDGMENT OF PARENTHOOD

Julie Shatz and Victor Lawrence hereby acknowledge that they are the biological parents of Leslie Shatz, born April 18, 19__, in Eugene, Oregon.

Julie Shatz and Victor Lawrence further state that they've welcomed Leslie Shatz into their lives and that it is their intention and belief that they've taken all steps necessary to fully legitimate their child for all purposes, including the right to inherit from and through Victor Lawrence.

Julie Shatz and Victor Lawrence further expressly acknowledge their legal duty to properly raise and adequately support Leslie Shatz.

Dated: _____   Signature: _____
                                        Julie Shatz

Dated: _____   Signature: _____
                                        Victor Lawrence

---

2. Lesbians Having Children by Artificial Insemination

Artificial insemination isn't artificial from the point of view of reproduction, and for this reason and others, many people now refer to artificial insemination as alternative or donor insemination. Sperm is injected into the uterus and, if it fertilizes an egg, a child develops. The woman doesn't have intercourse. For lesbians, artificial insemination is a highly desirable—and probably the most common—way to become a parent.[4]

Artificial insemination is often used when a married woman is unable to become pregnant through sexual intercourse with her husband. If her husband is able to produce sperm, she will be inseminated with his semen. If he is not, she will be inseminated with the semen of a donor (often chosen because he has characteristics similar to the husband's). The donor has no legal rights to or obligations toward the child—the husband is legally considered the father.

Although this is the position today, it took 200 years to get there. Artificial insemination was first used by women at the end of the 18th century. Many churches declared it sinful. The Catholic Church's views were expressed by Gannon F. Ryan, Chaplin, St. Thomas More Chapel, Syracuse University, discussing whether the church would ever condone artificial insemination:[5]

We reply no and under no circumstances, because the evil of both masturbation and adultery are involved, thus making the procedure most repugnantly wicked. The agreement of all parties doesn't alter the immorality of the procedure. We cannot vote to violate the Laws of God. Even a desirable end,

such as children in the home, cannot justify an evil means to achieve it. This is elementary.

While churches wrestled with moral issues, courts faced the question of whether the husband was the father of the child. It took them nearly 20 years to say "yes."

- In 1954, an Illinois court found that the husband was not the legal father: "With or without consent of the husband [it] is contrary to public policy and good morals, and constitutes adultery on the part of the mother. A child so conceived isn't a child born in wedlock and is therefore illegitimate."[6]

- In 1973, a New York Court found that the husband, who had consented to the insemination by a donor, was the lawful father: "a child born of consensual artificial insemination by a donor during a valid marriage is a legitimate child entitled to the rights and privileges of a naturally conceived child of the same marriage."[7]

For lesbians, there are many advantages to conceiving by artificial insemination. It can be done without medical personnel or any great expertise. Also, unlike adoption, artificial insemination avoids entanglement with the state; no social worker comes snooping into your life. Finally, if the woman uses a sperm bank, the identity of the donor can be (and usually is) kept secret, thus eliminating future problems of custody and visitation.

But if she uses a known donor, is he considered the father? If she had a husband, clearly the answer would be no. For lesbians, there is no easy answer. Artificial insemination laws vary from state to state—most states' laws apply only to married women. Several states don't have any laws.

a. Do We Really Have to Learn Law Just to Choose a Donor?

If you want to eliminate the potential possibility that your donor will assert himself as the father, go the route of an anonymous donor. You can contact a sperm bank yourself or you can ask your doctor to obtain sperm from a sperm bank for you. Sperm banks are often associated with medical schools and donors are usually medical students. You can specify race, religion, complexion and often even height. The donors are asked to provide a thorough medical history (including illnesses of parents and grandparents) and are tested for diseases—both personal (such as syphilis and AIDS) and hereditary (such as sickle-cell anemia). The donor remains anonymous and will never have the rights or obligations of a parent.

Some women object to using a sperm bank—it's impersonal, it usually requires that a doctor get involved and if, heaven forbid, the child should have a rare illness that the sperm bank never tested for, it might be impossible to find the donor. If you want to use a known donor, we highly recommend that you get a copy of *Artificial Insemination: An Alternative Conception*, which covers finding donors, screening them, getting medical information, planning the time of the insemination and arranging for the delivery of the semen.[8] But keep in mind that if you don't use a sperm bank, you are taking a risk that the donor will assert himself as the father.

A few states offer you some protection. In Oregon, for example, the law states that a man who donates his semen for use in artificial insemination with a woman other than his wife loses all parental rights. A court interpreting this law held that it is valid as long as the woman and the donor did not have an agreement giving him rights to parenthood. If they had made such an agreement, the court ruled, then this statute would unconstitutionally take away his right to be a father.[9]

In Colorado, the statute states that the "donor of semen provided to a licensed physician for use in artificial insemination in a woman other than the donor's wife" is not considered the legal father. In a case interpreting its statute, the court focused on the absence of the word "married" before the word "woman" in the law. The court held the law to be ambiguous with respect to known donors and unmarried women, and therefore examined the mother and the donor's conversations, understandings and agreements.[10] This case emphasizes the need to be clear and consistent in your dealings with any known donor.

If you will use a known donor, you have basically two ways to select him:

• You can use a man you know or are introduced to who has assured you that he doesn't want to be the father. This requires tremendous trust and is very risky.

In a New York case, for example, a lesbian couple had two children using different donors. The first donor waived all parental rights. So did the second donor (a gay man), but he agreed to be available if the child asked about her biological origin. The child did and the donor eventually sued for paternity. New York has no relevant statute and the mother and donor did not write down their agreement. Although the court ruled against the donor—upholding the rights of lesbians to create their own families—the case was an emotional drain, lasting two years, and has lead to much dissension in New York's lesbian and gay community.[11]

• Have a friend select the donor. You and the donor remain anonymous to each other, but your friend knows both identities. Often people take the added precaution of having the intermediary pick up semen from more than one donor and mixing it together so even the intermediary isn't sure whose sperm actually fertilized the egg. This may lessen the chances of conception, however, as antigens in the two semen samples may conflict and inhibit fertilization.

In Section c, below, we provide agreements you can use if you go the route of a known (either to you or to an intermediary) donor.

b. Must a Doctor Do the Insemination?

In a few states, using an unknown donor isn't the only way to protect yourself from a man who later claims to be dad. In California, Colorado and Illinois, for example, the statutes state that the "donor of semen provided to a licensed physician for use in artificial insemination in a woman other than the donor's wife" is not considered the legal father. If you select the donor but have him deliver his semen to your doctor who performs the insemination, the donor won't be considered the father. But you must use the doctor. In one California case, a court held that where a licensed physician hadn't been used, the donor known to and chosen by the mother, was the legal father of the child, entitled to full parental rights and responsibilities.[12]

Several other states have similar laws; however, those states insert the word "married" before the word "woman," leaving open the questions of what happens when a doctor is or isn't used to inseminate an unmarried woman. And in Georgia and Idaho, anyone *but* a licensed physician is prohibited from inseminating a woman. It's considered practicing medicine without a license.

Conclusion: Except in a few states where the law is clear, if you don't want the donor to be considered the father, nothing is guaranteed. Your safest approach is to use a doctor and have the doctor obtain the semen from a sperm bank. But the honest reality is that only 10% of physicians nationally will inseminate an unmarried woman. So if you want to use a doctor, you may have to shop around. Contact any feminist clinic or a Planned Parenthood office for a possible referral. If you want (or have no choice but) to use a known donor or not use a doctor, be aware of all of the potential risks involved.

Time Out for a Story

Our friends Regina and Susan wanted to have a child. They talked a long time about bringing a baby into their relationship, and were satisfied that the difficulties would be more than balanced by the joy and fulfillment. Regina wanted to bear the child, which was fine with Susan. Neither woman wanted to bring a fourth person (a father) into the relationship.

At one point, Susan suggested that her friend Tom, who was attractive, intelligent, healthy and had nice teeth (she liked the idea of her child having nice teeth), would be wonderful. But Regina pointed out that, no matter how sure they were that Tom didn't want to be involved in raising the child, there would always be the possibility that he would change his mind and seek visitation. And there was no way to guarantee to Tom that neither Regina nor the state would ever ask him for child support. The best they could offer Tom would be a written agreement, saying he wouldn't be financially responsible, but they knew it might not be enforceable.

Finally, Regina and Susan decided that Regina would have a child by artificial insemination, with the donor never being involved. They considered saving the doctor and sperm bank fees by having a friend act as a liaison. This made sense, but Regina decided that because she lives in California, she'd use a doctor for the insemination.

Regina and Susan were reassured by the doctor that the donor had no history of inheritable mental or physical illness, or communicable disease. They gave hair, skin and eye color, as well as racial and ethnic background, preferences. After five months of inseminations, Regina became pregnant. She was fortunate to find two other women who had been inseminated about the same time and they started a weekly "support group." They discussed questions common to all mothers and some unique to lesbian mothers who have children by artificial insemination. All were concerned about what they would tell their children in later years.

Susan and Regina went to classes on natural childbirth. Finally the great day arrived. Regina gave birth to a beautiful, healthy girl in a San Francisco hospital. They were surprised that their child was a girl, however, since they knew that 75% to 80% of children conceived by artificial insemination are boys. The family is doing very well.

c.   *Artificial Insemination Agreements*

Below are agreements for a woman and a donor whose identity is not known to her, who want to ensure that the donor isn't the legal father of the child. You can use the same agreements, with some modifications, if you know the donor. Remember that only a few cases have been decided in this area, and so the enforceability isn't certain. And let us remind you: Courts do not look favorably upon a woman who argues: "We agreed he wouldn't be the father. Yes, I let him visit the child after the child was born, but I never intended him to be the father." If you don't want him to be the father, then say no to any contact. You can never predict when his monthly Sunday visits will lead to his mother coming around to see her "grandchild."[13]

ARTIFICIAL INSEMINATION DONOR'S AGREEMENT

I, [name of donor], have been given the opportunity to donate my semen for the purpose of artificial insemination of a woman whose identity is unknown to me, and wish to protect my interests and those of all concerned. In furtherance of this desire, I freely state that:

1. I understand the purpose of such artificial insemination is to produce a child or children.

2. I don't expect to have divulged to me the identity of the woman, or of the child or children who may be produced as a result of such insemination, nor do I expect to learn whether such insemination(s) result in the birth of a child or children.

3. I agree not to seek the identity of the child or children, or of the mother, and I waive all parental rights which I might have regarding the child.

4. I donate my semen with the understanding and agreement that the person who's responsible for its collection will undertake to keep my identity confidential and unknown to anyone except those directly involved in the collection.

5. I agree to submit to a physical examination carried out by a qualified medical doctor, as well as to tests for the detection of any inheritable disease or other defects, after each test and procedure is explained to me; I further agree to supply true and full answers to the doctor in connection with all relevant questions bearing upon my health and family background. It's my understanding that such information will be treated in confidence, and not linked to my identity in any documents outside the confidential files of the doctor (or intermediary) responsible for the semen collection.

6. I understand that any and all financial compensation I receive will be payment for the expenditure of my time in medical examination and semen collection, as well as reimbursement for loss of income and travel expenses because of my donation. This amount is estimated to be $_____. [If the donor wants no compensation, eliminate this clause.]

Date: _____ Donor Signature: _____

Date: _____ Doctor (or Intermediary) Signature: _____

RECIPIENT'S AGREEMENT

I, [your name], hereby engage the services of [name of doctor or intermediary] to collect semen [**if doctor is collecting add:** and perform one or more artificial insemination procedures on me from an unknown donor]. I make this agreement in order to fully protect the interests of myself, any child born as the result of such artificial insemination, the donor, the doctor(s) and any laboratory used in supplying the semen.

In this connection I agree that:

1. I understand that the purpose of the insemination is to attempt to produce a pregnancy in me; that any pregnancy involves the risk of a miscarriage or other complication, difficulties in delivery and birth defects; and that the risk of such problems is also present in pregnancies resulting from artificial insemination.

2. The doctor (or intermediary) engaged by me to collect the semen will obtain the necessary semen from a donor who won't be advised of my identity, nor of the success or failure of the insemination, and who'll agree in writing not to seek out my identity or the identity of any child who may be born from the insemination. Furthermore, I acknowledge that the identity of the donor isn't to be divulged to me and I agree not to seek out his identity.

3. I hereby authorize the doctor, in [her/his] sole and absolute discretion, to use fresh or frozen semen from one or more unidentified donors, to select the donor(s), and to select the laboratory that has collected, processed and stored frozen semen.

4. I fully understand that the doctor performing the insemination procedure isn't responsible for the physical or mental characteristics of any child so produced and do hereby absolve and release the doctor, [her/his] collaborating colleagues, the institution in which [she/he] practices, the donor(s), and the laboratory involved in sperm collection from any liability whatsoever arising out of, or resulting from, the collection and processing of semen or from any other aspect of the artificial insemination procedure.

5. I agree that the nature of this agreement is such that it must remain confidential and, therefore, agree that the sole copy of it may be given to the doctor for [her/his] confidential files.

Date: _____   Donor Signature: _____

Date: _____   Doctor (or Intermediary) Signature: _____

3. Having a Child Using a Surrogate Mother

The *Baby M.* case brought the possibility and problems of surrogate motherhood to public attention.[14] In *Baby M.*, a married couple (Elizabeth and William Stern) chose not to try to have a child because Elizabeth had multiple sclerosis, and pregnancy, in some MS patients, poses a serious health risk. They contracted with Marybeth Whitehead for her to be impregnated with William Stern's semen, to carry the baby to term, and then to give up the child to be adopted by Elizabeth for the Sterns to raise. All went well until baby M (Melissa) was born, and Marybeth didn't want to part with her. The Sterns sued Marybeth to enforce the contract.

The legal question was whether the contract was enforceable. The trial judge said yes, terminated Marybeth's parental rights, allowed Elizabeth to adopt Melissa and ended the case. The New Jersey Supreme Court reversed, invalidating the contract:

> *... because it conflicts with the law and public policy of this state. While we recognize the depth of the yearning of infertile couples to have their own children, we find the payment of money to a "surrogate" mother illegal, perhaps criminal, and potentially degrading to women. Although in this case we grant custody to the natural father, the evidence having clearly proved such custody to be in the best interests of the infant, we void both the termination of the surrogate mother's paternal rights and the adoption of the child by the wife/stepparent.*

Baby M. is binding only in New Jersey. In response, however, legislatures and courts of other states have struggled with the problems of surrogacy. Surrogacy contracts are now illegal in Arizona, the District of Columbia, Indiana, Louisiana, Michigan, Nebraska, New York and Utah. They are permitted in Florida, Kentucky, Nevada, New Hampshire, North Dakota, Virginia and Washington if no money is exchanged. Only Arkansas and West Virginia have laws expressly allowing surrogacy contracts when money is paid. Political groups wrestle with their concerns, too. Some feminists are concerned that surrogacy arrangements exploit women and turn them into baby-making machines. Others see a woman's choice to be a surrogate mother as one of the freedoms a woman should have and be able to choose if this is what she wants.

We know that the debate will only get more heated as the number of married couples and gay men who seek surrogate mothers to help them parent increases. For a gay man, it's his only hope (other than co-parenting with a lesbian friend) of having his own child. When it works (and it does), the surrogate mother carries the child to term and gives it to the father after the birth. The mother's medical care and expenses are paid by the father. In states granting second-parent adoptions, the surrogate mother's parental rights (if the law in that state considers her to have any) may be terminated and the child adopted by the father's lover.

Often, the father requires that the surrogate mother go through a psychiatric evaluation before being accepted by the father, and already have children of her own. The father's fear is that the mother will want to keep the child. On the other hand, the mother's fear is that the father will *not* want to take the child.

4. Practical Issues When You Have a Child by Artificial Insemination or Surrogacy

Several practical issues come up when you have a child by artificial insemination or surrogacy as an unmarried parent.

a. What Name Can I Give My Child?

You can name your child anything you want. Many couples give the child the last name of the nonbiological parent, whether or not that parent will be considered a legal parent. In fact, when the nonbiological parent *won't* be considered a legal parent, giving the child that parent's last name can provide additional evidence that the partners fully intended to be equal parents.

b. How Do We Fill in the Birth Certificate?

If you have a child by artificial insemination, you may feel a little odd when you see the "Father's Name" blank on the hospital form used to request the birth certificate staring at you. Similarly, gay men who use a surrogate mother to bear their children may feel like a renegade when it comes time to fill in "Mother's Name." Here are your options.

- Don't put the name of the donor (if known) or the surrogate mother, unless you want that person to have rights or responsibilities. Remember our message

to be consistent in your behavior toward and about the donor/surrogate mother.

- Don't put your lover's name (even if it's sex-neutral, like Chris or Lee). This is illegal and could raise many eyebrows.

- You can put "unknown."

- Many people simply write in "Name withheld."

- If you want to be bold, you can write by "artificial insemination" or "surrogate mother," but consider any later embarrassment for the child.

- One creative—though technically criminal—option is to invent a fictitious name. In most hospitals, no one will carefully read the name—but providing incorrect information is a misdemeanor.

Californians Have Another Option

In September of 1993, the California Department of Vital Records and Statistics began issuing new birth certificates. Instead of blanks for "Mother" and "Father," the Department now designates the blanks "Mother/Parent" and "Father/Parent." Now you *can* list your lover in the other blank. At the time of the adoption, when you fill out the Court Record of Adoption (Form V544), put the biological mother's name in the "Mother" slot and the other mother's name in the "Father" slot. When the Department of Vital Records and Statistics types up the birth certificate, they will replace "Mother and "Father" with "Parent" and "Parent."

You can mark the hospital form "Do Not Report" so that the information isn't given to the newspaper "Births" columnist.

c. What If the Child Wants to Find the Donor or Surrogate Mother Later?

Several women ask if it's possible to have the best of all worlds—anonymity now, with the possibility that little Justin will be able to find the donor later, perhaps when he's a teenager or older. This is a good question, especially given that many adopted children seek to meet their biological parents. But we have no real answer. If you want to be sure of no interference by the donor and want to assure him he'll never be liable for support, you must maintain anonymity.

If you use a liaison, that person can keep all records secret, but this is no sure thing. Records could be subpoenaed by the state or someone acting on behalf of the child in a paternity-support lawsuit. If the donor, mother and child might be able to find each other in the future, be sure you disclose all risks.

We've never heard of this issue coming up with surrogate mothers, but that's probably because the case law and literature on the topic is in its infancy. Virtually all children get curious about their roots. There's no reason to think a child born by a surrogate mother will be any different.

D. Adopting a Child

The most permanent way of becoming a nonbiological parent is to adopt. If you adopt a child, you become the legal parent of that child. As part of the process, the biological parents' rights are terminated. (Except when you adopt your lover's child—but that kind of adoption is covered in Section A, above.) An adopted child has

the right to inherit from you—not from the biological parents—and the child can sue you for child support if you fail to provide it. After an adoption, the biological parents have no such obligation.

Adoption is an ancient practice, used in Roman, Babylonian, Assyrian, Greek and Egyptian societies, primarily to provide an heir for the adoptive parent (read: father). Adoptions were equally important in feudal times, when land could be passed to only a male heir, often with the consent of the local king or duke. If a landholding baron or knight had no male heir, adopting a son was the one method to keep the property in his family.

Today, adoptions involve a court. Prior to the adoption, the court terminates the biological parents' rights (this may be done minutes, weeks, months or years before the adoption); then the adoption occurs, and the court issues an order declaring the child adopted and stating that you're the legal parent. Before you go to court, an official agency (usually social services or juvenile probation) will investigate you and your home. In most adoptions, the investigating agency recommends whether you'll be allowed to adopt. If the biological parents' rights were terminated prior to the adoption, the adoption won't usually be contested. And unless the judge won't permit an adoption by a lesbian or a gay man, the court proceeding will be routine, with the judge following the agency's recommendation.

If you want to adopt, you will need an attorney. Adoptions aren't very complicated, but a judge will be reassured by the presence of a lawyer, and probably disturbed by the absence. To utter the obvious, a lesbian or gay man adopting a child wants the judge to be as acquiescent as possible. Also, a lawyer with good local connections, who has handled gay and lesbian legal issues before, will know the ropes to get a good social worker or to disqualify a hostile judge.

As of January 1996, only New Hampshire and Florida expressly prohibit lesbians and gay men from adopting. And as we go to print, a challenge to the Florida ban is pending before a state court. Other states are not necessarily supportive of lesbians and gays who want to adopt; bills are regularly introduced into state legislatures to bar such adoptions. Thankfully, most are defeated.

Although several states no longer officially deem lesbians and gay men "unfit" to raise a child, many lawyers feel it's easier to get second-parent adoptions than initial adoptions by a gay man or lesbian. (See Section A, above, for information on second-parent adoptions.)

California was one of the first states to allow an openly gay man living with his lover to adopt a child. Ohio was one of the most recent states to grant such an adoption. Although there are no statistics about gay parent adoptions, single people are adopting in increasing numbers. Surely some, perhaps many, of these people are gay.

The increase in single-parent adoptions hasn't solved the major problem with adoption today: The number of children available for adoption is very low. Birth control has reduced the number of "illegitimate" children, traditionally the major source of adopted children. And the stigma

against having a child outside of marriage is gone, increasing the number of unwed mothers who keep their children. Agencies are trying to find homes for "hard-to-place" children—usually disabled or older kids. Don't be discouraged, but be realistic. Adoption is a difficult process. Your chances of adopting a perfectly healthy newborn are slim. But lesbians and gays have done it, and if you long for a child and cannot, or choose not to, give birth, explore adoption.

Start with a local lesbian or gay organization. Its members will know what's been done and what's possible in your area. If you proceed, find a friend in the adoption agency—someone sympathetic to your cause. Even in the best situations, be prepared to wait about two years between the initial application and the placement of a child in your home.

1. Methods of Adoption

There are basically four ways to adopt:

- through a public or private agency
- through the mother (or an intermediary)
- through an international agency—that is, a foreign adoption, or
- as a second parent (see Section A, above).

a. Agency Adoptions

Most gay men and lesbians adopt through an agency. The agency—either a state agency, such as the county welfare department, or a private adoption agency—locates children available for adoption. (Foster children are often adopted by foster parents this way; in fact, foster parenting is one of the most common avenues for adopting in many states. See Section E, below, on foster parenting.)

Would-be adoptive parents are interviewed by the agency, which has obtained consents to adopt from the biological parents. The agency recommends to the court who the adoptive parent(s) will be. Traditionally, agencies favor married couples over single parents. No agency we know of "favors" lesbians or gays, though some treat them like any other single people or like a married couple. (See Section A, above, for information on joint adoptions by gay and lesbian couples.) Unfortunately, however, many agencies will rule out gay and lesbians from adopting. There are, however, advantages to using an agency:

- An agency adoption provides maximum assurance that a child's biological parents won't change their minds.
- The procedures are established, and the agency is known to the court, which means the judicial procedure should go smoothly.

b. Private Adoptions

In a private adoption, you find the child yourself, or with the aid of a private adoption firm or an individual intermediary (where legal). No state agency gets involved, except to investigate the home and report to the court. Private adoptions are legal in most states and are common for adopting infants. The adopting parents normally pay the biological mother's medical expenses and sometimes her living expenses, in addition to paying the legal fees. Paying any other "fee," however, is illegal.

In a case where a couple obtained a child by paying a lawyer a substantial sum, the judge discovered the truth, angrily ordered the infant removed from the home in which he'd lived for a year and placed him in a state institution. Fortunately, an appeals court recognized that this was literally throwing the baby out with the bathwater, reversed the trial judge's decision and allowed the baby to stay in the home.

In many states, it's illegal to advertise for an adoption, and using an intermediary to locate or place an adopted child is questionable. In Virginia and Washington, an intermediary may place a child; in Arizona, the intermediary may assist the biological mother in the placement. In California, however, it's a misdemeanor for anyone except a parent or a licensed agency to place a child.

Once you locate a baby, you'll need the consent of the biological mother, and the biological father, if his identity is known and he hasn't abandoned the child or otherwise forfeited his rights. The biological parent(s) sign a consent-to-adopt form, and an adoption proceeding is filed in court. The law may require, or the judge may order, an investigation into your home and a report. And although your attorney and friends can help you decide whether the child's biological mother should be told of your sexual orientation, there's usually no reason to tell the agency.

⚠ Beware of "black market" adoptions. Almost everyone has heard the term "black market adoptions." The idea of people skulking down dark alleys to buy a baby from a mother or an intermediary isn't pleasant. These are illegal. One way this "adoption" works is to have the biological mother register at a hospital in the name of the adoptive mother so that the birth certificate contains the "adopting" parent's name. However handled, it leaves the adoptive parent open to blackmail and the risk of losing the child should the biological mother change her mind and try to reclaim the child.

c.   Foreign Adoptions

It may be possible to adopt a child from another country. U.S. immigration laws provide a special visa for a child who's to be adopted by an American citizen. There are two methods of adopting an "alien" child. (That's what our government calls any foreigner.)

• The child may be adopted in his or her own country. The child must be personally seen by the adoptive parent(s) before the adoption is completed.

• The child may be admitted to the United States for adoption if the adopting parent(s) have met the pre-adoption requirements of their state of residence.

In either case, it's sometimes possible for a single person to qualify as an adopting parent. Many countries, however, strongly prefer—and even require—that infants be adopted by married couples. Also, the United States isn't alone in its societal bias against lesbian or gay adoptions. So if you are involved in a foreign adoption, you may need to keep your sexual identity private.

Although adoptions by lesbians or gay men going abroad are rare, they are not as rare as they used to be. You must locate the would-be adoptive child yourself, and then travel to the child's country and go through its adoption procedures. This can sometimes—perhaps oftentimes—become quite difficult. The adoption "laws" of many countries are murky at best. In Peru, for example, they seem to consist of finding the right person to pay money to. And Tibetan refugees in India can be adopted only if the Dalai Lama says they can.

Despite these difficulties, we know people who have adopted outside of the U.S. You must be at least 25 years old (adopting as a single parent) and any investigation of you must be done before the Immigration and Naturalization Service (INS) will issue an immigration visa for the child. Many countries don't quickly issue final adoption decrees. Chile, for instance, issues an interim decree, and requires a two-year wait for a final decree. You must obtain a special visa for the child from the INS to bring the child to the U.S. before the adoption is final.

Foreign adoptions through an agency in your state are slightly more feasible than traveling to a foreign country. Some agencies can, and do, locate foreign orphans to be adopted by U.S. citizens. The prospective adoptive parent is investigated by the adoption agency. If it determines that you are suitable, it certifies to the INS that the state's pre-adoption standards have been met, and INS issues a visa so the child can be brought to the U.S. In general, agencies aren't being asked to find homes for children from Europe, North America or Japan.

Foreign adoptions are costly. You must pay:

- the child's transportation to the United States
- the fees of the adoption agency in the child's country
- the fees of the U.S. adoption agency, and
- attorneys fees and INS charges.

Foreign adoptions, however, have been successful for gay and lesbian people. In a New York case, a gay man was granted certification as an adoptive parent by the Justice Department to adopt a Russian child. This case was an appeal from an INS rejection of his application. As a result of this case, the Justice Department (and now the INS) will not deny an orphan visa petition just because an adoptive parent is gay and lives with a lover who will co-parent.[15] Be prepared to be very patient and persevering.

2. Legal Aspects of Adoption

The following information is general. State laws vary considerably; treat what you read here as a starting place for your research.

Age limits. Some states have age restrictions for the adoptive parent. In California, the adoptive parent must be at least ten years older than the adopted child. Other states, such as Delaware, require the parent to be over 21, and some states, such as Rhode Island, simply state

"any person older than the child may adopt."

Residence. You, and normally the child, must reside in the state where the adoption case is filed. Many states require that adoptive parents bringing a child into the state for adoption notify the state or a county adoption agency. These laws don't apply if the biological parent brings the child into the state. If a child you want to adopt resides in another state, you may have to establish residence in that state before adopting.

Who may be adopted. Interreligious and interracial adoptions used to be, and sometimes still are, refused by adoption agencies and therefore courts as not considered in the "best interests of the child."

Betty, a Native American friend of ours, informs us that federal law requires preference be given to the following people in the adoption or foster placement of an Indian child:

- a member of the child's family
- other members of the child's tribe, or
- other Indian families.

She also notes that the law requires that the tribe be notified of most foster-adoption placements, and warns that some state adoptions can be set aside by tribal courts.

Change of name. All states permit the adoptive parent(s) to change the child's last name at the time of adoption.

Records and birth certificates. Nearly all states seal adoption records, allowing them to be inspected only if the court so orders. Adoptive parents can obtain a new birth certificate with the child's new name and which substitutes the adoptive parents for the biological parents.

Consent of the adopted child. Once the child reaches a certain age, his or her consent is required for an adoption. The age varies from age ten (Michigan) to age 14 (Texas). In a few other states, such as West Virginia and Vermont, the adopted person may have an adoption vacated by filing a dissent within one year after it's final.

E.   Foster Parenting a Child

If you have an urge to be a parent, foster parenting may accomplish your goal.

Growing numbers of foster-home placement agencies are placing children with gay and lesbian foster parents. Who winds up in foster homes? Children who, for one reason or another, have been dumped into the cold lap of Mother State. Many kids have emotional difficulties. Usually, either the child is considered delinquent (incorrigible) or the parent is delinquent (abused or neglected the child, or in jail).

Some of these kids may fall into one of the following categories.

• Gay teenagers who can't get along with their parents—often the underlying problem is the teen's emerging sexual identity. Sometimes these teens are kicked out; often they run away, and occasionally, their parents just seem to have evaporated. These kids, if possible, should be placed in stable gay households.

• Children of gay or lesbian parents removed from the parents' home because of neglect, substance abuse or another problem. These children, too, should be placed in homes resembling the homes they are growing up in—that is, with a gay or lesbian couple.

In some cities, such as New York, San Francisco, Los Angeles and Trenton, agencies have actively recruited gay foster parents for such placements and juvenile judges recognize the appropriateness of making such placements. On the other hand, Nebraska will not place foster children with lesbian or gay parents. Massachusetts and New Hampshire, where nontraditional households are given low priority, have made it very difficult for a lesbian or gay person to be a foster parent. In Massachusetts, the applicant must state his or her sexual orientation. And North Dakota allows only married couples to become foster parents.

A foster parent is only a temporary guardian of a child. The state has simply granted you a license to be a foster parent. The ultimate goal is the reunification of the child with his or her parents, not the adoption of the child by you. You may get the opportunity to adopt, but it will take years of the state trying to bring the parents and child back together. You have no legal relationship with the child. The child won't inherit from you unless you provide for him or her in your will. The placement might be emergency placement for two days, or might last years.

States pay foster parents a monthly amount for support of each foster child. The amount varies among states, but in many urban areas the range is $200 to $275 per

month. Clearly this isn't generous, and we can't imagine that anyone becomes a foster parent for the pay. Still, if you become a foster parent, the monthly allotment can help.

1. Applying for a Foster Child

Single people (except in North Dakota) and, in many states, "roommates" can get foster parents' licenses. And some openly gay households have been licensed. So, if a gay or lesbian couple wants to become foster parents, should one of them apply to the licensing agency as a single person, or should they apply as a couple? We can't tell you how to apply, but we can give you information to help you decide.

If you want to keep your relationship private, have one person apply as a single individual. A single adult, sharing space with another adult, can become a licensed foster parent in most states. But foster care placement is at the agency's or court's discretion, so social workers will march into your home to look about. They have an odd view that the right to privacy is exercised only by people who have something to hide. Of course, they don't put it that way, and instead turn people down because of "lack of openness." At any rate, plan in advance how "open" to be. And when you decide, be consistent; if there's one thing you can count on when dealing with social workers, it's that they'll be back.

In some instances, it may be foolish to tell a foster agency that you're gay or lesbian. Generally, however, maintaining secrecy and applying for a child is risky. The agency may find out the truth; more likely, the child will, and it's not appropriate to ask the child to lie. The question of "to be, or not to be—out" is raised often in this book. However you answer that question for your own life, kids should be dealt with honestly. And once a foster kid knows the truth, it's going to be hard to keep it secret. If you can locate a sympathetic social worker, you may be able to resolve your coming-out dilemma informally and personally.

2. Placing Gay Kids (and Kids of Gays) in Gay Homes

As we've said, some agencies will approve stable, caring, gay households for placement of gay-identified (the agencies' term) teenagers or children of gay or lesbian parents. These agencies realize that few heterosexual foster parents can adequately deal with gay teenagers and that children of gay and lesbian parents should remain in that environment for their foster placement. With gay teens especially, these agencies know that placing gay kids in large group homes could be problematic.

It's often easier for a gay person or couple to become licensed foster parents than it is to actually have children placed in their home. And because foster placement is always considered temporary, the child can be removed at his or her request, your request, or the request of the agency or government probation officers. So there are uncertainties to being a foster parent, especially for a lesbian or gay foster parent.

The changes in gay foster parenting have been largely brought about by the dedicated work of many lesbian and gay people. Several years ago, Sue Saperstein worked with the director of the San Francisco

Department of Social Services to get a gay caseworker in the department to handle the foster placement of gay kids. In response, the San Francisco Foster Licensing Division of the Department of Social Services has licensed lesbian and gay foster homes.

Linda Graham worked with Project Lambda in Boston, helping place gay teenagers in gay households. Amazingly, Project Lambda was funded by an agency of the United States Department of Justice and was very successful for a few years. Now, of course, Massachusetts makes it nearly impossible for gays or lesbians to be foster parents.

And in Los Angeles, Gay and Lesbian Adolescent Social Services (GLASS) certifies gay and lesbian people to become licensed foster parents. GLASS also runs four group homes to place gay, lesbian and HIV-positive teens.[16]

Alternative Family Services of San Francisco and Sonoma counties licenses the homes of lesbians and gay men, single people, unmarried heterosexual couples and groups.[17] This private foster-care agency places gay teenagers in gay homes and provides follow-up support. Prior to placement, Alternative Family Services provides three weeks of orientation and five weeks of "skills" training for prospective foster parents. After the eight weeks, an agency social worker matches foster parents with foster children, considering race, sexual orientation and religion. There's an initial meeting between the parents and the teenager, and then a trial visit. If all goes well, the foster parents and kid sit down and work out a detailed agreement.

On the average, a teenager stays in a foster home between six months and a year. Yes, this will shatter your image and dreams of a foster parent-child relationship becoming lifelong with "lots of homemade cookies and adorable grandchildren." But the shortness isn't an indication of failure. The reality is that any teenager's life, and especially a foster teenager's life, is chaotic and changing; "success" of a placement isn't measured by duration, but by the love between the foster parent and the child, and the teenager's growth toward self-sufficiency.

3. Practical Steps to Becoming a Foster Parent

There's a foster-home division in almost every county welfare department. Call it and ask for a list of agencies, both state-operated and private, that license foster homes. Finding an agency willing to place gay-identified teenagers with lesbian and gay couples may take a little work. Ask a local lesbian or gay organization which agencies are sympathetic to placing gay-identified teenagers in gay homes. Agencies or particular social workers willing to make such placements often keep a low profile, believing themselves to be more effective that way.

Because most states have several agencies that place foster children and because you can be licensed by only one agency at a time, investigate carefully. Once you select an agency, the licensing process itself is usually quite simple. You fill out an application, are interviewed by an employee of the agency who is, or should be, concerned only with whether you'd make a

good foster parent and are visited at home. In addition:

- you should have a separate room for the child

- you must have a medical exam

- you must be fingerprinted—ex-felons and ex-sex offenders aren't eligible, and

- if you're asking for a young child, you must demonstrate that you have time to care for the child, or have arranged for child care.

But the most important criteria are stability and responsibility.

You may have a choice of becoming licensed as a foster home for a particular child or getting a general foster-home license and having the agency place a child. When on the general list, you have the option of refusing a child if you and the child don't hit it off. Becoming licensed for a specific child works differently.

Example: Michael and Ron had befriended Scott, a gay boy of 14. Scott was living at an institution and on weekend days caught a bus to Michael and Ron's. They drove him back in the evenings. On Thanksgiving, Scott said to Ron, "Wouldn't it be great to live here all the time?" Ron sighed. "It'd be wonderful—but it's impossible. We all know that." Later, Michael and Ron wondered if it really was impossible. They contacted Scott's social worker, who agreed that placing Scott in Michael and Ron's home would be good for him. The social worker sent Michael and Ron the application forms, and a license was granted. Scott lived happily in Michael and Ron's home.

Getting licensed as a foster parent takes some paperwork. Usually the agency will assist you with it, so you shouldn't need an attorney. If, however, you want some help or think you're being discriminated against, you may need a lawyer. See Chapter 10.

F. Becoming a Guardian of a Child

A guardian is an adult other than a legal parent responsible for taking care of a minor.[18] Usually, the adult gets physical custody of the child, and is sometimes given authority to manage the minor's assets. In most states, a guardian isn't legally or financially responsible for a child's actions. For example, if a child causes damage by vandalism, a parent (in most states) is liable, but a guardian isn't. There's usually an exception if the guardian agrees, on the child's driver's license application, to be financially responsible for any damage the child causes while driving.

Some guardianships are informal; others are court-appointed. We cover only uncontested guardianships, where the legal parents consent to the arrangement. Contested guardianships are birds with different (and usually nasty) chirps. Almost by definition, contested guardianships are messy and bitter. Someone—the parent or the proposed guardian—is charged with being unfit. It's unusual for a lesbian or gay couple to gain a child through a contested guardianship, but it has happened.

Informal guardianships are temporary and can be changed at the decision (or whim) of whoever placed the child. They're commonly used when, because of illness, jailing or extended travel, a parent asks a relative or friend to temporarily take over parenting. There is no legal case. The parent simply delivers the child to the guardian with a document of authorization.

Formal guardianships involve court proceedings. An adult wanting to be appointed guardian files a petition and the court decides whether the guardianship is "in the best interests of the child." As long as everyone agrees, the judge usually grants the guardianship and issues an order establishing its terms.

1. Informal Guardianship

An informal guardianship is almost always preferable to a court proceeding. Going to court—even in a nonadversarial setting—is always a crap shoot. It is possible that the judge will be outraged at the idea of a child living with gay adults. If you hide your sexual orientation from the judge and it comes out during the proceedings, the judge will probably be angry with you.

If a child is eligible for welfare, the welfare benefits usually follow the child to the guardian's home, but be sure to check your state's laws. Normally, if the guardian is a close relative or meets the welfare department formalities (which are less rigid than with formal guardianships), the benefits will follow. If you're confused or anticipate trouble, find a friendly social worker and casually explain your problem. We've found that for every welfare rule saying you can't do something, there's another saying you can.

An Informal Guardianship

Ben, a gay man, and Paula were old friends. Paula's son Mark had confided in Ben the summer before coming out to his mother. Paula wasn't shocked to learn that Mark was gay, but was finding him hard to handle. Mark wrote Ben the following letter.

Mark's letter

Dear Ben:

Remember how we talked last summer about my parents' divorce? Well, I find there's another reason I want to come to Boston to go to school. I am gay. I just told mother and she said, "No 15-year-old can be gay!"

Can you write her and ask if I can come stay with you for the school year? I can't even get any studying done around here! She respects you. Please!

Love,
Mark

Paula wrote to Ben at almost the same time. She had no intention of relinquishing custody or abandoning her duties as Mark's mother. She just knew they needed time apart. Her letter was a little different.

Paula's letter

Dear Ben,

I need to talk to you. Mark has just been impossible lately, and nothing I can do or say seems to help. Of course I have known that he's gay for a long time, but he has come out to me very belligerently and accuses me of never understanding him. Frankly, right now, I don't. He has been talking about writing you. I sure hope he does.

Love,
Paula

Paula reflected on the various possibilities and concluded that allowing Mark to live with Ben, a long-time friend and mature gay man, made sense. Fortunately, it made sense to Mark and Ben, too. And Mark's father readily agreed—he'd taken little interest in raising Mark for years and was for any solution that didn't involve work or money on his part. A court proceeding was unnecessary and undesirable. Paula's concern was with Mark's well-being. And going to court could produce a nasty reaction from a judge. So Mark lived happily with Ben during the school year, and returned to his mother during the summer.

2. Informal Guardianship Documents

While written documents aren't essential to establish an informal guardianship, they're desirable. To continue our story, suppose Mark suffered a deep cut on his arm while at Ben's. The wound would have been sewn up by a doctor, under laws authorizing doctors to do what's necessary in an emergency. But what if the doctor also recommended plastic surgery, surgery that had to be done (if at all) within 24 hours? As this is "elective," not "emergency" surgery, the doctor would require Mark's parents' permission before operating. If Ben had no document authorizing him to make medical decisions for Mark, he'd have an obvious problem if he could not find Paula. Or, to switch to a more pleasant example, suppose Mark wanted to go on a school picnic and needed written permission to attend. Ben would need written authorization in order to give permission.

And then there's the question of support. Who pays Mark's living expenses? Paula and Ben discussed it, and wrote down their agreement. They also covered school attendance, curfews and the like. And because Mark is a teenager, he was in on the discussion and signed the agreement. After all, if Mark doesn't like what Paula and Ben decide, he can vote with his feet.

Below is a sample form. To prepare one of your own, adapt the form to your specific situation. Make at least four originals: one for the school, one for the hospital and others for the unexpected. These forms aren't court orders. Have them notarized; you may also want an attorney to look at them. We believe they're valid, and should suffice when a school official, doctor or someone similar needs proof that the guardian can act for the child. If someone refuses to honor a form, point out that you have the legal authority to act for the child. After all, that's what the agreement says. If that doesn't work, call the child's parents fast. And if a school or other public agency insists that you use its form, use it.

TEMPORARY GUARDIANSHIP AGREEMENT

We, Paula Ruiz of 1811 Main Street, Cleveland, Ohio, and John Ruiz of 493 Oak Street, Cincinnati, Ohio, are the parents of Mark Ruiz, born to us on August 18, 19__. We hereby grant Ben Jacobs, of 44 Tea Road, Boston, Massachusetts, temporary guardianship of Mark Ruiz. We grant to Ben Jacobs the power to act in our place as parents of Mark Ruiz, to authorize any medical examination, tests, operations or treatment that in Ben Jacobs's opinion are needed or useful to Mark Ruiz.

We also hereby grant to Ben Jacobs the power to act in our place as parents of Mark Ruiz in connection with any school, including, but not limited to, enrollment and permission for activities.

During the period while Ben Jacobs acts as guardian of Mark Ruiz, the costs of his/her upkeep and living expenses shall be paid as follows. *[Insert what has been agreed on.]*

Dated: _____   Signature: _____
                                         Paula Ruiz

Dated: _____   Signature: _____
                                         John Ruiz

Dated: _____   Signature: _____
                                         Mark Ruiz

Dated: _____   Signature: _____
                                         Ben Jacobs

Notarization

AUTHORIZATION TO CONSENT TO MEDICAL, SURGICAL, OR DENTAL
EXAMINATION OR TREATMENT OF A MINOR

I, Paula Ruiz, being the parent with legal custody of Mark Ruiz, born August 18,
19__, hereby authorize Ben Jacobs, into whose care Mark Ruiz has been entrusted, to
consent to any X-ray, examination, anesthetic, medical or surgical diagnosis, or
treatment and hospital care to be rendered to Mark Ruiz under the general or special
supervision and upon the advice of a physician or surgeon licensed to practice
medicine in any state of the United States, or to consent to an X-ray, examination,
anesthetic, dental or surgical diagnosis, or treatment and hospital care to be rendered
to Mark Ruiz by a dentist licensed to practice dentistry in any state of the United
States.

This authorization is valid from September 1, 19__ to June 30, 19__.

Dated: _____   Signature: _____
                                                        Paula Ruiz

Dated: _____   Signature: _____
                                                        Ben Jacobs

Notarization

3. Court-Appointed Guardianships

A court-ordered guardianship makes sense if the parent is mentally ill or incarcerated, or if a third party (usually a relative) may try to intervene and get custody. It also may be necessary to obtain benefits, deal with school authorities or manage the child's money. (An adult must be legally authorized to care for the child's financial assets.)

As mentioned above, we don't cover contested guardianships, where relatives or other persons object to the guardianship. In this situation, you'll need an attorney's help. If you anticipate problems with the guard-ianship process, you should see an attorney before you begin.

The court proceeding and the social service investigation for an uncontested guardianship vary from state to state. Be sure to discuss your situation with a knowledgeable lawyer sympathetic to, and aware of, lesbian and gay concerns. Unless you're convinced you won't face a biased, hostile judge, don't file a formal guardianship. And while heterosexual couples can safely handle their own guardianships, you'll probably want to hire a lawyer. The patina of respectability that an "Esq." carries will help you gain your result, however much of an illusion that patina really is.

G. Arrangements Between a Teenager and the Adults Who'll Care for the Teen

When a teen comes to live with gay or lesbian adults—through foster parenting or a guardianship—the teen and the adults need an agreement. The purpose isn't to sue each other if the garbage isn't dumped, but to formulate understandings and expectations. Our sample agreement concerns Eric, a sixteen-year-old who has come to live with John and David.

CONTRACT BETWEEN A TEENAGER AND THE ADULTS HE WILL LIVE WITH

1. FIRST THINGS

General: Eric's coming into John and David's home; we are making this agreement to help make our family life together as harmonious and enjoyable as possible. We realize that circumstances change and we agree to review this agreement every six months.

Disputes: All disputes will be carried out in English. This means no punching. It also means that we will do our best to communicate openly and not assume that the others "ought to know what concerns us."

Eric's Parents: Eric's parents will be encouraged to visit if they wish to do so and will be made as welcome as possible.

2. FINANCES

John and David will receive $300 from the welfare department as stipend for Eric's support. The money will be used as follows:

$100 for rent

$100 for food

$50 for clothing

$50 for Eric for spending money.

John and David will contribute more to Eric's support than they are compensated by welfare. Further, Eric's $50 per month spending money isn't conditioned upon his doing chores. John will be the banker.

3. HOURS

Eric agrees to be home by 7:00 pm on school nights and by 1:00 am on weekends. He agrees to let John and David know what he's doing. He also agrees to call home by 6:30 pm on school nights and by 9:00 pm on weekends to request any later hours.

John and/or David agree to be home by 6:30 pm on weeknights and by 1:00 am on weekends, and agree to leave a note on the refrigerator and/or call if there's any change.

4. MEALS

Dinner is considered a special time, and will be served around 7:30 pm. Everyone is expected to be present if at all possible.

5. DRUGS

Eric will obey all laws regulating drug use.

6. SCHOOL

Eric will be enrolled in public school and agrees to attend regularly.

7. CHORES

Eric will keep his room neat—but it's his room and as long as he confines his mess to this area, there will be peace. Eric won't spread his belongings around the rest of the house. If he does, they will be placed in his room.

John and David will shop, do the general cleaning, cook, keep the household accounts, do the wash and do the maintenance around the house.

Eric's responsible for his own room; he will clean up after dinner and wash dishes twice a week. He will also take out the garbage—without being asked—and pitch in on small chores and large cleaning jobs. Yard work will be divided.

8. TIME TOGETHER

John agrees to be home at least two nights a week and David agrees to be home two nights a week. Tuesday night and Saturday afternoons are times together and no plans can be made unless they include everyone—except if we all agree otherwise.

9. STEREO EQUIPMENT

The stereo equipment is David's. He admits he's fanatic about it, but it was expensive. So everyone agrees only David will use it. He will attempt to either play music everyone enjoys or use earphones. He's willing to put albums, tapes and CDs on for others. The radio and TV can be used by all, and the volume is to be kept at a moderate level.

10. SMOKING

Smoking is permitted only in the back room.

11. SPACE

Eric has his room and is free to lock it if he chooses. John and David have their room, and they may lock it if they choose. Everyone's privacy is respected.

12. GUESTS

John and David aren't used to sharing their home with a lot of people so Eric is permitted only one guest at a time and only when someone else is home unless other arrangements have been made; Eric is responsible for his guest's behavior.

No guests after 9 pm without agreement.

13. SOCIAL WORKER

We agree to meet with Jeff Lakely, the social worker, every other week and candidly discuss our joys and problems.

14. LENGTH OF THIS AGREEMENT

Eric, David and John understand that their living together must be enjoyable for everyone, and that they must all give a lot for it to work. If one person can't make it work, they will terminate the agreement and it will expire.

Dated: _____   Signature: _____
                                            Eric Farmer

Dated: _____   Signature: _____
                                            David Roberts

Dated: _____   Signature: _____
                                            John Torres

Endnotes

[1]See especially, *Considering Parenthood: A Workbook for Lesbians,* by Cheri Pies (Spinsters Ink, 1985) (contains an excellent annotated bibliography).

[2]Available from Cambridge Documentary Films, P.O. Box 385, Cambridge, MA 02139, (617) 354-3677. We are also aware of the growing psychological literature declaring children raised by two mothers or two fathers to be just as psychologically healthy as children raised by heterosexual parents.

[3]Not Cole Porter.

[4]For a thorough discussion of the legal issues involved in artificial insemination, see *Lesbians Choosing Motherhood: Legal Implications of Alternative Insemination and Reproductive Technologies,* available from the National Center for Lesbian Rights, 870 Market Street, Suite 570, San Francisco, CA 94102, (415) 392-6257. Also, a history and current state of the law of artificial insemination is available in "Artificial Insemination and Legal Reality," by Julia J. Tate, published by the American Bar Association (1992).

[5]7 Syracuse L. Rev. 96, 101 (1955).

[6]*Doornbos v. Doornbos,* 40 U.S. Law Week 2308; No. 54-S-14981 Super. Ct. Cook County, Illinois (1954).

[7]*Adoption of Anonymous,* 345 N.Y.S.2d 430 (Super. Ct. 1973).

[8]Write to the San Francisco Women's Center, 3543 18th St., San Francisco, CA 94110.

[9]*McIntyre v. Crouch,* 780 P.2d 239 (1989).

[10]*In the Interest of R.C.,* 775 P.2d 27 (1989).

[11]*Thomas S. v. Robin Y.,* 599 N.Y.S.2d 377 (1993).

[12]*Jhordan C. v. Mary K.,* 179 Cal.App.3d 386 (1986).

[13]This was precisely the situation in a recent North Carolina case, *In re Jane Doe,* in which the court refused to terminate the donor's parental rights. The court did not award him custody, however, and the mother did not object to the limited visitation arrangement ordered by the court.

[14]537 A.2d 1227 (N.J. Supreme Court 1988).

[15]*Gressin v. Slattery.* Contact Lambda Legal Defense and Education Fund at its New York office (the address and phone number are in Chapter 10, Section E) for the case citation or for more information.

[16]GLASS is located at 650 North Robertson, Suite A, West Hollywood, CA 90069, (310) 358-8727.

[17]Alternative Family Services has two locations: 25 Division Street, Suite 201, San Francisco, CA 94103, (415) 626-2700 and 5 Keller Street, 2nd Floor, Petaluma, CA 94952, (707) 765-2700.

[18]For more information in California, see *The Guardianship Book,* by David Brown and Lisa Goldoftas (Nolo Press). ∎

CHAPTER 4

Medical Emergencies and Financial Matters: Delegating Authority

Every lesbian and gay man, whether in a couple or not, should consider what will happen if they become seriously ill or suffer a medical emergency. Ask yourself several questions: Who do you want to have authority to act for you if you are incapacitated and cannot make your own health care decisions? Who do you want to be allowed to visit you in intensive care? Who do you want to have legal authority to handle your financial affairs if you can't?

You can control these matters by preparing some simple legal documents which will ensure that your desires are carried out if you become incapacitated. Using different documents, discussed below, you can provide for your health care and treatment, and management of your finances.

Unfortunately, if no advance preparation has been done, tragedy can strike. In a well-known case from Minnesota, Karen Thompson was forbidden to have any contact with, or authority to act for, her incapacitated lover, Sharon Kowalski. Sharon was seriously injured in a car accident. Her mother and father ran to court to remove her from Karen's care after learning that the women were lovers. Karen and her lawyer persisted, however, and after a seven-year battle, the Minnesota Court of Appeals finally named Karen as Sharon's legal guardian. By then, however, Sharon had lost years of Karen's aid in her recovery, which can never be made up.

Many other situations involve people with AIDS. Often, the lover and other people the patient regards as "family" are excluded from visiting him in the hospital by his biological family. Sometimes, biological family members have religious—and medical—ideas that the ill person rejects. Because hospitals and doctors conventionally look to the immediate family for authority to act (absent a document giving the lover that power), the lover is sometimes forced to look on in horror while the doctor is instructed in ways which the lover knows are contrary to his mate's wishes.

There are more than just medical care decisions to make when a person is ill or incapacitated. Someone must pay bills, deposit checks and take care of the other financial matters. The authority to make financial decisions traditionally belongs to a spouse, not a lover or friend. Until a few years ago, a court hearing was usually necessary to authorize anyone else to handle financial matters. Now, you can use what is called a durable power of attorney for finances to handle these matters.

This chapter explains how you can handle medical and financial matters during a medical emergency. The materials are both for people caught in an emergency, and for people foresighted enough (which we hope all our readers are) to prepare documents in the event an emergency develops.

Medical emergencies have, tragically, become realities for many gay people, and the legal documents we discuss in this chapter are of vital importance for people with AIDS and all life-threatening illnesses. As we are all sadly aware, the AIDS epidemic has been responsible for the incapacity and deaths of thousands of gay men. AIDS has made people aware of their mortality and their need to be responsible to themselves and their loved ones. We provide a list of referrals to organizations that provide legal assistance or legal referrals for people with HIV or AIDS in Chapter 10, Section F.

All medical emergencies are frightening and stressful. Our close friend Jan was diagnosed with AIDS. Within about a week and one-half after diagnosis, he had recovered sufficiently to leave the hospital. We were all so elated that he was out of the hospital and doing better that we didn't want to consider death. We became jubilant as he improved. His mother baked a dozen pies and after a week his parents flew back home. Within a month, however, Jan had to go back into the hospital. Because his fever was so high, he was unable to make any personal, let alone business, decisions. His parents flew out again.

We knew we had to prepare for future times when Jan would be unable to make medical or business decisions. We also had to prepare for his death. We were fortunate because Jan's parents talked with and listened to Jan's lover, business partner and friends. We had to figure out who would have the power to decide business and financial matters, medical care, hospital visitation and burial plans if Jan didn't recover sufficiently to make his own decisions. When Jan became coherent, we urged him to consider this and to prepare the necessary documents.

Jan died in the summer. No legal papers can lessen that tragedy. The documents we provide here, though, can help to prevent needless additional pain and confusion, as well as the denial of ill gay and lesbian people's wishes.

Terminal Illnesses and Hospices

In recent years, hospice programs, including AIDS hospices, have been set up throughout the country to help terminally ill people maintain control over how they live and ultimately die. There are over 2,000 hospices in the U.S. Cancer patients make up the highest proportion of users of hospices. In addition, approximately 17,000 AIDS patients use hospices each year.

Typically, the terminally ill person stays at home, where care is provided by family, close friends and medical professionals. Special counseling is given to the terminally ill person and those close to him. Hospice programs help ensure that a terminally ill person doesn't end up on life support systems, which is likely to happen if he dials 911 or enters a hospital facility.

Information about hospices throughout the country can be obtained from the National Hospice Help Line, 800-658-8898.

A. Health Care Decisions

The increasing use of life-sustaining medical technology over the last decades has raised fears in many that our lives may be artificially prolonged against our wishes. The right to die with dignity, and without the tremendous agony and expense for both patient and family caused by prolonging lives artificially, has been addressed and confirmed by the U.S. Supreme Court, the federal government and the legislatures in every state.

This individual right also protects against the situation where doctors might wish to provide a patient with less extensive care than he would like. For example, a doctor may be unwilling to try experimental treatments or maintain long-term treatments on a patient who she feels has slim chances of recovering.

In 1990, the United States Supreme Court held that every individual has the constitutional right to control his own medical treatment. The Court also expounded that "clear and convincing evidence" of a person's wishes must be followed by medical personnel—even if those wishes are directly opposed by the patient's family.[1]

1. Documents Protecting Choices of Medical Care

In response to the legal right to control one's own medical treatment, every state now has laws authorizing individuals to create a simple document that provides the "clear and convincing evidence" of that person's wishes concerning life-prolonging medical care. Depending upon the state, the document may be called by one of several different names: Living Will, Medical Directive, Directive to Physicians, Declaration Regarding Health Care or Durable Power of Attorney for Health Care.

The directions expressed in the document are to be followed if an individual is no longer capable of communicating to medical personnel his choices regarding life-prolonging and other medical care.

It is important to note that many of these documents take effect only when a patient is diagnosed to have a terminal condition or to be in a permanent coma. These documents are not used when a person is able to communicate her wishes to doctors in any way or is only temporarily unconscious.

The document specifically called a durable power of attorney for health care, however, can become effective whenever the person who creates it (the "principal") decides. You can prepare one now, to become effective only if you become incapacitated. This is called a "springing" durable power of attorney. Or you can prepare one that becomes effective once you sign it.

2. Differences Among Types of Medical Care Documents

The two basic types of documents to direct medical care are a Living Will and a Durable Power of Attorney for Health Care. A Living Will is not a will at all, but a document stating a person's decision to receive or not to receive certain medical treatment.

The basic difference between the two types of documents is simple. The Living Will is a statement made by you directly to medical personnel which spells out the medical care you do or do not wish to receive if you become terminally ill and incapacitated. It functions as a contract with the treating doctor, who must either honor the wishes for medical care that you have expressed—or transfer you to another doctor or facility that will honor them.

In a Durable Power of Attorney, you appoint someone else (your "attorney-in-fact") to see that your doctors and health care providers provide you with the kind of medical care you wish to receive. You can specify in the document what type of care you want or don't want. In some states, you can also give the person you appoint the broader authority to make decisions about your medical care on your behalf.

In An Emergency: DNR Orders

In addition to your Living Will and Durable Power of Attorney for Health Care, you may want to secure a Do Not Resuscitate order, or DNR order. A DNR order documents the wish that you not be administered cardio-pulmonary resuscitation (CPR) and will alert emergency medical personnel to this wish. DNR orders were first used in hospital settings to alert hospital staff that CPR should be withheld from a patient, but now they are frequently used in situations where a person might require emergency care while outside of the hospital.

You may want to consider a DNR order if:

- you have a terminal illness
- you are at an increased risk for cardiac or respiratory arrest, or
- you have strong feelings against the use of CPR under any circumstances.

In most states, any adult may secure a DNR order. But some states, such as South Carolina and Utah, allow you to create an order only if you have been diagnosed as having a terminal illness.

If you want a DNR order, or you want more information about DNR orders, talk with a doctor. A doctor's signature is required to make the DNR valid—and in most states, he or she will obtain and complete the necessary paperwork. If the doctor does not have the form or other information you need, call the Health Department for your state and ask to speak with someone in the Division of Emergency Medical Services.

If you obtain a DNR order, discuss your decision with your lover or other caretakers. They should know where your form is located—and who to call if you require emergency treatment. Even if you are wearing identification, such as a bracelet or necklace, keep your form in an obvious place. Consider keeping it by your bedside, on the front of your refrigerator, in your wallet or in your suitcase if you are traveling. If your DNR order is not apparent and immediately available, or if it has been altered in any way, CPR will most likely be performed.

When Your State Form Is Not Enough

When it comes to medical directives, there are many state differences in the forms and formats used. Some state laws mention that a specific form must be followed for a directive to be valid. Because the Supreme Court ruled in the *Cruzan* case that every individual has a constitutional right to direct his or her own medical care, however, the most important thing for you to keep in mind is that your directions should be clear and in writing to doctors and other medical personnel. If you feel strongly about a particular kind of care—even if your state law or the form you get does not address it—it is a good idea to include your specific thoughts in your written document. If you are using a specific state form that does not adequately address your concerns, write them in on the form with the additional request that your wishes be respected and followed.

3. What to Include in a Medical Directive

The trend in the laws controlling health care directives is to allow individuals to direct their own medical care both if they are diagnosed to be in a permanent coma or if they have a terminal condition. Another trend is to allow individuals the right to direct what "comfort care"—care which doctors feel may alleviate pain and which may or may not prolong life—should be provided or withheld.

The problem many people have in filling out their state forms on directing health care is that they are not sure how to fill in the blanks—and are not sure what much of the terminology means. Although medical technology and treatments are evolving over time, filling out the forms is not as difficult

as it may seem at first. In most health care documents, you can direct:

- that all life-prolonging procedures be provided
- that all life-prolonging procedures be withheld, or
- that some be provided, while others are withheld.

The following medical procedures and treatments are usually considered to be in the category of "life-prolonging."

- *Blood and blood products.* Partial or full blood transfusions may be recommended to combat diseases that impair the blood system, to foster healing after a blood loss or to replenish blood lost through surgery, disease or injury.

- *Cardiopulmonary resuscitation.* (CPR) is used when a person's heart or breathing has stopped. CPR includes applying physical pressure, using mouth-to-mouth resuscitation, using electrical shocks (if available), administering intravenous drugs to normalize body systems and attaching you to a respirator.

- *Diagnostic tests.* Diagnostic tests are commonly used to evaluate urine, blood and other body fluids and to check on all bodily functions. Diagnostic tests can include X-rays and more sophisticated tests of brainwaves or other internal body systems. Some diagnostic tests, including surgery, can be expensive and invasive.

- *Dialysis.* A dialysis machine is used to clean and add essential substances to the blood—through tubes placed in blood vessels or into the abdomen—when kidneys do not function properly.

- *Drugs.* The most common and most controversial drugs given to seriously ill or comatose patients are antibiotics—

administered by mouth, through a feeding tube or by injection. Antibiotics are used to arrest and squelch infectious diseases. Drugs may also be used to eliminate or alleviate pain. Because high doses of pain control drugs can impair respiration, such drugs sometimes hasten death in a seriously ill patient.

• *Respirator.* A mechanical respirator or a ventilator assists or takes over breathing for a patient by pumping air in and out of the lungs. These machines dispense a regulated amount of air into the lungs at a set rate— and periodically purge the lungs. Patients are connected to respirators either by a tube that goes through the mouth and throat into the lung or that is surgically attached to the lung.

• *Surgery.* Surgical procedures such as amputation or a brain shunt are often used to stem the spread of life-threatening infections or to keep vital organs functioning. Major surgery such as a hysterectomy or a heart bypass are also typically performed on patients who are terminally ill or comatose.

• *Comfort care.* The laws of most states assume that people want relief from pain and discomfort and specifically exclude pain-relieving procedures from definitions of life-prolonging treatments that may be withheld. If that was all there was to it, most people would agree with this and welcome the relief. But the medical community disagrees over how much pain or discomfort people feel when they are close to death from a terminal illness or in a permanent coma—and whether providing food and water or drugs to make a person comfortable or alleviate pain will also have the effect of prolonging the person's life.

Some people are so adamant about not having their lives prolonged when they are

comatose or likely to die that they choose to direct that all comfort care and pain relief be withheld in those circumstances even if a doctor thinks those procedures are necessary. Other people are willing to have their lives prolonged rather than face the possibility that discomfort or pain would go untreated.

• *Artificially administered food and water.* If you are close to death from a terminal condition or in a permanent coma and cannot communicate your preferences, it is likely that you will also not be able to voluntarily take in water or food through your mouth. The medical solution is to provide you with food and water—as a mix of nutrients and fluids—through tubes inserted in a vein, into your stomach through your nose or into your stomach through a surgical incision.

Intravenous feeding, where fluids are introduced through a vein in an arm or a leg, is a short-term procedure. Tube feeding through the nose (nasogastric tube), through the stomach (gastrostomy tube), intestines (jejunostomy tube) or largest vein, the vena cava (total parenteral nutrition), can be carried on indefinitely.

To make an informed decision about which procedures you do and do not want, as well as about others which might pertain to your particular medical condition, it may be a good idea to discuss your medical directive with your physician. She can explain the medical procedures more fully and can discuss the options with you. You will also find out whether your doctor has any medical or moral objections to following your wishes. If she does object and will not agree to follow your wishes regardless of those objections, you will probably want to change doctors.

4. Using a Durable Power of Attorney for Health Care

Even when you have specified your wishes in a medical directive regarding life-prolonging and comfort care medical treatment, certain decisions may still be difficult to resolve.

- when, exactly, to administer or withhold certain medical treatments
- whether or not to provide, withhold or continue antibiotic or pain medication, and
- whether to pursue complex, painful and expensive surgeries which may serve to prolong life but cannot reverse the medical condition.

To deal with these situations, in most states you can use a Durable Power of Attorney for Health Care (sometimes called a Health Care Proxy or Patient Advocate Designation) to appoint someone who understands your wishes and whose judgment you trust to make these decisions in accordance with your wishes and in your best interest. To help the appointed person make and carry out these decisions, the power of attorney or proxy form may include specific authorizations:

- to give, withhold or withdraw consent to medical or surgical procedures
- to consent to appropriate care for the end of life, including pain relief
- to hire and fire medical personnel
- to visit you in the hospital or other facility even when other visiting is restricted
- to have access to medical records and other personal information, and
- to get any court authorization required to obtain or withhold medical treatment if, for any reason, a hospital or doctor does not honor the document.

The most important factor in choosing your attorney-in-fact is to select a person you totally trust. Most readers will choose their lover. If your lover can't serve because of health reasons, be sure you pick a person who truly understands you and your life, and who, of course, you can rely on totally.

It is also a good idea to appoint a second person as a backup or replacement attorney-in-fact to act if your first choice is unable or unwilling to serve. Make it clear, however, that the second person is only a back-up. It is not a wise choice to appoint co-proxies: two people who must make decisions would only complicate the process.

 Do Not Appoint Your Doctor As Attorney-in-Fact. Although your doctor is an important person for your attorney-in-fact to consult concerning all health care decisions, you should not appoint your doctor to act as attorney-in-fact. The laws in most states specifically forbid treating-physicians from acting in this role—to avoid the appearance that they may have their own interests at heart and may not be able to act purely according to your wishes.

5. Legal Rules and Conditions

Each state makes its own rules concerning health care directives. Here are some of the rules and conditions of which you should be aware.

Required form. In some states, you must use a form specifically required by special provisions in state law. (See Section 6 below.)

No proxy. Many states recognize living wills but do not have any legal provision for the appointment of a proxy in their health care directive. In these states, if you want to appoint someone to supervise your care and make sure that your wishes are followed, you must prepare a durable power of attorney for health care in addition to a living will. Make sure that your description of the medical treatment you do or do not want is exactly the same in both documents. Or, in your durable power of attorney, simply state that you grant your attorney-in-fact full authority to enforce the instructions you set out in your Living Will, and attach the power of attorney to the Living Will.

6. Preparing Your Health Care Documents

In most instances, you do not need to consult a lawyer to prepare a living will, power of attorney for health care or other medical directive form. The forms are usually quite simple. The Appendix contains six durable power of attorney for health care forms—Forms 2 through 7. Five of the forms are state-specific statutory forms for the states with the estimated largest numbers of lesbian and gay residents: California, Florida, Illinois, New York and Texas. If you live in one of those states, use your state's form.

The sixth form, Form 7, is a general durable power of attorney form, valid in many, but by no means all, of the other states. DO NOT USE THIS FORM in the five states listed above, or in the following states: Kansas, Kentucky, Minnesota, Mississippi, Nevada, New Hampshire, Oklahoma, Oregon, Rhode Island, South Carolina, Utah, Vermont, West Virginia and Wisconsin. In each of these states, laws require that a specific form be used to create a valid durable power of attorney for health care.

We simply don't have space to print every state's specific form in the Appendix. If you live in a state that requires a specific form which we don't include, you can obtain your state-specific form from any of the following:

• Any large hospital. By law, any hospital which receives federal funds must provide patients with appropriate durable power of attorney forms. Check with the Patient Representative of the hospital.

• Most state medical associations will provide the form for a minimal fee. Try calling directory assistance in your state capitol to obtain the phone number of your state's medical association.

• Choice in Dying, 200 Varick Street, New York, NY 10014, (800) 989-9455, will provide you with a form for your state.

• Nolo's *WillMaker* computer program (version 5.0 or later) includes all state-specific medical directive forms.

• National Center for Lesbian Rights, 870 Market Street, Suite 570, San Francisco, CA 94102, (415) 392-6257, can provide you with a durable power of attorney form for your state, along with supporting documents (such as a glossary and information on selecting medical personnel). The form and supporting documents are available for a nominal fee.

7. What to Do With Your Completed Documents

Once you have completed the documents directing your medical care, there are several steps you should take with them.

Signing, witnessing, notarizing. Every state law requires that you sign your documents—or direct another person to sign them for you—as a way of verifying that you understand them and that they contain your true wishes.

Most state laws also require that you sign your documents in the presence of witnesses. The purpose of this additional formality is so that there is at least one other person who can attest that you were of sound mind and of legal age when you made the documents.

Some states also require that you and the witnesses appear before a notary public and swear that the circumstances of your signing, as described in the documents, are true. In some states, you have the option of having a notary sign your document instead of having it witnessed.

Making and distributing copies. Ideally, you should make an effort to make your wishes for your future health care widely known. Keep a copy of your health care directives, and give other copies to:

- any physician with whom you now consult regularly
- any attorney-in-fact or health care proxy you have named, including any back-up
- the office of the hospital or other care facility in which you are likely to receive treatment, and
- any other people or institutions you think

it's wise to inform of your medical intentions, such as a hospice program.

Qualifications for Witnesses

Many states require that two witnesses see you sign your health care documents and that they verify in writing that you appeared to be of sound mind and signed the documents without anyone else influencing your decision.

Each state's qualifications for these witnesses are slightly different. In many states, for example, a spouse, other close relative or any person who would inherit property from you (this most likely includes your lover) is not allowed to act as a witness for the document directing health care. And many states prohibit your attending physician from being a witness.

The purpose of the laws restricting who can witness your documents is to avoid any appearance or possibility that another person was acting against your wishes in encouraging specific medical care. States that prevent close relatives or potential inheritors from being witnesses, for example, justify their restrictions by noting that these people may have a conflict of interest.

---

8. Sample Completed Durable Power of Attorney for Health Care Form

We've found it can help some people to see what a completed health care form looks like. Below is a completed durable power of attorney form, signed and witnessed using Form #7 from the Appendix.

Durable Power of Attorney for Health Care

To my family, friends, physicians, health care providers, community care facilities and any other person who may have an interest in my medical care:

I, _Virginia Vitale_ , being of sound mind, voluntarily create this Durable Power of Attorney for Health Care.

1. Appointment of Attorney-in-Fact

If I become unable to make health care decisions for myself, I appoint the following person as my attorney-in-fact with authority to make health care decisions for me as I direct in this document:

Name:_Edna McNulty_

Address:_2461 Derby St., Lincoln, Nebraska_

Day Phone: _402-555-6011_   Evening Phone: _402-555-6011_

2. Appointment of Alternate Attorney-in-Fact

If that person is unable or unwilling to act as my attorney-in-fact for the purpose of making health care decisions, I appoint the following person to serve:

Name: _Sandra Smith_

Address: _47 Opal Drive, Lincoln, Nebraska_

Day Phone: _402-555-6994_   Evening Phone: _402-555-2204_

3. When Effective

This durable Power of Attorney for Health Care shall:

• become effective when I sign it

• not be affected by my subsequent disability or incompetence, and

• remain in effect until my death, or until I revoke it.

4. Authority I Grant My Attorney-in-Fact

My attorney-in-fact shall have all lawful authority permissible to make health decisions for me, but must also carry out and enforce any specific directions or limitations I provide in this Power of Attorney.

5. Specific Directions and Limitations

I specifically direct that _____ I wish to live as long as I can enjoy life, but I do not wish to receive medical treatment which is futile or will provide no benefit to me. I have discussed my desires with my attorney-in-fact and trust that she will make health care decisions consistent with those desires. I specifically ask that my life not be prolonged and that life-sustaining treatment be withheld or withdrawn: (1) if I am in an irreversible coma or persistent vegetative state; or (2) if I have an incurable injury or am terminally ill and the application of life-sustaining treatment would serve only to delay artificially the moment of my death.

_____ My attorney-in-fact understands that I consider life-sustaining treatment to include (but not be limited to): the use of nasogastric or gastrostomy or other feeding tubes for food or fluids; intravenous therapy for feeding or hydration; the use of ventilators or respirators; dialysis; antibiotic therapy; and cardiopulmonary resuscitation.

_____ I want my attorney-in-fact to consider the relief of suffering and the quality as well as the extent of the possible extension of my life in making decisions concerning life-sustaining treatment. I ask that I be provided with caring and supportive nursing and medical care to relieve pain and suffering, including narcotics to relieve pain even if respiration is depressed by such treatment.

Executed this _____18_____ day of _____December, 1995_____ at _____Lincoln_____, _____Nebraska_____.

Virginia Vitale
Principal's signature

Declaration of Witnesses

I am at least 18 years old. I declare that the person who signed or asked another to sign this document in my presence is personally known to me, and appears to be of sound mind and acting willingly and free from duress.

I also declare that I do not have a claim against the person, am not the person's heir or beneficiary under his or her will or other document, and am not:

- related to the person by blood, marriage, or adoption
- an employee for a life or health insurance provider for the person
- an employee of a health facility that's treating the person, or
- an employee of a nursing or group home where the person resides.

Nancy Dubois
signature

Nancy Dubois
print name

Residence Address: _____23 Piedmont Lane, Lincoln, NB_____

Date: _____December 18, 1995_____

Jezebel Waters
signature

Jezebel Waters
print name

Residence Address: __23 Piedmont Lane, Lincoln, NB__

Date: ____December 18, 1995____

Notarization

State of: ____Nebraska____

County of: ____Lancaster____

On this _____ day of _____ in the year _____, before me, a Notary Public, State of _____, duly commissioned and sworn, personally appeared _____, proved to me on the basis of satisfactory evidence to be the person whose name is subscribed to the within instrument, and acknowleged to me that he or she executed the same.

In witness whereof, I have hereunto set my hand and affixed my official seal in the State of ____Nebraska____ County of ____Lancaster____ on the date set forth above in this certificate.

Notary Public

State of _____

My commission expires _____

9. Revoking a Durable Power of Attorney

You can revoke your durable power of attorney at any time, as long as you are competent. While oral revocation may be possible, you are better off revoking it in writing and giving copies of the revocation to the former attorney-in-fact as well as doctors, hospitals, banks and other people and institutions you gave copies of your power of attorney.

You might want to revoke a durable power of attorney for any number of reasons—for example, you and your lover split up or your lover has become ill and is in no position to serve as your attorney-in-fact. Even if you want to change something in your durable power of attorney—for example, your wishes about life-sustaining procedures or how you want your attorney-in-fact to handle a new piece of property you've inherited—you'll need to revoke the old one. There is no accepted form that can be used to simply amend a durable power of attorney.

Below is a sample revocation. It should be witnessed and notarized. If the durable power of attorney was recorded with the county recorder's office, the revocation must also be recorded.

REVOCATION OF POWER OF ATTORNEY

Recording requested by and when recorded mail to
Josie Jones
154 Main Avenue
Jackson, Wyoming 83001

NOTICE OF REVOCATION OF [RECORDED] POWER OF ATTORNEY

I, Josie Jones, of 154 Main Avenue, City of Jackson, County of Teton, State of Wyoming, executed a power of attorney dated July 10, 1990, appointing Jane Smith, of 154 Main Avenue, City of Jackson, County of Teton, State of Wyoming, my true and lawful attorney-in-fact with full power to act for me and in my name as specified [and such power of attorney was duly recorded on July 10, 1990, in Book 98, at Page 104 of the Official Records, County of Teton, State of Wyoming.]

I hereby revoke the power of attorney given to Jane Smith and all power and authority contained therein.

Dated: August 20, 1996

Josie Jones
_____
Josie Jones, Principal

WITNESSES

Annie Wilson

Annie Wilson of 221 Shattuck Ave., Jackson, Wyoming

Mavis Tarrall

Mavis Tarrall of 9113 Byron Street, Jackson, Wyoming

NOTARIZATION

State of: _____Wyoming_____)
County of: ___Teton___) SS
)

On this __20th__ day of __August__ in the year 1996 ,
before me, a Notary Public, State of Wyoming , duly commissioned and
sworn, personally appeared _Josie Jones_ , proved to me on the basis of
satisfactory evidence to be the person whose name is subscribed to the within
instrument, and acknowleged to me that he or she executed the same.

In witness whereof, I have hereunto set my hand and affixed my official seal in
the State of __Wyoming__ County of __Teton__ on the date set forth above
in this certificate.

Notary Public

State of _____Wyoming_____

My commission expires __June 30, 1997__

B. Self-Deliverance and the Right to a Natural Death

We know of people with AIDS and other terminal illnesses who have wanted to obtain information about self-deliverance or suicide as a means of regaining control over the last part of their lives. Attempting suicide is illegal in most states; similarly, it's illegal for friends, family or medical personnel to aid a suicide attempt. So, practical information about self-deliverance is hard to come by. The best source of information we know of is *Let Me Die Before I Wake,* the Hemlock Society's Book of Self-Deliverance for the Dying, by Derek Humphrey (available from The Hemlock Society, P.O. Box 66218, Los Angeles, CA 90044).

C. Burial and Body Disposition

Burial and body disposition are potential problems for the survivors of someone whose medical emergency results in death. We know of a biological family that claimed the body of a person who died from AIDS and refused to give the service and disposition the deceased had wanted. Instead, they gave their own, which conflicted drastically with the deceased's spiritual values. We even know a surviving partner who was excluded entirely from a burial service. In the past few years, a number of states have passed laws making it illegal for family members to violate a deceased person's wishes as to burial services and body disposition. Whether or not you live in one of these states, however, many painful situations can be avoided by proper planning and advance discussions, so lovers, friends and biological families know what's wanted.

1. Written Instructions

After death, a body must be disposed of quickly. If you haven't left written instructions, nearly every state gives control to your blood relatives—your lover can be excluded. If your lover has the resources to sue to gain control over your body, he may succeed, but these cases are messy and expensive. One man who sued and won was Michael Stewart. When his lover died leaving no instructions, the family took the body and prepared for a religious funeral. Michael sued, arguing that he knew what his lover wanted—and a religious funeral wasn't it. The court gave Michael the right to stop the funeral, due to their spouse-like relationship.[2]

In most states, written body disposition instructions are binding. Written instructions let you state your wishes and name someone to carry them out. Contrary to what many believe, your will is not the best place to leave these instructions. A will is not likely to be found and acted upon until quite some time after your death. If you anticipate objections from your family, make sure to write your instructions in a separate document, then sign and date it. Here are two examples:

Example 1:

I have made arrangements with the Tri-City Funeral Society regarding my funeral and burial. I appoint Alfred Gwynne to be responsible for implementing these arrangements regarding my death.

Example 2:

I have made the following arrangements regarding my death:

1. I have made an agreement with Hillman Hospital, San Francisco, California, to donate any of my organs or body parts needed by the hospital.

2. After any such donation, I direct that my remains be cremated, and my ashes scattered at sea. I have made written arrangements with the Nicean Society regarding my cremation.

3. I direct that Anna Rodriguez, my good friend and executor, be solely responsible for ensuring that these instructions are carried out.

2. Choices Regarding Disposition of the Body

In preparing for your death, you have a number of choices regarding disposition of your body, including esoteric ones like cryonics—body-freezing with the hope of being brought back to life sometime later. The major ones are:

- A traditional funeral at a commercial mortuary or funeral home, which can include embalming. It may also include burial.

- A funeral that you arrange with the help of a funeral society. These exist in many states and provide information about low-cost funerals and burials, and simple, dignified memorial services.

- Cremation, either through a specialized for-profit cremation company, mortuary or funeral home.

- Donation of your body to a medical school.

- Donation of body parts and organs to hospitals or organ banks. People with AIDS cannot donate body parts and organs to hospitals and organ banks. They can often, however, donate their bodies to a medical school.

For decades, funerals and burials were controlled by commercial funeral parlors, which were both secretive and expensive. The business of funerals first came under attack in the 1960s, especially through Jessica Mitford's fine book *The American Way of Death*. Since then, reforms have been instituted in most states. Today it's usually possible to find good funeral services at a reasonable price if you ask knowledgeable friends for recommendations, and monitor costs closely—and most importantly, plan in advance to target the services that fit in with your budget.

We don't have space to give you an exhaustive rundown on each alternative, but here are a few significant points:

- Embalming is generally not legally required.

- Commercial funerals can cost many thousands of dollars. So shop around— compare services offered and check the prices charged by nonprofit funeral societies.

- Burial is also expensive—especially given the high costs of "perpetual care" that many cemeteries charge for maintaining the gravesites.

- Funeral societies exist in most major urban areas. Membership fees are minimal, about $15 to $25. Most funeral societies don't handle funerals or burials themselves, but have contractual arrangements with cooperating local funeral parlors to provide inexpensive services to their members.

- Donation of your body to a medical school requires specific arrangements in advance. In many areas, there's no pressing need for bodies. In all of California, for example, only about 1,000 bodies are needed a year. Bodies donated to medical schools are normally not returned for funerals.

- Donation of body parts is a much more pressing need. Thousands of people in this country are kept alive by dialysis machines while waiting months or years for a kidney transplant. Other organs are needed—eyes, heart tissues, even knee parts have been transplanted. Some states have adopted the Uniform Anatomical Gift Act, which lets you authorize the donation of body parts simply by carrying a short, signed donor card with you. It's useful, though, to arrange with a hospital or organ bank to receive, and use, your donation. Bodies from which organs have been transplanted may be returned for burial—or may be cremated in a designated plot.

- Cremations have increased over the past few years. Cremation is the burning of the body, followed by the inurnment or scattering of the ashes. Some state laws allow ashes to be scattered over private land; other states forbid it. Cremations are offered by most commercial funeral homes and by for-profit organizations such as the Neptune Society or Telephase. Be careful how you specify the service you want. Some funeral homes provide—and charge for—the presence of a coffin at the memorial service, even if you have been cremated.

- Many funeral-burial businesses have couple rates, allowing a couple to pay for services in advance. We know of a business that refused to give its couple rate to a gay couple. This discrimination is legal. Otherwise, we haven't heard of discrimination against lesbians or gay men in the funeral business, although some funeral parlors have refused to handle the bodies of people who died from AIDS. (Support your local gay undertaker!)

D. Estate Planning Note

In preparing for a possible medical emergency, consider what will happen to your property after you die. This is what lawyers call "estate planning," and it's particularly important for seriously ill people. After someone dies, his property is transferred either by his estate planning documents, such as a will, living trust or joint tenancy document, or by laws imposed by his state. No other method is possible. Oral statements about who should get his property made before his death have no legal effect. A durable power of attorney ceases to be effective when the principal dies, so the attorney-in-fact can't transfer the property. Even while the principal is alive, an attorney-in-fact doesn't have the power to make a will or estate plan for the principal.

Without estate planning documents, your lover has no rights over any aspect of what happens to you and your property after your death. Unless you've made written instructions, your lover can't receive any of your property, decide how it's disposed of or arrange for your burial and body disposition.

These dire consequences can be avoided by proper estate planning, which we discuss in Chapter 5. Here we want to stress how important estate planning can be. If you do nothing else, at least prepare a will, so you, not your state's laws, determine who gets your property.

E. Durable Power of Attorney for Finances

A person with a medical crisis is frequently incapable of managing her financial affairs. Exhaustion, recurring dementia, long periods of treatment and many other reasons leave people unable to handle practical matters. During the periods of incapacity, however, bills must be paid, checks drawn, taxes filed, insurance requested and benefits applied for. Also, the ill person may need someone to run her business or buy her Christmas presents.

As we've said, you can authorize someone to handle money matters for you by using a durable power of attorney for finances. You can include any reasonable limitation on the attorney-in-fact's authority, as well as set forth any specific direction. For example, you could restrict your attorney-in-fact from having the power to sell your home, or require him to use money from specified bank accounts to pay certain bills.

Clearly, the most important decision when creating a durable power of attorney for financial affairs is the choice of the attorney-in-fact; most readers will choose their lover. Choose an alternate as well, in case your original choice can't serve. The people

selected should be people you fully trust and who have good business sense.

All 50 states and the District of Columbia permit some form of durable power of attorney for finances. Form 1 in the Appendix is a general durable power of attorney for finances form, good in all states (and the District of Columbia). As you'll see when you look at the form, you first appoint an attorney-in-fact. You then grant or limit financial powers to her simply by writing, or leaving out, your initials in Section 6, where the powers are listed. Each power is defined later in Section 17. For example, Section 6b authorizes powers for "real estate transactions." What this means—and what real estate is included—is defined in Section 17b.

To prepare your own durable power of attorney for finances using Form 1, simply complete the form, typing in the requested information, and making appropriate choices where indicated—such as whether the power of attorney becomes effective when you sign it, or only if you become incapacitated. (If you want the power of attorney to take effect only if you become incapacitated, you power of attorney is called a "springing" durable power of attorney.) You and two witnesses must sign the form before a notary public. The notary notarizes your signatures.

The following states have adopted some specific version of a "statutory short form" durable power of attorney for finances:

Alaska	Indiana	New York
California	Minnesota	North Carolina
Colorado	Montana	Texas
Connecticut	Nebraska	Wisconsin
Illinois	New Mexico	

Although using a state-authorized form is not mandatory, these forms may be more familiar and acceptable to financial institutions than our generic form.

In general though, our financial durable power of attorney will be readily accepted by government agencies, insurance companies, banks and other financial institutions as long as the document has been:

• properly filled in

• signed and dated by the principal

• notarized

• witnessed by at least two people who are not entitled to inherit under the principal's will, and

• recorded with the county recorder's office, if the attorney-in-fact will be handling real estate matters.

On the next pages are an example of a durable power of attorney for finances. A blank version of this form is included in the Appendix. If you use this form, be sure you include the "warnings" at the beginning of it.

Durable Power of Attorney for Financial Management

WARNING TO PERSON EXECUTING THIS DOCUMENT

THIS IS AN IMPORTANT LEGAL DOCUMENT. IT CREATES A DURABLE POWER OF ATTORNEY. BEFORE EXECUTING THIS DOCUMENT, YOU SHOULD KNOW THESE IMPORTANT FACTS:

This document may provide the person you designate as your attorney-in-fact with broad powers to manage, dispose, sell and convey your real and personal property and to borrow money using your property as security for the loan.

THESE POWERS WILL EXIST FOR AN INDEFINITE PERIOD OF TIME UNLESS YOU LIMIT THEIR DURATION IN THIS DOCUMENT. THESE POWERS WILL CONTINUE TO EXIST NOTWITHSTANDING YOUR SUBSEQUENT DISABILITY OR INCAPACITY.

THIS DOCUMENT DOES NOT AUTHORIZE ANYONE TO MAKE MEDICAL OR OTHER HEALTH CARE DECISIONS FOR YOU.

YOU HAVE THE RIGHT TO REVOKE OR TERMINATE THIS POWER OF ATTORNEY.

IF THERE IS ANYTHING ABOUT THIS FORM THAT YOU DO NOT UNDERSTAND, YOU SHOULD ASK A LAWYER TO EXPLAIN IT TO YOU.

1. Attorney-in-Fact

I, _____Jonathan Chen_____ of _____147 Iris St., Detroit, Michigan_____, appoint _____Lucas Wilkes_____ of _229 Apple St., Detroit, Michigan_____ as my attorney-in-fact to act for me in any lawful way with respect to the powers delegated in Part 6 below. If that person (or all of those persons, if more than one is named) does not serve or ceases to serve as attorney-in-fact, I appoint _____Edward Chen_____ of _2461 Derby St., Lincoln, Nebraska_____to serve as attorney-in-fact.

2. More Than One Attorney-in-Fact

a. Authorization

If more than one attorney-in-fact is designated, they are authorized to act:

☐ jointly. ☐ independently.

b. Resolution of Disputes

☐ If my attorneys-in-fact cannot agree on a decision or action under the authority delegated to them in this durable power of attorney, that dispute shall be resolved by binding arbitration. The arbitration shall be carried out by a single arbitrator, who shall be _____ _____, if available. The arbitration shall begin within five days of written notice by any attorney-in-fact to the arbitrator that a dispute between the attorneys-in-fact has arisen. The details of the arbitration shall be determined by the arbitrator. The written decision of the arbitrator shall be binding on all my attorneys-in-fact.

3. Delegation of Authority

My attorney-in-fact ☐ may ☐ may not delegate, in writing, any authority granted under this durable power of attorney to a person he or she selects. Any such delegation shall state the period during which it is valid and specify the extent of the delegation.

4. Effective Date

This power of attorney is effective:

☐ immediately, and shall continue in effect if I become incapacitated or disabled.

☒ only if I become incapacitated or disabled and unable to manage my financial affairs.

5. Determination of Incapacity

For purposes of this durable power of attorney, my incapacity or disability shall be determined by written declarations by ☐ one ☐ two licensed physician(s). Each declaration shall be made under penalty of perjury and shall state that in the physician's opinion I am substantially unable to manage my financial affairs. If possible, the declaration(s) shall be made by _____ _____. No licensed physician shall be liable to me for any actions taken under this part which are done in good faith.

6. Powers of Attorney-in-Fact

I hereby grant to my attorney-in-fact power to act on my behalf in the following matters, as indicated by my initials by each granted power or on line a, granting all the listed powers. Powers that are **not** initialed are **not** granted.

INITIALS

_____	a.	ALL POWERS (b THROUGH m) LISTED BELOW.
___JC___	b.	Real estate transactions.
___JC___	c.	Tangible personal property transactions.
___JC___	d.	Stock and bond, commodity, option and other securities transactions.
___JC___	e.	Banking and other financial institution transactions.
___JC___	f.	Business operating transactions.
___JC___	g.	Insurance and annuity transactions.
_____	h.	Estate, trust, and other beneficiary transactions.
___JC___	i.	Claims and litigation.
___JC___	j.	Personal and family maintenance.
___JC___	k.	Benefits from Social Security, Medicare, Medicaid, or other governmental programs, or civil or military service.
_____	l.	Retirement plan transactions.
___JC___	m.	Tax matters.

Note: These powers are defined in Part 17, below.

7. Special Instructions to the Attorney-in-Fact

_____

_____

_____

_____

8. Compensation and Reimbursement of the Attorney-in-Fact

[X] The attorney-in-fact shall not be compensated for services, but shall be entitled to reimbursement, from the principal's assets, for reasonable expenses. Reasonable expenses include reasonable fees for information or advice from accountants, lawyers or investment experts relating to the attorney-in-fact's responsibilities under this power of attorney.

☐ The attorney-in-fact shall be entitled to reimbursement for reasonable expenses and reasonable compensation for his or her services. Reasonable compensation shall be determined exclusively by the attorney-in-fact.

☐ The attorney-in-fact shall be entitled to reimbursement for reasonable expenses and compensation for his or her services of $_____ per _____.

9. Nomination of Conservator or Guardian

If, in a court proceeding, it is ever resolved that I need a conservator, guardian or other person to administer and supervise my estate or person, I nominate my attorney-in-fact to serve in that capacity. If my attorney-in-fact cannot serve, I nominate the successor attorney-in-fact nominated in Part 1 to serve.

10. Personal Benefit to Attorney-in-Fact

☒ My attorney-in-fact may buy any assets of mine or engage in any transaction he or she deems in good faith to be in my interest, no matter what the interest of or benefit to my attorney-in-fact.

☐ My attorney-in-fact may not be personally involved in or benefit personally from any transaction he or she engages in on my behalf, except _____

_____.

☐ My attorney-in-fact may not be personally involved in or benefit personally from any transaction he or she engages in on my behalf.

11. Commingling by Attorney-in-Fact

My attorney-in-fact ☒ may   ☐ may not   mix (commingle) any of my funds with any funds of his or hers.

12. Bond

The attorney-in-fact shall serve without bond.

13. Liability of Attorney-in-Fact

My attorney-in-fact shall not incur any liability to me, my estate, my heirs, successors or assigns for acting or refraining from acting under this document, except for willful misconduct or gross negligence. My attorney-in-fact is not required to make my assets produce income, increase the value of my estate, diversify my investments or enter into transactions authorized by this document, as long as my attorney-in-fact believes his or her actions are in my best interests or in the best interests of my estate and of those interested in my estate. A successor attorney-in-fact shall not be liable for acts of a prior attorney-in-fact.

14. Gifts by Attorney-in-Fact

My attorney-in-fact may not (i) appoint, assign or designate any of my assets, interests or rights directly or indirectly to himself or herself, or his or her estate or creditors, or the creditors of his or her estate, (ii) disclaim assets to which I would otherwise be entitled if the effect of the disclaimer is to cause such assets to pass directly or indirectly to my attorney-in-fact or his or her estate, or (iii) use my assets to discharge any of his or her legal obligations, including any obligation of support owed to others (excluding me and those whom I am legally obligated to support).

15. Reliance on This Power of Attorney

I agree that any third party who receives a copy of this document may rely on and act under it. Revocation of the power of attorney is not effective as to a third party until the third party has actual knowledge of the revocation. I agree to indemnify the third party for any claims that arise against the third party because of reliance on this power of attorney.

16. Severability

If any provision of this document is ruled unenforceable, the remaining provisions shall stay in effect.

17. Construction of Powers Granted to the Attorney-in-Fact

The powers granted in Part 6 above authorize the attorney-in-fact to do the following.

b.   Real estate transactions

Act for the principal in any manner to deal with all or any part of any interest in real property that the principal owns at the time of execution or thereafter acquires, under such terms, conditions and covenants as the attorney-in-fact deems proper. The attorney-in-fact's powers include but are not limited to the power to:

(1) Accept as a gift, or as security for a loan, reject, demand, buy, lease, receive or otherwise acquire ownership of possession of any estate or interest in real property.

(2) Sell, exchange, convey with or without covenants, quitclaim, release, surrender, mortgage, encumber, partition or consent to the partitioning of, grant options concerning, lease, sublet or otherwise dispose of any interest in real property.

(3) Maintain, repair, improve, insure, rent, lease, and pay or contest taxes or assessments on any estate or interest in real property owned, or claimed to be owned, by the principal.

(4) Prosecute, defend, intervene in, submit to arbitration, settle and propose or accept a compromise with respect to any claim in favor of or against the principal based on or involving any real estate transaction.

c.   Tangible personal property transactions

Act for the principal in any manner to deal with all or any part of any interest in personal property that the principal owns at the time of execution or thereafter acquires, under such terms as the attorney-in-fact deems proper. The attorney-in-fact's powers include but are not limited to the power to:

Lease, buy, exchange, accept as a gift or as security for a loan, acquire, possess, maintain, repair, improve, insure, rent, lease, sell, convey, mortgage, pledge, and pay or contest taxes and assessments on any tangible personal property.

d.   Stock and bond, commodity, option and other securities transactions

Do any act which the principal can do through an agent, with respect to any interest in a bond, share, other instrument of similar character or commodity. The attorney-in-fact's powers include but are not limited to the power to:

(1) Accept as a gift or as security for a loan, reject, demand, buy, receive or otherwise acquire ownership or possession of any bond, share, instrument of similar character, commodity interest or any instrument with respect thereto, together with the

interest, dividends, proceeds or other distributions connected with it.

(2) Sell (including short sales), exchange, transfer, release, surrender, pledge, trade in or otherwise dispose of any bond, share, instrument of similar character or commodity interest.

(3) Demand, receive and obtain any money or other thing of value to which the principal is or may become or may claim to be entitled as the proceeds of any interest in a bond, share, other instrument of similar character or commodity interest.

(4) Agree and contract, in any manner, and with any broker or other person and on any terms, for the accomplishment of any purpose listed in this section.

(5) Execute, acknowledge, seal and deliver any instrument the attorney-in-fact thinks useful to accomplish a purpose listed in this section, or any report or certificate required by law or regulation.

e. Banking and other financial institution transactions

Do any act that the principal can do through an agent in connection with any banking transaction that might affect the financial or other interests of the principal. The attorney-in-fact's powers include but are not limited to the power to:

(1) Continue, modify and terminate any deposit account or other banking arrangement, or open either in the name of the agent alone or in the name of the principal alone or in both their names jointly, a deposit account of any type in any financial institution, rent a safe deposit box or vault space, have access to a safe deposit box or vault to which the principal would have access, and make other contracts with the institution.

(2) Make, sign and deliver checks or drafts, withdraw by check, order or otherwise funds or property of the principal from any financial institution.

(3) Prepare financial statements concerning the assets and liabilities or income and expenses of the principal and deliver them to any financial institution, and receive statements, notices or other documents from any financial institution.

(4) Borrow money from a financial institution on terms the attorney-in-fact deems acceptable, give security out of the assets of the principal, and pay, renew or extend the time of payment of any note given by or on behalf of the principal.

f. Business operating transactions

Do any act that the principal can do through an agent in connection with any business operated by the principal that the attorney-in-fact deems desirable. The attorney-in-fact's powers include but are not limited to the power to:

(1) Perform any duty and exercise any right, privilege or option which the principal has or claims to have under any contract of partnership, enforce the terms of any partnership agreement, and defend, submit to arbitration or settle any legal proceeding to which the principal is a party because of membership in a partnership.

(2) Exercise in person or by proxy and enforce any right, privilege or option which the principal has as the holder of any bond, share or instrument of similar character, and defend, submit to arbitration or settle a legal proceeding to which the principal is a party because of any such bond, share or instrument of similar character.

(3) With respect to a business owned solely by the principal, continue, modify, extend or terminate any contract on behalf of the principal, demand and receive all money that is due or claimed by the principal and use such funds in the operation of the business, engage in banking transactions the attorney-in-fact deems desirable, determine the location of the operation, the nature of the business it undertakes, its name, methods of manufacturing, selling, marketing, financing, accounting, form of organization and insurance, and hiring and paying employees and independent contractors.

(4) Execute, acknowledge, seal and deliver any instrument of any kind that the attorney-in-fact thinks useful to accomplish any purpose listed in this section.

(5) Pay, compromise or contest business taxes or assessments.

(6) Demand and receive money or other things of value to which the principal is or claims to be entitled as the proceeds of any business operation, and conserve, invest, disburse or use anything so received for purposes listed in this section.

g. Insurance and annuity transactions

Do any act that the principal can do through an agent, in connection with any insurance or annuity policy, that the attorney-in-fact deems desirable. The attorney-in-fact's powers include but are not limited to the power to:

(1) Continue, pay the premium on, modify, rescind or terminate any policy of life, accident, health, disability or liability insurance procured by or on behalf of the principal before the execution of this power of attorney. The attorney-in-fact cannot

name himself or herself as beneficiary of a renewal, extension or substitute for such a policy unless he or she was already the beneficiary before the principal signed the power of attorney.

(2) Procure new, different or additional contracts of health, disability, accident or liability insurance on the life of the principal, modify, rescind or terminate any such contract and designate the beneficiary of any such contract.

(3) Sell, assign, borrow on, pledge, or surrender and receive the cash surrender value of any policy.

h.   Estate, trust, and other beneficiary transactions

Act for the principal in all matters that affect a trust, probate estate, guardianship, conservatorship, escrow, custodianship or other fund from which the principal is, may become or claims to be entitled, as a beneficiary, to a share or payment.

i.   Claims and litigation

Act for the principal in all matters that affect claims of or against the principal and proceedings in any court or administrative body. The attorney-in-fact's powers include but are not limited to the power to:

(1) Assert any claim or defense before any court, administrative board or other tribunal.

(2) Submit to arbitration or mediation or settle any claim in favor of or against the principal or any litigation to which the principal is a party, pay any judgment or settlement and receive any money or other things of value paid in settlement.

j.   Personal and family maintenance

To do all acts necessary to maintain the customary standard of living of the principal, the spouse and children and other persons customarily or legally entitled to be supported by the principal. The attorney-in-fact's powers include but are not limited to the power to:

(1) Pay for medical, dental and surgical care, living quarters, usual vacations and travel expenses, shelter, clothing, food, appropriate education and other living costs.

(2) Continue arrangements with respect to automobiles or other means of transportation, charge accounts, discharge of any services or duties assumed by the principal to any parent, relative or friend, contributions or payments incidental to membership or affiliation in any church, club, society or other organization.

k. Benefits from Social Security, Medicare, Medicaid, or other governmental programs, or civil or military service

Act for the principal in all matters that affect the principal's right to government benefits. The attorney-in-fact's powers include but are not limited to the power to:

(1) Prepare, execute, file, prosecute, defend, submit to arbitration or settle a claim on behalf of the principal to benefits or assistance, financial or otherwise.

(2) Receive the proceeds of such a claim and conserve, invest, disburse or use them on behalf of the principal.

l. Retirement plan transactions

Act for the principal in all matters that affect the principal's retirement plans. The attorney-in-fact's powers include but are not limited to the power to:

Select payment options under any retirement plan in which the principal participates, make contributions to those plans, exercise investment options, receive payment from a plan, roll over plan benefits into other retirement plans, designate beneficiaries under those plans and change existing designations.

m. Tax matters

Act for the principal in all matters that affect the principal's local, state and federal taxes. The attorney-in-fact's powers include but are not limited to the power to:

(1) Prepare, sign and file federal, state, local and foreign income, gift, payroll, Federal Insurance Contributions Act returns and other tax returns, claims for refunds, requests for extension of time, petitions, any power of attorney required by the Internal Revenue Service or other taxing authority, and other documents.

(2) Pay taxes due, collect refunds, post bonds, receive confidential information, exercise any election available to the principal and contest deficiencies determined by a taxing authority.

I understand the importance of the powers I delegate to my attorney-in-fact in this document. I recognize that the document gives my attorney-in-fact broad powers over my assets, and that these powers will become effective as of the date of my incapacity (or sooner if specified in this document) and continue indefinitely unless I revoke this durable power of attorney.

Signed this ____14____ day of ___May_____ 19___94___.

State of _____Michigan_____ County of ____Wayne_____

__Jonathan Chen_____   123-45-6789_____
      Your Signature   Your Social Security Number

Witnesses:

On the date written above, the principal declared to me that this instrument is his or her durable power of attorney for financial matters, and that he or she willingly executed it as a free and voluntary act. The principal signed this instrument in my presence.

Name:____Abigail Sweet_____ Name:_____Ira Wembly_____

Address: __4022 Washington Ave.__ Address:____17 Fox Hill Road_____

_____Detroit, Michigan_____ _____Bloomfield Hills, Michigan_____

Certificate of Acknowledgment of Notary Public

State of _____

County of _____

On _____, 19 _____ , before me, _____

_____, a Notary Public, personally appeared _____,

_____ personally known to me or proved to me on the basis of satisfactory evidence to be the person whose name is subscribed to this instrument, and acknowledged that he or she executed it.

_____

(NOTARY SEAL)   Notary Public for the State of _____

                My commission expires: _____

Endnotes

[1]*Cruzan v. Director, Missouri Dept. of Health*, 497 U.S. 261.

[2]*Stewart v. Schwartz Brothers–Jeffer Memorial Chapel, Inc.*, 19 Family Law Reporter 1544 (1993). ∎

Looking Ahead: Estate Planning

Few people look forward to the day when they will die; making plans for that inevitable time can seem dull, even macabre. But it's vitally important that lesbians and gays—especially those who are coupled—plan what they want to happen to their property after they die. This is called estate planning. Generally, if you die without a will (or living trust or other legal means for transferring property), your property will be distributed under your state's "intestacy" laws. These laws require that *all* your property pass to certain specified relatives, namely a spouse, children, parents and siblings. State death laws don't recognize lesbian and gay relationships.

If you have a living together contract, you may think you've done enough. But that's not the case. A living together contract defines how a couple owns property while both partners are alive. It's not a substitute for a will or living trust, documents which validly and legally specify what happens to a person's property after he or she dies.

If you don't take steps to "plan your estate"—that is, you don't draft a will, create a living trust or follow any of the other suggestions in this chapter—your surviving lover can try to obtain your property by arguing, or litigating, that your living together agreement (even an oral one) gives her rights to that property. But it's far from certain that her claim would succeed.

She might have to sue, which will be time-consuming, expensive and nasty. Don't risk it. Rather, be sure to specify, in an appropriate legal document, what will happen to your property at your death. If you and your partner have mixed property and it's unclear who owns what, you can resolve that in a clearly defined living together contract.

We know quite a few horror stories involving people's families suddenly swooping down on a surviving lover to claim all the deceased person's property. Some years ago, an article in *Christopher Street* magazine described the plight of one man whose lover died and left no will. The deceased's family quickly appeared and started removing property from the couple's apartment. "His mother took the pillows and pillowcases off the bed," the lover said. "I ended up having to fight for my own clothes. We wore the same size."

Deciding what you want done with your property after you die isn't the only benefit of estate planning. If you and your lover are raising a child together but only you are the recognized legal parent, you can nominate your lover as a guardian for your child. Further, you can appoint the person you want to be responsible for supervising the distribution of your property. You can also summarize your wishes for memorial services and body disposition or specify that the arrangements are to made by your lover, though we recommend that you do this in a document separate from your will (See Chapter 4, Section C, for a more detailed discussion of burial and body disposition.)

This chapter presents two approaches to estate planning. Section C covers wills, the most basic of all estate planning documents, and contains a sample completed will form. The same form is included, blank, in the Appendix. At a minimum, we urge you to prepare a will.

![warning icon] **The will in this chapter and the Appendix is only a "bare bones" basic will.** It is fully legal, if properly prepared, typed, signed and witnessed, as described below. You can leave your property to whomever you choose and name a guardian for your minor children. But many other needs you might have are not covered by this will, due to space constraints. For example, we don't cover how you can leave an item of property to be shared by more than one person. Similarly, we don't explain how you can leave property to your child but delay the age at which she becomes entitled to receive it.

Our main points are that you need a will and should prepare it soon, real soon. Use our will—it's better than having no will at all. But many readers can benefit from a thorough explanation of all that can be done in a will. If your situation is in any way complex—you want to make a shared gift, you want to appoint different guardians for different minor children, or you fear that your biological family will challenge your will—we urge you to consult one of Nolo's more detailed will preparation resources: *Nolo's Simple Will Book*, by Denis Clifford, or *WillMaker*, a computer program which allows you to write your own will on a computer. (Both resources are good in all states but Louisiana.) And if neither of these meets your needs, you can always consult a lawyer.

Section D covers more extensive estate planning. Transferring all your property by a will can have drawbacks, principally probate. Probate is a legal proceeding where your will is filed with a court, your assets identified, your debts paid and your property distributed to your heirs. Probate is usually expensive and time-consuming. By planning ahead, you can eliminate or lessen the need for probate, and sometimes save on death taxes. Section D can help you to decide whether your estate planning can end with a will, or whether more is warranted.

Before we plunge into particulars of wills and estate planning, let us acknowledge that giving attention to the practical consequences of death, while important, is quite minor when compared to the misery, grief and tragedy of the death of a loved one. We share the thoughts of a friend who lost his lover of nearly three decades.

A. Reflections on the Death of a Mate

Recognizing that one individual's reactions to death are no basis for generalization, I offer the following only as a personal response to a question about the feelings a survivor experiences when an abiding homosexual relationship is ended by the death of one of the partners. My only qualification for doing so lies in being such a survivor after a mutual love of nearly thirty years.

From what I perceive through observation, through literature, or by intuition, I strongly suspect that, except for easier distribution of property in a legally binding relationship, there may not be great differences of impact for the survivor whether the love has been homosexual or heterosexual. The death of a mate obviously leaves one emotionally and, in the case of a long illness, physically spent. What are the significant feelings that survive after the initial shock of finality has exhausted itself in the busy-work that ensues around the affairs of the decedent? Despair isn't quite one of them, for if a close relationship has endured two or three decades, each partner has already recognized and yielded to the necessity for mutual independence and steadfast self-reliance. Nonetheless, there's a transient sense of cosmic inquiry: "What am I doing here?" which may easily deteriorate to, "What am I doing anywhere?" But the daily business of living—and it may seem a business without profit—does supersede such disorientation.

The feelings that continue, and which most poignantly harbor the pain, can be identified, I believe, as essentially two. The first of these is the piercing loneliness of having no focus for one's affection after so long a time. The emptiness of not loving is an infinite void, and it summons the most painful recognition of loss. Such feelings, however, though perpetual, aren't near the surface and reveal themselves most forcefully in what seems to be the dullness of leisure or in the sadness of reflection.

Lying nearer the surface are the daily—sometimes hourly, for a little while perhaps constant—reminders that feed the second and more persistent pain, one that will never be totally consumed. Couples inevitably develop their own language, visual as well as verbal, based on shared experiences, shared jokes, mutual acceptance of difficulty, shared joys and sorrows, reciprocal devotion. Layers are thereby added to the relationship much as alluvial deposits are washed down to enrich life's texture in a less psychologically ornamented environment. The survivor continues to use that language, for it's a part of him, although he now lacks an auditor who grasps its overtones, undertones and essential meanings. When those symbols, and the figure in the carpet which they represent, appear—whether verbally, cerebrally or viscerally—and no one's there to recognize an allusion, to be counted on for sympathetic amusement at one's own folly, to recognize an earlier situation now cryptically cited to give sharpened meaning to the present, the vacancy is felt as the ebbing away of an adult lifetime.

For those of us who aren't artists, the structure which houses those symbols may be the closest we shall ever come to the creation of poetry. Like poetry, the form of communication and its underlying history make up an economical construct of imagery that distills experience. To borrow a verb from Gerard Manley Hopkins, the distillation "explodes" as mutual recognition, as ineffable joy, as reciprocal contemplativeness—in short, as the impact of art. The irreversible decay of the only context in which the construct obtained, and in which a man's life has been elevated out of the limitations of self-concern into felicitous union, is what I perceive to be the basis of grief. Although the "grief returns with the revolving year," it is, in the fullness of time, merged into a sense of one's own good fortune, into the joyful remembrances of things past, and into an appreciation for what the relationship still contributes to one's future.

B. Death and Living Together Contracts

In Chapter 6, we explain that most states enforce written living together contracts that cover property. If you have a contract stating that you're the half-owner of specific property, your partner has no power to dispose of your share, either during life or at death. And if your contract says that you become the sole owner of all co-owned property at your lover's death, this provision will normally be honored, unless he leaves a will to the contrary. If this occurs, a dispute is likely to ensue between the surviving lover and the beneficiary under the will over who gets the deceased person's one-half share of the property. This is something you and your lover obviously want to plan to avoid through good, shared estate planning.

If you and your lover have no written contract, and much of the property was in the name of the deceased, the survivor may claim that an oral or implied living together contract existed by which the couple had agreed to share property ownership equally.[1] But to prevail with this argument, the surviving partner would have to sue the heirs who inherit by will or intestate succession (automatic inheritance laws when the deceased had no will or trust) and prove that the oral or implied contract really existed, or that she should get the property under an equitable remedy.

No hard and fast rules govern how a survivor can prove that an oral or implied contract existed in order to get a share of the deceased's estate. But if you're the survivor of a person who left no will (or who left a will but disposed of property you believe is yours by contract), you may have a case if any of the following situations exist:

- You worked in the home and your lover earned the money, but you agreed to share everything. In some states, you may be able to claim property under an oral contract. In some other states, your claim might be under an implied contract or other equitable remedy on the theory that you worked with the expectation of being paid, which never happened.

- You and your lover bought items jointly, and had agreed that all property belonged to both, with the survivor taking 100% if the other died. With a written agreement you'd have little trouble prevailing, but even with an oral agreement, you may succeed, especially if friends and relatives will step forward and testify that they knew about your understanding. It will also depend, to some extent, on the attitude of the deceased's relatives otherwise entitled to inherit. If they are supportive of you, or will work out a compromise, a probate court will likely go along.

- You and your lover jointly contributed to the purchase of real property, but the property was put in only the deceased's name. In most states, it's difficult to rebut the legal presumption that the person whose name is on the deed is the legal owner, but you may be able to establish the legal grounds necessary to support an equitable remedy that would result in your receiving a portion of the property.

C. Wills

A will is a document in which you specify who gets your property when you die. These people and institutions are called your "beneficiaries." The advantages of a will are the following:

- A will is relatively easy to make.
- You can leave your property to anyone you wish. No laws prohibit you from leaving your property to your lover (or anyone else, for that matter).
- A will is easy to change or revoke; you're not stuck with it once you make it.
- Your will is your own business. Discussing it with your lover is probably a good idea, but you're not required to reveal its contents to anyone.

As we've mentioned, the considerable drawback to using a will is probate. After reading Section D, you may decide to take steps to avoid probate. Even if you do, you should also make a will. First, you may have property at your death that you hadn't thought of, or known of, when planning your estate, such as a suddenly inherited house, a gift of an expensive stereo or computer, big winnings at the races or a personal injury lawsuit recovery. If you have a will, you can simply pass the "residue of your property" (any property you own not specifically left to beneficiaries in your will or by other methods) to your lover. And, as we mentioned, in a will you can also name who will supervise distribution of your property and nominate a guardian for your minor child.

Once you decide what property you want to transfer by will, don't delay in preparing the document. There is no benefit to postponing the drafting of your will; delay only increases the risks of the consequences of an untimely death—that is, your parents or siblings inheriting all of your property, rather than your property going to whom you've chosen.

1. Who Can Make a Will?

Anyone who's legally an adult and "of sound mind" can make a valid will. An adult is anyone 18 years or older (19 or older if you live in Wyoming, and 19 or older for real estate in Alabama). You have to be very far gone before your will can be invalidated on the grounds that you weren't "of sound mind." If you're reading this book, you're competent to draft a will.

The will form in this book can be used by residents of all states except Louisiana, which has a different legal system than those of the other states. (Louisiana's law comes from French, not English, law.) If you live in Louisiana, you'll need to see a lawyer to prepare a will. (See Chapter 10, Section A.)

Most other people, however, don't need a lawyer. A will can readily be prepared without the assistance, and cost, of a lawyer. If you have a large estate and desire extensive estate planning (complicated trusts, "pour-over" wills—that sort of thing), you'll need to have your will prepared by a lawyer. But if you have a moderate estate and envision a straightforward distribution, you can very likely prepare your own will. Lawyers try to scare people into buying their expensive services by claiming that each will requires "expert, professional attention," then routinely have their secretaries use the same form-book wills, over and over and over again.

2. Providing for Your Children

There are many lesbian and gay couples whose relationships include a child or children, whether from donor insemination, an earlier marriage or adoption. (See Chapter 3 for more information.) Either member of such a couple can leave property to their own or their lover's children without problems. You simply name the children in your will and leave them whatever you want. Or, you and your lover can leave all property to each other, and then name the children as alternate beneficiaries.

Providing for your minor children, however, does inevitably raise concerns. If you die before they're grown, who will care for them and how will they be supported? Let's look at each of these concerns separately.

a. Custody

The legal parent or parents of a minor child are the person or persons entitled to custody of that child. If there is only one legal parent, that parent can direct, but not mandate, who will have custody of the child if the legal parent dies. When there are two legal parents (whether members of a same-sex couple, or the divorced parents of a child), each is entitled to custody. If one dies, the other automatically has sole custody.

Some lesbian and gay couples share legal custody of a child by adoption, including second-parent adoptions. But most lesbian and gay couples with a child do not have this joint legal protection. In most cases, only one member of the couple—the biological parent or sole adoptive parent—has custody rights.

If no competent and willing legal parent is available, another adult must have legal responsibility for caring for a minor child, unless the child is legally emancipated.[2] This adult is called the child's personal guardian. Only a legal parent can name a personal guardian in his or her will for a minor child.

The nomination of a minor child's personal guardian in a will is not legally binding. Children are not property and cannot be transferred by will as if they were. The final decision is made by a judge, using the standard of the child's "best interest." A personal guardian nominated by a parent is usually confirmed by a court, however. Normally, only if there is a contested custody proceeding, or some obvious flaw in the guardian (for example, she shows up drunk to court), will a court reject the guardian nominated by the parent.

With most lesbian or gay couples, only one parent has authority to name the minor's personal guardian. That parent can, and usually does, name her lover as the personal guardian. But if she does not do so, and she dies, the surviving lover will probably have, at best, an uphill battle to gain custody. The lover must convince a court that the person nominated or the deceased's relative is not the best person to raise the child, and that she, the lover, is.

The parent or parents who name a personal guardian for their minor child in a will can also name an alternate guardian, just in case the first choice can't serve.

b. Support

Either member of a lesbian or gay couple can leave property to the couple's minor child, regardless of who is the legal parent. Of course, before you can consider leaving money or property to a minor, you must have something to leave. If you have little beyond a big mortgage and car payments, you might consider buying a moderate amount of term life insurance to help provide for your child if you die, until he is on his own. Because term life insurance pays benefits only if you die during the covered period (often five or ten years), it's far cheaper than other types of life insurance.

Assuming you have property to leave to your children, your first concern is who will manage it if you die before your children are mature enough to have it. Except for property of little value, the law requires that an adult manage property inherited by minors until they turn 18. If you don't designate a manager in your estate plan, a court will appoint one for you. These court procedures are time-consuming, costly and may produce a result you wouldn't approve of. Here are several ways to do it yourself:

- *Leave property directly to your children's other parent.* You can use the will in this book to do this. It's an excellent approach if you've a close-knit family and the other parent is a competent financial manager. Especially if moderate amounts are involved, it often doesn't make sense to create a more elaborate plan.

- *Use the provisions of the Uniform Transfers to Minors Act (UTMA).* In most states, you can use the UTMA to name a custodian to manage property you leave to your minor children for their benefit until the children are either 18 or 21 (up to 25 in California, Alaska and Nevada). The UTMA works particularly well for leaving $100,000 or less, since chances are an amount of money or property in this range will have been spent for the child's education and living expenses by age 21. To use the UTMA, you can use one of Nolo's specialized estate planning or will-drafting products (see Estate Planning Resources box at the end of this chapter).

• *Create a child's trust.* For large estates, $100,000 or more, consider establishing a simple child's trust, in either your will or living trust. Like the UTMA discussed above, the trustee of a child's trust manages the money for your child and doles it out for education, health and other needs under the terms of the trust. The child's trust ends, and any remaining money is turned over to your child outright, at whatever age you designate. Again, see the Estate Planning Resources list at the end of the chapter.

 Name the same person to care for your child and any property you leave that child. It's wise to nominate the same person you nominated as personal guardian to serve as custodian of your children's money and other property (in your will, or under the UTMA or in a child's trust), unless that person doesn't have good financial sense. If you face this problem, you are better off naming different people to care for your child and manage her finances, but make sure your choices are personally compatible, as they will have to work together if you die before your child is an adult.

3. Typical Will Provisions

Some important matters you can take care of in a will include the following:

• You can leave anything you own to anyone or any institution you choose. You can leave money, book royalties or clothes. You never have to state your relationship to the beneficiary—it's no one's business. Once you draft your will, you don't have to hold onto property just because it's left to someone in your will. If you left your Renoir painting to your friend Bob in your will, but sell the painting before you die, Bob's out of luck.

• You can forgive debts owed to you.

• You can suggest a personal guardian for your minor children.

• You can name a property guardian to manage your minor children's property.

• You can set up simple trusts for your children or leave UTMA gifts.

• You can name the person who will super-vise the distribution of your property left by your will. This person is called your executor or, in some states, your personal representative. You can name your lover, or anyone you trust, to be your executor. Some states require that a bond be posted if your executor doesn't live in the state; so it is a good idea to name an executor who lives in the same state you do.

• You can disinherit people. You can't completely disinherit a spouse—but this is a problem few of our readers will face. If that issue does concern you, see *Plan Your Estate,* by Denis Clifford and Cora Jordan (Nolo Press).

Disinheriting

You can disinherit almost anyone by simply not mentioning him or her in your will. To disinherit a spouse or child (or child of a deceased child), however, requires more explicit action. We don't cover spouses here. To disinherit a child (or child of a deceased child), you can state the disinheritance expressly in your will—"I disinherit my son William Jones and direct that he receive nothing from my estate." The will form in this book provides a general clause that will result in a child's or children's disinheritance if you don't leave property to them. Specifically, the will states: "If I do not leave property in this will to one or more of my children or my grandchildren named above, my failure to do so is intentional." If you want to use an express disinheritance clause, you'll find samples in *Nolo's Simple Will Book*, by Denis Clifford.

Some states have laws, called "pretermitted heir" statutes, which are designed to prevent accidental disinheritance of children. These laws provide that if you fail to mention a child born after your will was made, that child receives a set percentage of your estate. So, if you have a child after writing your will, you should revise the will to leave something to that child.

4. Technical Requirements in Preparing a Will

For your will to be valid:

- It must be typed—or partially typed and partially printed.

- It must state that it's your will—"This is the will of (your name)" suffices.

- It must be signed and dated by you after declaring to witnesses that it's your will.

Some authorities recommend you say, "This is my will," and the witnesses answer, "He says it's his will." It sounds like Gilbert and Sullivan, but it can't hurt. More importantly, the witnesses must know the document is your will, but aren't expected (or required) to read it.

- It must be signed and dated by three witnesses who are not beneficiaries under the will. They sign after you. In many states, only two witnesses are required. Using a third, however, can't hurt and means the will is valid in all states.

5. Are Handwritten Wills Valid?

Handwritten wills are called "holographic." In some states they are valid; in others, they're not. Regardless of your state's rule, your will should be typed and witnessed, not handwritten (and unwitnessed). Holographic wills often receive suspicious treatment by courts. They must be letter-perfect and can't have any cross-outs, machine-printed dates or technical errors. If you're trapped in the woods and the wolves are coming to get you, write out a will and say your prayers. When you return to civilization, prepare a formal (typed) will and sign it before witnesses.

6. Are Joint Wills Valid?

A joint will is one document through which two people leave their property. After the first person dies, the joint will specifies what happens to the property of the second person when she dies. We don't recommend joint wills; the survivor, we believe, should have the freedom to dispose of her property. If you're thinking of using a joint will despite our recommendation, see a lawyer.

7. Is My Will Valid If I Move to a New State?

If you follow our advice, your will will be valid in any state except Louisiana. You might want to draft a new will after you move, however, if your executor now resides in a different state. To accomplish this change, you can revoke your will and write a new one, or add a "codicil" changing your executor. (See Section C.10, below.)

8. Preparing a Basic Will

The sample will form in the example below can be used by most people with a moderate-sized estate to prepare a basic will. We show the sample form after its initial completion, but not yet retyped into final form or signed and witnessed. We do this so you can see what a form looks like with blanks filled in and inappropriate sections crossed out. If you prepare your own will using the form in the Appendix, you'll need to fill in whatever requested information applies to you, make the necessary changes and eliminate the clauses that don't apply.

Here are some guidelines on preparing a basic will using the form in the Appendix.

Do it in two steps. After reading this chapter, prepare a rough draft of your will, using or adapting the form in the Appendix. Once you're satisfied you've covered everything, type the will on 8-1/2" x 11" white typing paper. (You can use a computer.)

Let us repeat—complete only the clauses that pertain to you. If you were never married, delete Clause II, "Prior Marriages." Then renumber the remaining clauses. Thus, clause "III: Children" would become "II: Children."

Use plain language and common sense. If you write "I leave my car to my sister Sue," she will receive whatever car you own when you die. If you write, "I leave my Toyota to my sister Sue," and sell it before you die and buy a Porsche, Sue gets no car. Courts try to give effect to the "intent" of the will writer, but they can't contradict clear words.

Don't make changes before you sign your will. If you want to change your will before it's signed and witnessed, don't just cross something out and initial the change. Instead, you'll need to retype it. And after the will has been completed—signed, dated and witnessed—you can make changes only by using a "codicil." (See Section B.9.a, below.)

Will

Will of _____Samuel Troplon_____

I, _Samuel Troplon_____, a resident of __New York____County, __Queens_____, declare that this is my will.

I. Revocation

I revoke all wills and codicils that I have previously made.

II. Prior Marriages

I was married to _____ and am now divorced.

III. Children

A. I have __1__ children now living, whose names and dates of birth are:
                                                                    is:

Name _Florette Jones-Troplon_____

Date of Birth _March 6, 1987_____

[Repeat as often as needed]

The terms "my children" as used in this will shall include any other children hereafter born to or adopted by me.

B. I have the following children of my deceased child_____.

Name_____

Date of Birth_____

[Repeat as often as needed]

C. If I do not leave property in this will to one or more of my children or my grandchildren named above, my failure to do so is intentional.

D. If at my death any of my children are minors, and a personal guardian is needed, I recommend that _____Martin Jones_____ be appointed guardian of the persons of my minor children. If ____Martin Jones_____ cannot or refuses to serve, I nominate _my brother Aaron Troplon_____ as guardian of the persons of my minor children.

E. If at my death any of my children are minors and a property guardian is needed, I name ____Martin Jones_____ to be appointed guardian of the property of my minor children. If _____Martin Jones_____ cannot or refuses to serve, I name _____my brother Aaron Troplon_____ to be appointed guardian of the property of my minor children.

IV. Gifts

A. I make the following gifts of money or personal property:

1. I give every child or grandchild listed in Clause III $1.00 (one dollar) in addition to any other property I may give them elsewhere in this will, or otherwise.

2. I give the sum of $ ____5,000____ to _____my friend Alice Beckwith_____ if ~~he~~/she/~~it~~ survives me by 60 days; if ~~he~~/she/~~it~~ doesn't, this gift shall be made to __Tim Grayson_____.

[Repeat as often as needed]

3. I give __my 1990 Ford Fiesta_____ to __June Rochelle_____ if ~~he~~/she/~~it~~ survives me by 60 days; if ~~he~~/she/~~it~~ doesn't, the gift shall be made to _Leo Portnoy_____.

[Repeat as often as needed]

4. I forgive and cancel the debt of $_1,000__ owed to me by __Peter Block____.

[Repeat as often as needed]

B. I make the following gifts of real estate:

1. I give my interest in the real estate in ___Queens, New York___, commonly known as ___423 75th Avenue, Forest Hills___, to ___Martin Jones___ if he/~~she/it~~ survives me for 60 days. If he/~~she/it~~ doesn't survive me for 60 days, that property shall be given to ___Florette Jones-Troplon___.

[Repeat as often as needed]

V. Residue

I give the residue of my property subject to this will as follows:

A. To ___Martin Jones___, if he/~~she/it~~ survives me by 60 days.

B. If not, to ___Florette Jones-Troplon___ if he/~~she/it~~ survives me by 60 days.

C. If neither ___Martin Jones___ nor ___Florette Jones-Troplon___ survives me by 60 days, then to ___my brother Aaron Troplon___.

VI. Executor

A. I nominate ___Howard Black___ as executor of this will, to serve without bond. If ___Howard Black___ shall for any reason fail to qualify or cease to act as executor, I nominate ___Rachel Robertson___ to serve without bond.

B. I grant to my executor the right to place my obituary of ~~her~~/his choosing in the papers ~~she~~/he thinks appropriate.

VII. No Contest

If any person or persons named to receive any of my property under my will in any manner contests or attacks this will or any of its provisions, that person or persons shall be disinherited and shall receive none of my property, and my property shall be disposed of as if that contesting beneficiary had died before me leaving no children.

VIII. Simultaneous Death

If ___Martin Jones___ and I should die simultaneously, or under such circumstances as to render it difficult or impossible to determine who predeceased the other, I shall be conclusively presumed to have survived _____Martin Jones_____ for purposes of this will.

I subscribe my name to this will this _7th_ of ___March___, ___1996___, at _New York_, _Queens_, _New York_.

___Samuel Troplon___

IX. Signature and Witnessing

On this _____ of_____, _____, _____ declared to us, the undersigned, that this instrument was [his/her] will, and requested us to act as witnesses to it. [He/she] thereupon signed this will in our presence, all of us being present at the time. We now, at [his/her] request, in [his/her] presence, and in the presence of each other, subscribe our names as witnesses and declare we understand this to be [his/her] will, and that to the best of our knowledge the testator is competent to make a will, and under no constraint or undue influence.

We declare under penalty of perjury that the foregoing is true and correct.

Witness's Signature _____
Address _____

Witness's Signature _____
Address _____

Witness's Signature _____
Address_____

Completing the Will Form

Here we cover some basics of how to complete the clauses of the will in the Appendix.

Your Name and Address

Use your full name and use it the same way throughout the will.

Your address is important because if, at the time of your death, you had connections with more than one state, each state may try to impose death taxes. Giving your residence will help minimize this, and will help establish in which county your will is to be probated. (It's probated in the county where you made your home.) If you have real ties to more than one state, see a lawyer to figure out how to keep more than one from trying to impose death taxes.

I. Revocation

This clause applies to and covers all prior wills, including any handwritten document that could possibly be construed as a will.

II. Prior Marriages

Fill in this clause only if you've ever been married. If you have, mention the marriage(s) and that it (they) ended (obviously, we're assuming it has). If you are still legally married, you will want to see a lawyer before completing your will.

III. Children

If you have any children, list them all, and all children of any child of yours who has died. Your children are those for whom you are a legally recognized parent—that is, children you have given birth to, biologically fathered or adopted. If you are co-parenting, but are not legally recognized as a parent, you would not include the children here. Instead, you can provide for them in Clause IV.

As previously mentioned, if you wish to disinherit a child using this will, you can do so by leaving nothing to that child. The child will be disinherited under the terms of Clause III.C.

If you have custody of minor children, you can nominate a personal guardian for those children in Clause III.D. Lesbian and gay parents are usually very concerned with who will get custody of their minor children when they die. State laws strongly favor granting custody to a surviving legal parent over everyone else. Many divorced gay parents want their lovers, not their ex-spouses, to have custody. But the law is clear. Parents cannot "will" their children. If the only legal parent dies, a judge decides who will have custody of the child. The parent, however, can nominate a person in the will, and the judge will usually give that nomination considerable weight. For more information on wills and custody of minor children, see *Nolo's Simple Will Book,* by Denis Clifford.

You can also use Clause III.E to name a property guardian for your minor children; this person will manage any property you leave your children and can manage any other property they acquire before they become 18. In most situations, children receive inherited property when they turn 18. If you want your children to get the property later, you can use something called a child's trust. In it, you specify the age the minor must reach before she receives the property, and name the trustee—the adult who will manage the property until the minor reaches that age. The trust also sets forth the terms of the trust, for example, that trust income can be used for the minor's education. Nolo's *WillMaker* software allows you to create a will with a child's trust on your home computer, and *Nolo's Simple Will Book* includes child's trusts in the will forms.

Stand-By Guardians

When a child has only one legal parent, the child may be placed in foster care after the parent dies but before the judge appoints the guardian.

Illinois, New York and a few other states get around this by letting the legal parent appoint a stand-by guardian—likely to be the same person nominated to be the legal guardian—to have custody immediately after the parent dies. The child avoids foster care and is placed with the adult with whom she is likely to live.

IV. A. Gifts of Money or Personal Property

In Clause A, you name beneficiaries for your money and personal property. Your personal property is everything but your real estate, which you give away in Clause B. Clause A lets you make direct, unconditional gifts to a single beneficiary, either a person or organization. If you want to leave a certain item of property to be shared by two or more people, see Nolo's other will resources or a lawyer. And, if you want to place conditions on a gift—for example, "I leave my boat to Ronald but only if he graduates from culinary school"—you'll need to see a lawyer.

If you leave someone money, you might want to add to the bequest "but in no event more than [number] percent of my (net or probate) estate" just in case there's not as much there as you'd planned.

You can also name an alternate beneficiary if the beneficiary doesn't survive you. If you don't name such a person, and the beneficiary dies before you, your property becomes part of your "residue" in Clause V, and goes to your residuary beneficiary.

Many people don't want to leave something to someone who will never benefit from it, and so they require the beneficiary to survive them by some specified period of time. We require the beneficiary to survive you by 60 days in order to receive the property. You can specify any other reasonable period you want, such as 30 or 100 days (two years isn't reasonable).

If you plan to give specific items of property to a beneficiary, describe them with sufficient detail so there is no question as to what property you mean. If you want to leave many small items to someone, however, and you don't want to list them all, you can state that you give "all my furniture [or "my tools" or "my records"] to [name]." If you don't care who gets your minor pieces of personal property, you can add a clause stating that these items "are to be distributed as my executor deems proper."

In Clause IV.A.4, you can also forgive (forget) debts owed you. Forgiving a debt is in reality making a gift to the debtor, who would otherwise owe the money to your estate.

IV. B. Gifts of Real Estate

In Clause B, you name beneficiaries for your real estate. As with personal property, it's wise to include a survivorship period, and to name an alternate beneficiary if the primary beneficiary doesn't survive the survivorship period. If the beneficiary (and alternate beneficiary, if you name one) doesn't survive you, the real estate becomes a part of your residue.

When you make a gift of real estate, all mortgages and other debts (such as tax liens) on the property go with it. If you want to give real estate free of a mortgage, see one of Nolo's other will resources.

V. Residue

The "residue" in your will is exactly what it sounds like—all property subject to your will remaining after the specific gifts in Clause IV have been distributed. You can select any person(s) or organization(s) you want to receive the "residue" of your estate. It's prudent to name an alternate beneficiary for your residue. If you want to be really careful, you can name a second alternate beneficiary to receive your will residue if the first two don't survive within the 60 (or however many you choose) days. Many people simply leave the bulk of their estate to their residuary beneficiary, rather than list all their property in Clause IV.

VI. Executor

Your executor should be someone you trust and can rely on, and who will be available and competent when you die. You should name at least one successor executor in case your first choice dies before you, declines to serve or is incompetent when you die. (If your will names no executor or no alternate when an alternate is needed, the probate court appoints one.)

If you don't state that the executor is "to serve without bond," the probate court will probably require the executor to post a sum of money. This means either that a large amount of cash from the estate is tied up or that the estate must pay a bondsman's fee (usually 10% of the amount of the bond).

If you name an out-of-state executor, the court may require a bond, even if you stated "to serve without bond."

VII. No Contest

Clearly, this clause is designed to discourage will contests. We have not included any general disinheritance clause, or a clause giving $1 to all nieces and nephews. As discussed, children are a special case and can be disinherited specifically if you want or you can do so under the terms of the will by not leaving them property. There's no need to specifically exclude other people; most will drafters and contemporary will-form books omit a general disinheritance clause.

A lawyer can help you if you think anyone in your family will challenge your will. If your relatives object to your sexual orientation, it's possible that they will challenge your will on grounds that you were incompetent, or under "undue influence," when you made your will, especially if you have considerable money. This may be even more likely if you leave your property to your lover, other gay or lesbian friends or a gay and/or lesbian organization. Although will contests are rare, they do happen, especially in cases of people with AIDS. Anyone diagnosed with AIDS should prepare a will as early after diagnosis as possible, to minimize the chance that the will will be successfully challenged on the grounds the you weren't mentally competent when you signed it.

If there's any real possibility that a relative will challenge your will, take action to establish that you are competent and not under undue influence when you sign it. If worse comes to worst, this evidence can be used in court after your death.

One possibility is to have your will prepared by and signed in front of a lawyer, who can testify that you were obviously competent. Another possibility is to write your will yourself and pay a lawyer only for review and the signing. If you're truly concerned about a challenge, explore various possibilities. Consult a lesbian/gay attorney service which can provide lawyers experienced with will contests. Consider using a lawyer who's familiar with videotaping, so when you sign your will, you can look into the camera and tell the world how sane you are. Or follow the approach of one lawyer who advises her lesbian and gay

clients to insert a clause like the following, which shows you considered leaving your property to your relatives:

> *I don't make my gifts to Ben Tymons out of any lack of love for my parents, sister, brother, Aunt Susan, Uncle Jonathan, cousin Cynthia, cousin Harold or other relatives, but rather because my relatives are adequately cared for and I specifically wish to benefit my friend Ben who has been a source of great love and comfort to me over many years.*

VIII. Simultaneous Death

This clause covers the unusual situation in which you die at the same time as your lover or other beneficiary. Most states have adopted the Uniform Simultaneous Death Act. This law presumes that when two people die together, and it's impossible to know who died first, the beneficiary is presumed to have died first. This way, the will writer's property passes to his or her alternate beneficiaries, and not to the briefly surviving lover and then to the lover's beneficiaries. If you name alternate beneficiaries with survivorship periods, this shouldn't be a problem. Even so, it doesn't hurt to include this provision in your will.

If you own property in joint tenancy, and you and the other joint tenant died simultaneously, you're presumed to have died last. Thus your share passes through your will (in this will, through your residuary clause) and the other joint tenant's share passes in her or his will. (See Section D.2.c, below, for more information on joint tenancy.)

If you own insurance, and you and the beneficiary die simultaneously, the proceeds of the policy are distributed as if the beneficiary had died before you—that is, to any alternate beneficiary named in the policy or under the residuary clause of your will.

IX. Signature and Witnessing

Sign and date your will in front of your three witnesses, who then sign the witness clause in front of each other.

In many states, a will can be witnessed by what's called a "self-proving affidavit," which can simplify or even eliminate witnesses' need to go to court after the will writer dies. Explanations of self-proving affidavits and sample forms are in *Nolo's Simple Will Book* and *WillMaker*.

9. Storing and Copying Your Will

Store your will in a safe place, one that your executor has ready access to. A safe deposit box is generally not a good idea because your executor probably won't have access to the box after you die.

You can make copies of your will for any person you want to have one. But do not sign any copies directly (photocopies of your signature on the original are okay). The reason for this is to prevent any possibility of duplicate wills, which can cause trouble later if you revoke or amend your will.

10. Changing or Revoking Your Will

Suppose you want to make a minor change in your will. For example, Mary died, and the library of lesbian fiction you were going to leave her you now want to leave to Martha. Or suppose you want to revoke your will entirely—let's say you and your lover just split up. What do you do?

a. Changing Your Will

When you should change your will is a matter of common sense. Don't make impromptu changes. At the same time, you can't just ink out a provision in your will or handwrite a change in the margin. Changes must be made formally.

The form used to make legal changes to a will is called a "codicil." You can use a codicil to make an addition, modification or deletion after your will is drafted, signed and witnessed. A codicil is a sort of legal "P.S." to a will, and must be executed with the same formalities. If possible, it should be typed on the last page of the will itself, or on an additional page or pages. It must be dated and signed by the will writer and three witnesses. They don't have to be the ones who witnessed the will, but try to use them if they're available.

Codicils are usually used for relatively minor matters, like the change of the beneficiary for the lesbian fiction library in the example above. If you want to make a major revision, don't use a codicil. A will that has been substantially rewritten by a codicil is confusing, awkward to read, and may not clearly show the relationship of the codicil to the original will. For major revisions, draft a new will; the first provision in our will—"I revoke all wills and codicils that I have previously made,"—will revoke your earlier will and any codicils to it. (See Section b, below, for information on revoking a will.)

Below is a sample codicil shown in completed draft stage, like the sample will

above. This is the codicil form we provide in the Appendix. Follow our same instructions for completing your will. When you're done, make several copies and attach the original codicil to your original will. Attach a copy of the codicil to each copy of your will.

Codicil

___First___ **Codicil to the Will of** ___Samuel Troplon___ **dated** ___March 7, 1996___

I, ___Samuel Troplon___, a resident of _____ County, ___New York___, declare this to be the first codicil to my will dated ___March 7, 1996___.

First. I revoke Item ___A2___ of Clause ___IV___, and substitute the following:

___I give the sum of $5,000 to my friend Tim Grayson, if he survives me by 60 days; if he___

___doesn't, this gift shall be made to Becky Alwith.___

Second. I add the following new Item ___5___ to Clause ___IV.A___ :

5. I give the sum of $5,000 to the Gay Men's Health Crisis Center.

Third. In all other respects I confirm and republish my will dated ___March 7, 1996___, this ___18th___ day of ___October, 1997___, at ___Queens, New York___.

___Samuel Troplon___

On the date written below, ___Samuel Troplon___ declared to us, the undersigned, that this instrument, consisting of _____ pages, including this page signed by us as witnesses, was the first codicil to [his/~~her~~] will and requested us to act as witnesses to it. [He/~~she~~] thereupon signed this codicil in our presence, all of us being present at the same time. We now, at [his/her] request, in [his/her] presence, and in the presence of each other, subscribe our names as witnesses, and declare we understand this to be [his/her] will, and that to the best of our knowledge the testator is competent to make a will, and under no constraint or undue influence.

Executed on _____, at _____, _____.

We declare under penalty of perjury that the foregoing is true and correct.

Witness's Signature_____

Address _____

Witness's Signature_____

Address _____

Witness's Signature_____

Address _____

b.   Revoking Your Will

Wills can be revoked easily. A will writer who wants to revoke her will or codicil should do so by:

- writing a new will, expressly stating that she's revoking all previous wills, or
- destroying the old will—burn, tear, conceal, deface, obliterate or otherwise destroy it with the intent to revoke it. If you destroy your will, do it in front of witnesses. Otherwise, after you die, it may be difficult to determine if you really intended to destroy it, or in fact, if you did. Someone may have a copy and claim the original will was unintentionally lost, and your would-be inheritors would have a real mess, and probably a lawsuit, on their hands.

D.   Estate Planning Beyond a Will

Lesbians and gay men who own substantial amounts of property can often obtain significant benefits for their surviving beneficiaries—their lover and other friends or relatives—by more extensive estate planning than simply writing a will. If you have little property, planning beyond a will is probably not necessary. Likewise, if you are young (under age 40) and healthy, you can probably wait until later in life to bother with further estate planning. Our rough rule is that anyone over 40 or ill at any age, with more than $50,000 in assets, can probably benefit from some estate planning beyond a will, which means determining and setting up the least expensive and most efficient method(s) of transferring your property after death.

As we've discussed, property that passes through your will must go through probate. Probate can be expensive. These fees are taken out of your property and reduce the amount your beneficiaries receive. If you leave your property to be transferred by an estate planning device which avoids probate, you can eliminate probate fees.

In this section, we provide you with an overview of the primary estate planning methods. If you want to look further, be assured that estate planning need not be as forbidding as many "professionals" would have you believe it is. They have a financial interest in making what they do seem as complicated (expensive) as possible. People with moderate estates, roughly under $625,000, can normally do most of the planning themselves, if they have good information.[3]

1.   Estimate the Value of Your Property

The first step for many people is to take stock of their net worth. You can estimate the net value of what you own by creating a list of your assets and debts and their values. This should help you determine if your estate will owe federal estate taxes, which are assessed for a net estate worth more than $625,000 in 1996. This tax threshold will rise by $25,000 per year through 2001, when only an estate over $750,000 will be subject to tax. Also, a list may help your survivors identify and locate of all your property.[4] Here is an example of a net value list.

NET ESTATE OF LESLIE GRAYSON

Personal Property	Value	Location or Description
Cash	$500	Safe Deposit Box
Savings accounts	$2,500	Tyson Bank
Checking accounts	$1,500	Tyson Bank
Government bonds	$0	
Listed (private corporation) stocks and bonds	$5,000 $2,000	Matco Corporation Break-Monopoly Company
Unlisted stocks and bonds	$0	
Money owed me including promissory notes, mortgages, leases and accounts receivable	$5,000	Jason Michaels (sold him my car)
Vested interest in profit-sharing plan, pension rights, stock options, etc.	$7,000	Death benefit from Invento Corporation pension
Automobile and other vehicles (include boats and recreation vehicles; deduct any amounts owed)	$3,000 $7,000	Honda motorcycle Toyota
Household goods, net total	$10,000	In my house
Art works and jewelry	$1,000	3 lithographs in my bedroom
Miscellaneous	$3,000	Silver set
Real estate (for each piece owned)		
Current market value	$175,000	1807 Saturn Drive Newkirk, Delaware
Mortgages and other liens	$85,000	
Equity (current market value less money owed)	$90,000	
My share of equity (assuming co-ownership)	$45,000	

Personal Property	Value	Location or Description
Business/property interests including patents & copyrights (for each business)		
Name and type of business		Invento Corporation; maker of small telephone related inventions
Percentage owned		33%
When acquired		1980
Estimate of present (market) value of interest	$250,000	
Life insurance (for each policy list)		
Company and type (or number) of policy		AETCO, No. 12345B
Name of insured		Leslie Grayson
Owner of policy		Leslie Grayson
Beneficiary of policy		Robin Anderson
Amount Collectible	$50,000	
Cash surrender value, if any	$1,000	
Total value of assets	$392,500	
Debts (not already calculated such as real estate mortgage)	$3,000	
Taxes (excluding estate taxes)	$12,000	
Total (other) liabilities	$15,000	
Total net worth	**$377,500**	

2.   Probate Avoidance

As we discussed earlier, probate is a court proceeding where your will is filed (or your property transferred under "intestate" laws if you didn't write a will or arrange for a transfer of your property by other methods), assets identified, debts and taxes paid, and remaining property distributed to your beneficiaries. Probate is expensive. Lawyers and executors receive fees, often substantial fees, for what's usually routine, albeit tedious, paperwork. Probate also takes considerable time, normally a minimum of several months. By contrast, property transferred outside of probate can usually be received by the beneficiaries within a few days of the deceased's death.

Probate has acquired a rather notorious aura. Most people may not know exactly what it involves, but they sense it's a lawyer's rip-off.[5] There's a lot of truth in that. Probate is largely an institutionalized racket. No European country has the expensive, form-filled probate process America has. Even in England, where our probate system got its start in feudal times, probate was simplified in 1926. Now, only in case of conflict does a court and lawyers get involved.

The several well-established methods of transferring property to avoid probate include:
• revocable living trusts
• informal bank account trusts
• joint tenancy, and
• life insurance.

Each has advantages and drawbacks, which we briefly discuss below.

a.   Revocable Living Trusts

A revocable living or "inter vivos" (Latin for "among the living") trust is usually the best way for a lesbian or gay person to avoid probate.[6] A revocable living trust is created by establishing a trust document and giving the trust a name (such as "The R. P. Payne Living Trust"). Because the trust states that it is revocable, you have the right to revoke or change any portion (or all) of it at any time before you die, as long as you are still mentally competent.

In the trust document, you name yourself as both the grantor (the person setting up the trust) and the initial trustee (the person managing the trust property). You list the property owned by the trust. You name your beneficiary or beneficiaries—the people you want to receive the trust property after you die. You also name a successor trustee to manage the trust after

you die or become incapacitated. (The successor trustee can be a beneficiary.) You must sign the trust document and have it notarized. It doesn't have to be witnessed or recorded. Finally, you must transfer all trust property with documents of title into the trustee's name. For example, if you place your house in the trust, you must execute and record a new deed transferring the house from you to yourself as trustee of the trust.

When you die, your successor trustee transfers your trust property to your beneficiaries without any court proceeding. While you are still alive, the trust is essentially a paper transaction, with no real-world effects. You maintain full control over the property in the trust (you can spend, sell or give it away) and can end the trust whenever you want. Trust transactions are reported as part of your regular income tax return; no separate tax forms are required. The only real downside is that property with a legal document title, such as real estate and stocks, must actually be transferred into the trustee's name.

Example: Wayne creates a living trust with himself as the initial trustee and his lover, Mark, as successor trustee. In the trust, Wayne makes several small gifts to friends, and names Mark as the beneficiary of Wayne's principal assets—a house and an apartment house. Wayne then executes and records deeds transferring title to the house and apartment house into the name of the trustee. When Wayne dies, Mark, acting as successor trustee, distributes the small gifts to Wayne's friends, and executes new deeds transferring the house and apartment house to the beneficiary—that is, himself.

Using a Charitable Trust

A charitable trust allows you to make a gift to charity (such as a lesbian and gay group or an AIDS organization) and also name someone to receive income from the donated property. Here's how it works. You donate property while you live to a charity, or charities, you select. Then the charity makes set payments, as defined by you in the trust document, to a beneficiary, or beneficiaries, you've named (called the "income beneficiary"). This beneficiary can be you, or another person, or both, such as you and your lover. The payment can be either a fixed sum or a set percentage of the value of the trust assets. The payments can be made for a set year period, or for the life of the income beneficiary(s). After this period expires, all remaining trust income is turned over to the charity.

You have to want to make a gift to a charity to bother with a charitable trust. But if you do want to make a charitable gift, this type of trust offers other benefits. First, the person who creates the trust receives an income tax deduction for the worth of the donated property. Second, a charitable trust can be particularly desirable if property has appreciated. The charity can sell it for its current market value, without having to pay capital gains tax. The money the charity receives from the sale becomes part of the trust property.

Third, for someone whose estate will be liable for federal estate taxes (on estates over $600,000), all the donated property is removed from the estate, thereby lowering those taxes.

This type of trust is called, in legalese, a "charitable remainder trust." For more information, see the third edition of *Plan Your Estate*, by Clifford and Jordan (Nolo Press).

b.   Pay-on-Death Bank Accounts

A "pay-on-death" bank account is an informal bank trust (sometimes called a "Totten trust") which avoids probate. You manage the account as you would any other bank deposit account. The only difference is that you name someone on the account form—such as your lover—as beneficiary of the account, to receive the balance after you die. During your life, you retain full and exclusive control over the account—you can remove any funds in the account for any reason, make deposits, close the account or whatever else you want.

There are no drawbacks to a pay-on-death bank account. Most banks have standard forms allowing you to create this type of trust—either by opening a new account or transferring an existing account. Pay-on-death account fees are normally no higher than the fees for other types of bank accounts.

c.   Joint Tenancy

Joint tenancy is a form of shared property ownership. What makes it unique is the "right of survivorship." Right of survivorship means that when one joint tenant dies, his share in the joint property automatically passes to the surviving joint tenant(s). (If there's more than one survivor, each acquires an equal share of the deceased tenant's original interest.) It's not possible to leave your share of joint tenancy property to someone other than the joint tenant(s) when you die. If you attempt to leave joint tenancy property in a will, the will provision will be ignored.

Any property can be bought and owned in joint tenancy, although it's most commonly used with real estate. (Joint tenancy is also covered in Chapter 7, Section D.) Joint tenancy is a good probate avoidance device for property you acquire, 50-50, with your lover—assuming each of you wants her share to pass to the other after death. You can also create joint tenancy ownership in property you own alone by transferring title of the property from yourself to yourself and someone else as joint tenants. You may owe gift taxes, however, if you give property worth more than $10,000 to the new joint tenant. Usually, a living trust is a better probate avoidance device than a transfer into joint tenancy for solely owned property.

Joint tenancy has drawbacks. Any joint tenant can sell his interest in the joint tenancy at any time, thereby destroying the joint tenancy. If a joint tenant sells (or gives away) his share, the new owner and the remaining owner(s) are called "tenants in common." Tenants in common don't have rights of survivorship. If a tenant in common dies, her share passes by her will, or by state law if she died without a will. Another drawback of joint tenancy is that joint tenants must own equal shares of the property. If you own unequal shares, joint tenancy won't work.

d.   Life Insurance

Normally, life insurance proceeds are paid directly to the policy's beneficiary (whom you've chosen), without going through probate. The proceeds of a life insurance policy are subject to probate, and included in the value of the probate estate, only if the beneficiary is the "estate" itself, not a specific person or organization. Only in the rare case of a large estate with no other assets to pay the death taxes and probate costs is there any reason to name the estate as the beneficiary.

3.   Death Taxes

All property owned at the time of death is subject to federal estate (death) taxes. Also, a number of states impose state death taxes as well. Death taxes are imposed whether the property is transferred by will (through probate) or by another device (outside of probate). Death taxes are harder to reduce or avoid than are probate fees, but there are some ways to achieve savings.

a.   *Federal Estate Taxes*

Federal estate taxes are assessed against the net worth of the estate (called the "taxable estate") of a person who died. A set amount of property is exempt from tax, depending on the year of death. As you can see from the list below, this exemption increases yearly through 2001, and may increase thereafter.

Year	Exempt Amount[7]
1996	$625,000
1997	$650,000
1998	$675,000
1999	$700,000
2000	$725,000
2001	$750,000
After 2001	$750,000 plus an adjustment for any annual cost of living change, rounded to the nearest $10,000.

Federal law also authorizes "marital deduction," exempting all property left to a surviving spouse. This is one reason lesbian and gay couples want to be allowed to marry.

Federal law exempts some items specifically from federal estate taxes, including:

• expenses of your last illness, burial costs and probate fees and expenses

• certain debts, in particular any state death taxes assessed, and

• all gifts made to tax-exempt charities.

Keep in mind these rules:

• All property you legally own will be included in your federal taxable estate.

• The worth of a house, or any other property, is your equity in it, not (necessarily) the full market value.

• Property which you have transferred but still control (such as property you placed in a living trust) will be included in your estate.

• The total value of all property held in joint tenancy will be included in your taxable estate, minus the portion the surviving joint tenant can prove he contributed. The government presumes that the deceased person contributed 100% of any joint tenancy property, and the survivor contributed nothing. If the survivor can prove he contributed all or some of the money for joint tenancy property, the taxable portion will be reduced accordingly.

Example 1: Eighteen years ago, Joe and Ben bought a lemon-yellow Jaguar XKE together, and have preserved it in mint condition. It's always been owned in joint tenancy, but the records proving that each person contributed half the purchase price have long since been lost. Joe dies. The government will include the current market value of the entire car in Joe's taxable estate unless Ben can somehow prove that he contributed half the cost.

Example 2: The same facts, except Ben contributed all the money used to buy the car and maintain it, and kept the records. Joe dies. Even though the car was owned in joint tenancy, none of its value is included in Joe's taxable estate because Ben can prove that Joe didn't contribute any money to buy or maintain it.

The tax rates on property that is not exempt from estate tax are stiff. The technical workings of estate tax calculations are complex; they require the services of an estate lawyer or other tax expert. But the basic rules can be readily grasped. If an estate is over the exempt amount, the tax rate on the nonexempt portion is the rate for full value of the estate. Then the tax on the exempt portion is deducted. What this means is that the effective tax rate starts at 37%.

Example: Pete dies in 1996 with a net estate worth $725,000. The exempt amount for this year is $625,000. So $100,000 is subject to tax. But the tax rate applied is not the tax rate for an estate of $100,000 but that for estates of between $500,000 and $750,000, which is 37%. Then the tax due on the exempt portion of the estate is forgiven. In other words, the tax on the $100,000 is $37,000.

The estate tax rate is graduated, so the larger the estate, the higher the tax rate. The rate rises to 39% for estates worth between $750,000 and $1,000,000, and tops out at 55% for estates worth over 3 million.

b.   State Death Taxes

The states listed below impose no effective death taxes. If you live in one of these states, you don't need to worry about state death taxes:

States Without Death Taxes

Alabama	Hawaii	Oregon
Alaska	Idaho	Texas
Arizona	Illinois	Utah
Arkansas	Maine	Vermont
California	Minnesota	Virginia
Colorado	Missouri	Washington
District of Columbia	Nevada	West Virginia
Florida	New Mexico	Wyoming
Georgia	North Dakota	

If you live in any other state, your estate will be subject to state death taxes. Worse, many states' death tax rules discriminate against property left to anyone other than legal family. This is because many states provide different classes of death tax exemptions. The amount of exemption varies, depending on the legal relationship of the deceased person to the beneficiary. Usually, the largest exemption is for property left to a spouse, the next largest for property left to minor children, then for property given to other blood relatives, and finally to "strangers" (all others, including a lover). A few states—North Carolina, for example—don't provide any exemption at all for property left to "strangers." Finally, some states vary the tax rate itself, depending on whom the property is left to. Generally, the rate is lowest for property left to a spouse, highest for property left to "strangers."

What this means is that if you live in a state with death taxes and want to know their impact on your estate, you'll have to check your state's laws to determine the precise rules. (There's a state-by-state breakdown of death tax rules in *Plan Your Estate,* by Denis Clifford and Cora Jordan (Nolo Press)). The tax rate is much less than the federal tax rate, but, because "strangers" are taxed the most, the taxes will be much higher on property you leave your lover than they would be if you were married.

The state of your "domicile" (generally where you live) when you die is the state that imposes death taxes. If, however, you own real property (land, real estate) in another state that has death taxes, that state will impose its death taxes on the property in that state.

"Domicile" is a legal term of art, which refers to your principal residence—that is, where you intend to have your home. Usually, this is easy to figure out from voting records, your driver's license and many other forms that identify you. If you move around a lot, however, you risk having your estate subjected to more than one state's death tax. Pick one place and declare that your legal home. If you're very wealthy, get some legal advice on this point (like George Bush did about being a legal

resident of Texas, despite the fact that he's a New Englander through and through).

c. Avoiding or Reducing Federal and State Death Taxes

Estate tax planning is often thought to be a form of lawyer's magic, or chicanery, to escape death taxes. Certainly there's some gimmickry in many schemes used by the rich to escape or reduce death taxes, although not as much as there used to be. The sad truth, however, is that for most folks, death taxes aren't easy to escape. But there are a few ways to reduce death taxes, such as:

• Making tax-free gifts.

• Establishing trusts. Tax saving trusts are desirable only for net estates over the federal estate tax threshold ($625,000 for 1996). Because of the complex nature of tax savings trusts, a serious discussion is beyond the scope of this book. If you have a substantial estate, you may save considerably on estate taxes by using trusts, particularly if:

— The bulk of your estate will be left to a person who's old or ill and likely to die soon. When that person dies, the property you left her will be taxed again. If you set up a trust in your will leaving the old or ill person only the income from the trust and the right to use the principal only for an IRS-approved reasons (not, unfortunately, medical costs) during her life, with the principal going to someone else, this "second tax" can be avoided.

— You leave all your property to your children—it'll be taxed when you die and then taxed again when the children die. For years, one of the death tax dodges of the very rich was to leave their wealth in trust for their grandchildren, escaping taxation on the middle generation. Tax law changes curtailed this by introducing a "generation-skipping transfer tax." You can now leave up to $1,000,000 in a trust for your grandchildren and escape estate taxes on the middle generation. Any amount over this $1,000,000 is subject to federal estate taxes in each generation. So if you have children, grandchildren and a hunk of money, consider establishing a generation-skipping trust. If so, you'll definitely need to see a good estate planning lawyer.

• Transferring ownership of certain property, particularly life insurance, before death. Life insurance proceeds are not part of the deceased's federal taxable estate if he did not own the policy for at least three years before his death. If he did, the proceeds are included in his taxable estate. The IRS presumes you're trying to avoid taxes if you give the gift within three years of your death, and assesses taxes anyway. The IRS is strict in determining ownership. If you retained any significant power over an insurance policy (called, in insurance lingo, "maintaining incidents of ownership") within three years of death, you will be held to be the owner. Significant powers include the rights to:

—change, or name, the beneficiaries of the policy

—borrow against the policy, pledge any cash reserve it has or cash it in

—surrender, convert or cancel the policy

—select a payment option, such as lump sum or in installments

—make payments on the policy.

There are two basic ways an insurance policy can be owned by someone other than the insured. First, a person having what's called an "insurable interest" can take out, and pay for, a policy on the insured's life. Insurance companies don't allow lesbians and gays to have an "insurable interest" in their lovers; they require marriage, or a business (economic) relationship. Second, you can buy a policy and transfer ownership to another, even if they don't have an "insurable interest" in the insured. Of course, anyone has an "insurable interest" in his or her own life. So, you can buy a policy and assign it to your lover. Life insurance policies are usually transferred by making a gift to the new owner. Transfer forms should be available from your insurance company. It's the new owner who is now responsible for paying the premiums.

Once you give a gift of a life insurance policy, that's it. Gifts are final. If you break up, your ex-lover has the right to continue to own the policy. You couldn't compel him to cancel it. Thus, you can retain control over your life insurance policy, or reduce your taxable estate. But you can't do both.

4. Gifts and Gift Taxes

At first hearing, the concept of gift taxes may not sound fair. (You mean the feds even tax generosity?) Well, sort of. But think of it this way. If a rich person could "give" away all his property tax-free just before death, there wouldn't be any point to death taxes. So Congress has defined the point at which giving gifts becomes a matter for the tax collector. The rule, stated simply, is that gifts of up to $10,000 per person per year are tax-free. If Adrian gives $13,000 to Justin, gift taxes are assessed on $3,000; if

Adrian gives $10,000 to Justin and $10,000 to Jack, no gift taxes are assessed. Also, if Adrian gives $10,000 to Justin each year for three years, no gift taxes are assessed.

Because federal estate and gift taxes are unified, the same tax rates and dollar exemptions that apply to gift taxes apply to estate taxes. This is done through the mechanism of the "unified credit." For example, Adrian has never given a gift of more that $10,000. This year, he gives Justin $60,000. The first $10,000 is exempt from gift tax but the remaining $50,000 is subject to it. Adrian should file a gift tax return with the IRS, but instead he uses his unified credit against the gift tax that would have been owed on the $50,000. The result is that he owes no gift tax. If Adrian makes no other taxable gifts during his life, his estate will have used up $50,000 of his exemption at his death.

The $10,000 annual assessed gift tax exemption can be used to lower the eventual value of one's estate with estate planning.

> *Example: Sarah and Louise, both in their 60s, want their trusted young friend Marcy to have their summer house after they both die. The house is worth $100,000. They transfer title to Marcy for a "loan" of $50,000 each, at 8% interest. Payments are $10,000 a year. Marcy signs two promissory notes, secured by two mortgages. Each year, Sarah and Louise each make a "gift" of $10,000 to Marcy by forgiving the loan payment due, and continue to do this until the property is fully owned by Marcy with no tax liability. Obviously, this takes a lot of trust. Also, if either Sarah or Louise died, her estate might insist that the remaining loan payments be paid—although the debt could be forgiven in a will or living trust.*

If you're wealthy, other options are available that involve gifts. These include "pooled income" funds and charitable remainder annuity trusts. These devices aren't available for people with average incomes or estates, and so we don't cover them. Anyone making, or contemplating making, a substantial gift should check it out with a tax attorney or tax accountant.

Nolo's Estate Planning Resources

Nolo Press publishes the following estate planning guides:

- *WillMaker,* a software program for Macintosh, Windows and DOS , allows you to create, in a step-by-step, question and answer format, your own legally valid will.

- *Nolo's Simple Will Book,* by Denis Clifford, gives all the instructions necessary for drafting and updating a will.

- *Plan Your Estate,* by Denis Clifford and Cora Jordan, covers every significant aspect of estate planning. It is especially valuable for people with larger estates (over $625,000). Because of the broad scope of *A Legal Guide for Lesbian and Gay Couples,* we simply do not have space to deal in depth with many estate planning issues for people with large estates. *Plan Your Estate* picks up where we leave off.

- *Living Trust Maker,* a software program for Windows or Macintosh, allows you to create your own probate avoidance living trust. The program guides you step-by-step through the process. Legal help screens, an on-line glossary and a thorough manual explain all important legal terms.

- *Make Your Own Living Trust,* by Denis Clifford, provides a thorough explanation of this most popular probate avoidance device.

- *The Quick and Legal Will Book,* by Denis Clifford , contains forms and instructions for preparing a basic will.

- *Nolo's Law Form Kit: Wills,* by Denis Clifford and Lisa Goldoftas, provides you with a quick and easy, legally valid will.

- *Write Your Will and 5 Ways to Avoid Probate,* audio tapes by Ralph Warner.

Endnotes

[1]In some situations, a living together partner who receives little or nothing at death may also be able to claim part of the deceased person's estate based on equity (fairness). If a person—usually in a long-term living together relationship—would be cheated out of property she worked hard to purchase or create, a court may find this person has an equitable ownership right in at least a portion of the property.

[2]An emancipated minor is one who has achieved legal adult status. Emancipation usually comes at marriage, military service or by living independently with a court order of emancipation. Emancipation is rare. You cannot emancipate your child in your will. If you fail to name a guardian for your minor child, a judge will choose one for you.

[3]For extensive information on estate planning, start with *Plan Your Estate,* by Denis Clifford and Cora Jordan (Nolo Press).

[4]*Nolo's Personal Recordkeeper,* a computer program for Windows or Macintosh, can help you make your list.

[5]Fees are usually set by state law. Computation methods vary from state to state. In some states, fees are often based on the size of the estate. But however calculated, rest assured that the lawyer's fee will be generous. For example, the fees for both attorney and executor in California for a probate estate of $200,000 are roughly $10,300; court filing fees and appraisals can raise the total a good bit. If $100,000 is removed from the probate estate, the total attorney and executor fees saved $6,300.

[6]Anyone who wants to prepare a living trust should read the extensive discussion of it in *Make Your Own Living Trust,* by Denis Clifford (Nolo Press).

[7]Assuming none of the federal "tax credit" has been previously used for taxable gifts. See Section D.4, below. ∎

CHAPTER 6

Living Together Contracts for Lesbian and Gay Couples

A contract is no more than an agreement to do (or not to do) something. It contains promises made by one person in exchange for another's promises. Marriage is a contractual relationship. Saying "I do" commits a couple to a well-established set of state laws and rules governing, among other things, the couple's property rights. Although these rules are rarely explained to people before they reach the altar, they are available should disagreements arise during the relationship or if one mate dies or the couple splits up.

Unlike married couples, gay and lesbian couples inherit no contractual agreement when they start a relationship. Sure, gay and lesbians partners may have an obligation to a landlord or mortgage company if they rent or buy a place together, but that obligation would be no different if they were roommates. Getting together, in and of itself, does not create a contractual relationship. One reason a segment of the gay and lesbian community has fought to allow same-sex marriages has been to get the property rights that go along with marriage.

What typically happens to unmarried couples is that a couple buys property, mixes assets and invests together without writing down their intentions. If problems around money and property come up, they try to work out an understanding. Sometimes they visit a therapist or ask their friends to help. If they split up, they quietly divide their accumulations and go their separate ways.

But some couples can't quietly divide the property and move apart. They fight big time, in a courtroom. The first unmarried couples to bring their disputes to court were heterosexual couples. (Married couples do it all the time; it's called divorce.) Most courts responded by trying to figure out what the couple had agreed to and dividing their property accordingly. Legally, this means that courts ruled that unmarried couples generally have the right to create whatever kind of living together contracts they want when it comes to financial and property concerns.

A chapter on creating contracts so you can break up amicably would be pretty depressing—few people starting a relationship or wanting to protect the relationship they've built plan on splitting up. Instead, we present material on living together contracts to help you figure out what you intend, which, we hope, should lessen disagreements and misunderstandings when things are going well. And if you do happen to split up, having the agreement helps you avoid litigation (defined by Ambrose Bierce as "a machine which you go into as a pig and come out as a sausage"). The danger, trauma and expense of litigation are far less likely to be visited on those who have taken the time to define their understanding in an agreement.

A. Are Living Together Contracts Really Legal?

As mentioned, the legal rules governing living together contracts have been made by courts and judges, not by legislatures. The leading court case is called *Marvin v. Marvin*, and involved the actor Lee Marvin and the woman he lived with, Michele Triola Marvin. (She used his last name even though they were not married.) In the case, the California Supreme Court announced legal principles involving the right of unmarried couples to make contracts.[1] First, the court ruled that marital property laws do not apply to couples not legally married. Then, the court recognized that unmarried couples are here to stay, saying:

The fact that a man and a woman live together without marriage, and engage in a sexual relationship, doesn't in itself invalidate agreements between them relating to their earnings, property, or expenses. Neither is such an agreement invalid merely because the parties may have contemplated the creation and continuation of a nonmarital relationship when they entered into it. Agreements between non-marital partners fail only to the extent that they rest upon a consideration of meretricious sexual services.[2]

Finally, the court declared four contract principles:

- Unmarried couples may make written contracts.
- Unmarried couples may make oral contracts.
- If a couple hasn't made a written or oral contract, the court may examine the couple's life under the judicial micro-

scope to decide whether an "implied" contract exists.

- If a judge can't find an implied contract, she may presume that "the parties intend to deal fairly with each other" and find one lover indebted to the other by invoking ancient formidable legal doctrines.

Several cases since the *Marvin* decision have upheld the application of these principles to contracts made by gay and lesbian partners. Depending on the state, however, a court will follow different legal rules. Most states enforce contracts between gay and lesbian partners. Others prohibit contracts between unmarried couples; a few haven't considered the question. In a state where sodomy is illegal, a judge might refuse to enforce a contract on the ground that the underlying relationship is criminal. In fact, this is exactly what happened in a Georgia case. After a lesbian couple split up, one woman sued the other to enforce their written agreement. The trial judge refused because of their "illegal and immoral" relationship. The Supreme Court of Georgia reversed, saying that nothing in the agreement required them to engage in illegal activity.[3]

Furthermore, even in states where sodomy is legal, any contract that even hints of sex will be thrown out of court. A California appellate court refused to uphold a gay living together contract, declaring that it explicitly referred to rendering services as a lover in exchange for property, and was therefore an agreement for prostitution.[4] So in your contract, don't make any reference to sexuality. Identify yourselves as "partners," not "lovers." The less cute you are the better.

We're not suggesting that you not discuss your sexual relationship when preparing your contract. A force as powerful as passion can destroy, as well as enhance, any relationship. But discussing what's sexually expected, permitted, condoned or forbidden isn't the same as mentioning sexuality in a property contract. We aren't therapists, and we have nothing more to add about passion, except to note that it seems here to stay.

⚠ Enforcing your agreement. Most courts faced with enforcing a living together contract uphold written ones, reject implied ones, and fall somewhere in the middle with oral ones. When one partner says there was an oral contract while the other emphatically denies it, a judge is unlikely to find one, unless other evidence (such as a witness to a discussion about the contract) substantiates it. Paradoxically, when one partner dies and the other claims there was an oral contract entitling him to property, a judge is more likely to sympathize with the survivor and find a contract, especially if no one (except perhaps a relative of the deceased) refutes it.

As we emphasized above, however, the purpose of this chapter is to help you write down your understanding about your life as a couple. This chapter doesn't contain strategies on legally enforcing your living together contract in a courtroom. If it ever comes to that, you will need help beyond this book. (See Chapter 10.) And keep in mind that the fact that you have the right to rely on the doctrines of written contracts, oral contracts, implied contracts and fair dealing doesn't mean that you should. The law is still hostile to lesbians and gay men.

Going to court to prove your contract will be time-consuming, expensive and emotionally draining.

Example: Patti and Katherine move in together. After graduating from college, Patti enters dental school. Katherine, too, intended to finish school, but postponed her plans and supported them both until Patti finished. They had many conversations about their long-term plans, but wrote nothing down. After four years, Patti passed her dental boards. Katherine was ready to resume her education, but Patti fell in love with a classmate and moved out. Katherine was left with the flea market furniture, the flea-ridden dog and the feeling she was ripped off.

Remember—they had no contract. Assuming that Patti and Katherine intended to treat each other fairly, we can reasonably assume that because Katherine put Patti through dental school, Patti would reciprocate and pay Katherine's school expenses. Would a court find an implied agreement? Could Katherine prove an oral one? Maybe. It's not certain, even though Katherine has a sympathetic case.

B. When You Need a Living Together Contract

Obviously, you don't need a contract in a brief relationship. But in a long-term and serious relationship, whether you're basking in the glow of just having "joined forces" or you've been together 20 years, you should consider the legal consequences of how you live. If you mix assets or share expenses, put your agreement in writing, especially if significant money or property is involved. If you're both stone-broke NINKS[5] with no

property and little prospect of getting any soon, put away the pen and paper and take a nap in the sun.

Why should you put your contract a writing? The sooner you agree on how (and if) to share your property, the less confusion you are likely to face later. As the French legal scholar Beaumanoir wrote in *Coutumes de Beauvaisis* (1283): "For the memory of men slips and flows away, and the life of man is short, and that which isn't written is soon forgotten."

C. What to Include in a Living Together Contract

A living together contract can be comprehensive, covering every aspect of your relationship, or it can be specific, covering only your new house purchase. (Specific house purchase contracts are in Chapter 7.) These contracts need not be the fine-print monsters rammed down your throat when you buy insurance or a car. You can, and

should, design your contract to say exactly what you (both) want, in words that you (both) understand. A simple, comprehensible and functional document using common English is much better than one loaded with "heretofores" and "pursuants."

Let us make one suggestion: If you want your living together contract to include the day-to-day details of your relationship, make two agreements. The first should pertain to property and finances. If one of you ever sues the other in court, the property and finance terms should be the only ones a judge ever sees. Write up a second agreement about who will do the dishes, who will walk the dog, how many overnight guests you'll allow and whose art goes in the living room. A court won't—and shouldn't be asked to—enforce this kind of agreement. If you do just one agreement that includes the personal as well as financial clauses, a court might get caught up in the personal clauses, declare the contract illegal or frivolous, and refuse to enforce the financial clauses.

1.   Property and Finances Clauses

Your living together agreement should cover all of your property—the property you had before you began the relationship and the property you accumulate during it.

Property owned before living together. You each probably had some property before you met. Just because you move in together doesn't mean you can't continue to own your TV, oriental tapestry and floppy-eared cocker spaniel, while your lover holds onto her car and collected works of Virginia Woolf. If you'd prefer, you can each decide that some or all items will become jointly owned.[6] Whatever you decide, put it in writing. Making an agreement about the property you bring into the relationship may seem unnecessary, but it's not. Think about trying to separate it all ten years from now, when you've both been referring to everything around the house as "ours."

You can deal with use of valuable items as well as ownership. Who gets to use the property? Who pays for upkeep? For instance, Alan owns a boat which he'll want to keep it if he and Fred ever split up. Fred agrees to help with upkeep in exchange for using it without acquiring any ownership interest. It's up to you how detailed to get.

Property inherited or received by gift during the relationship. Many people will want to keep separate the property they inherit or receive by gift. Others will want to donate the property to the relationship. Again, it's up to you. Remember though, any property given to both of you is legally owned by both—this includes gifts you receive at your union ceremony or anniversary party, even if given by a relative or friend of just one of you. If you plan to keep inherited or gift property separate, don't forget to cover questions of use and control.

Property bought during the relationship. Many people make purchases item by item, understanding that whoever makes the purchase owns the property. George buys the kitchen table and chairs, and Ham buys the lamp and stereo. If they split up, each keeps the property he bought.

Purchases also can be pooled. Ham and George can jointly own everything bought during the relationship, and divide it all 50-50 if they separate. A consistent approach to property ownership may simplify things, but is required by neither law nor logic. Ham and George could choose a combination of the two methods. Some items may be separately owned, some pooled 50-50, and some shared in proportion to how much money each contributed toward the purchase price or how much labor each put into upkeep.

Expenses during the relationship. How will you divide the day-to-day costs for food, utilities, laundry, housing and the like, especially if prices go up or incomes go down? Even if you substitute margarine for butter, or vin ordinaire for Chateau Mouton-Rothschild, you must adopt a plan. We can't help you choose what you buy, but we have some suggestions of how to share expenses.

• Share and share alike. A few of our friends live like this. One couple has only one checking account. They both deposit their paychecks into it and pay all household bills out of it. Over the course of their relationship, they've each been in school or unemployed. Their incomes shift and who earns more varies year to year. They figure it all evens out in the end.

- Split 50-50. We know several couples who do this. Anytime one of them buys something for the house or pays a bill, he writes his name on the receipt and throws it into a jar. Every few months, they empty out the receipt jar and total up how much each has spent. One then writes the other a check to even things up.

- Each contributes in proportion to her income. This especially works well for people with great income discrepancies. We have two friends who live this way. One is wealthy and the other isn't. The woman with the churchmouse income was going crazy (broke, anxious and very dependent) trying to keep up with the queen-of-the-hill lifestyle of her lover. Finally, the two saw that they had a serious problem and adopted a plan under which all expenses were divided 80-20. It saved their relationship.

2. Cooling Off Clause

Consider including a clause to remind yourselves of your commitment should the stress of a moment threaten to drive you apart. We call this a "cooling off" clause. Although it's not enforceable in court, it's an excellent expression of intention. It can simply state that if one person wants to leave the relationship, he will take some time to cool off before grabbing the cat and the good wine glasses and heading for the hills. Imperfect souls that we are, we make a lot of hasty, irrational decisions when we're hurt or angry that we later come to regret. A

cooling off provision can break the routine and give you time to try to work things out.

Noel Coward understood the value—and the limits—of this kind of agreement in *Private Lives*. If either spouse called "Solomon Isaacs" during a fight, a truce would immediately begin. It worked well until one day, when the husband cried "Solomon Isaacs" and his wife broke a record over his head, shouting "Solomon Isaacs, yourself." Yes, cooling off clauses don't always cool people off.

Here are a few sample cooling off clauses:

Option 1. In the event either person is seriously considering ending the relationship, that person will take a vacation, finding another place to stay, whether with a friend or at a hotel, for at least three days before making a final decision. At least four more days will pass before we divide the property. In addition, we agree to attend at least one counseling session if either one of us wants it.

Option 2. Either of us can request a cooling off period for any reason, including that we are fighting. We will spend four days separately. At the end of four days, we will meet for a meal and try to discuss our difficulties rationally, and with affection for each other.

Option 3. At the request of either one of us, we agree to attend a minimum of four counseling sessions with a friend or professional before making any irrevocable decisions concerning our relationship.

Although our clauses don't, you can specify who will do the mediation-arbitration. Your choices are a professional mediator or arbitrator, your therapist, a trusted friend, a group of three colleagues, the minister of the local gay church or anyone else you know. Be creative to get the best person for the two of you. Several years ago, a New York couple split up. They needed help resolving a few issues and wanted someone who shared their experiences as African-American lesbians. They called the late poet/writer Audrey Lorde, who met with and assisted them. You might also look to see if a local gay and lesbian group has any organized mediation or arbitration services. (We discuss this in Chapter 9.)

3. Arbitration and Mediation Clause

If you split up and disagree over a provision in your contract, you have several ways to handle it. Traditionally, people went to court and let a judge decide. But happily there are alternatives to court. Our suggestion is mediation or, if necessary, arbitration. Both are cheaper, faster and usually less painful than litigation. You can include a mediation-arbitration clause in your contract and spell out exactly how you want to proceed.

Mediation is an informal process where you, your lover and the person or persons who will help you reach a compromise (the mediator(s)) work together to reach a mutually satisfactory decision. You then write out your agreement, agree to be bound by it and sign it. No decision is imposed on you. Many therapists do mediation work for couples splitting up.

Arbitration is a bit different. It, too, is informal, but you and your lover each present your version of the dispute to a person or persons you've named to make a

decision. Unlike mediation, an arbitrated decision is made and normally made final by the arbitrator. The parties usually agree in advance to be bound by the arbitrator's decision—otherwise, there's little point to the process. This means that if one of you sues in court, the court will enforce the arbitrator's decision. Business and labor disputes have been resolved through arbitration for years, partly because a dispute settled quickly is as important as who wins and who loses.

Below is a sample mediation-arbitration provision you can add to any agreement. If you don't like ours, take a look at other mediation and arbitration provisions at a local law library.

Meditation-Arbitration Clause

Any dispute arising out of this agreement shall be mediated by a third person mutually acceptable to both of us. The mediator's role shall be to help us arrive at our solution, not to impose one on us. If good-faith efforts to arrive at our own solution with the help of a mediator prove to be fruitless, either may make a written request to the other that our dispute be arbitrated. This shall be done as follows.

1. Either of us may initiate arbitration by making a written demand for arbitration, defining the dispute and naming one arbitrator.

2. Within five days from receipt of the demand, the other shall name the second arbitrator.

3. The two named arbitrators shall within ten days name a third arbitrator.

4. Within seven days, an arbitration meeting will be held. Neither of us may have a lawyer, but we may present evidence and bring relevant witnesses.

5. The arbitrators shall make their decision within five days after the hearing. Their decision shall be in writing and will be binding upon us.

6. If the person to whom the demand for arbitration is directed fails to respond within five days, the other must give an additional five days' written notice of his or her intent to proceed. If there is no response, the person initiating the arbitration may proceed with the arbitration before the arbitrator he or she has designated, and his/her award shall have the same force as if it had been settled by all three arbitrators.

D. Sample Living Together Contracts

At the back of this book are two tear-out contracts. One keeps a couple's property separate; the other combines it. Read them carefully, but hold off using them until you have read the specific agreements in this chapter. The contracts are designed to cover the major areas of concern to most lesbian and gay couples. One may meet your needs perfectly, but it's more likely you'll want to make some modifications to fit your circumstances. Here's how to do it.

Deletions. To remove clauses, or even a few words, simply cross them out and put both of your initials by each deletion. If you want to delete several provisions, retype the entire contract to avoid confusion.

Additions. Additions require a little more work. You must write or type the new clause and insert it into the contract. The small space before the signature lines is for minor additions. If you want to include several new clauses, type "Continued on Attachment 1" and then type all your additional clauses on a separate piece of paper labeled Attachment 1.

By the time you finish modifying one of our agreements, your changes may pretty much replace the original.

Congratulations! You've created your own contract. If you're at all nervous about the legality of the new document, especially if it refers to significant amounts of money or if property is involved, have a lawyer look at it. (See Chapter 10.) But be careful when dealing with attorneys. Many charge outrageous prices and have little experience with lesbian and gay couples. To find a lawyer who works with gay men and lesbians, look in a local gay or feminist paper or directory. Then call for the fee. Remember—you've already done the work; you're just asking the lawyer to check it over. You shouldn't be charged much more than $150.

Signing the contract. Whether you use one of our tear-out living together contracts or design your own, photocopy the final draft so you each have a copy. You and your lover each sign and date both copies. It makes no difference who keeps which—both are "originals." Having it notarized isn't necessary unless it covers real estate. If it does, you must notarize your signatures and record the agreement at your county records office. Notarization doesn't make the contract legal or enforceable. It simply proves that your signatures aren't forged.

Relax. Creating a contract that touches upon the very core of your relationship is bound to be an emotional experience. If either of you begins to feel overwhelmed, stop and regroup. Some couples will design a good agreement in an hour; other couples will take a month.

1. Short and Simple Living Together Contracts

The living together agreements we provide in the Appendix are quite thorough. For those of you who don't want such detailed agreements, we provide, below, two simple, one-page living together agreements.

KEEPING INCOME AND ACCUMULATIONS SEPARATE

Roosevelt Jackson and Alan Stein make the following agreement:

1. They are living together now and plan to continue doing so.

2. All property owned by either Roosevelt or Alan as of the date of this agreement remains his separate property and cannot be transferred to the other unless the transfer is done in writing.

3. The income of each person, as well as any accumulations of property from that income, belongs absolutely to the person who earns the money. Joint purchases are covered under Clause 7.

4. If Roosevelt and Alan separate, neither has a claim against the other for any money or property, for any reason, with the exception of property covered under Clause 7, or unless a subsequent written agreement specifically changes this contract.

5. Roosevelt and Alan will keep separate bank and credit accounts, and neither will be responsible for the debts of the other.

6. Living expenses, which include groceries, utilities, rent, and day-to-day household upkeep, will be shared equally. Roosevelt and Alan agree to open a joint bank account into which each agrees to contribute $750 per month to pay for living expenses.

7. If Roosevelt and Alan make joint purchases, ownership of each specific item will be reflected on any title slip to the property. If the property has no title slip, or if the slip is insufficient to record all details of their agreement, Alan and Roosevelt will prepare a separate, written, joint ownership agreement. Any such agreement will apply to the specific jointly-owned property only, and won't create an implication that any other property is jointly-owned.

8. This agreement sets forth Roosevelt and Alan's complete understanding concerning real and personal property ownership and takes the place of any and all prior contracts or understanding whether written or oral.

9. This agreement can be added to or changed only by a subsequent written agreement.

10. Any provision in this agreement found to be invalid shall have no effect on the validity of the remaining provisions.

Dated: _____   Signature:_____
                                               Roosevelt Jackson

Dated: _____   Signature:_____
                                               Alan Stein

COMBINING INCOME AND ACCUMULATIONS

Aline Jones and Mary Wiebel agree that:

1. We live together now and plan to continue doing so.

2. All property earned or accumulated prior to our living together belongs absolutely to the person earning or accumulating it, and cannot be transferred to the other unless it's done in writing.

3. All income earned by either of us while we live together and all property accumulated from that income belongs equally to both of us, and should we separate, all accumulated property will be divided equally.

4. Should either of us receive real or personal property by gift or inheritance, the property belongs absolutely to the person receiving the inheritance or gift and it cannot be transferred to the other unless it's done in writing.

5. In the event that either of us wishes to separate, we will divide equally all jointly-owned property under Clause 2.

6. Once we divide the jointly-owned property, neither of us will have any claim to any money or property from the other for any reason.

7. This agreement represents our complete understanding regarding our living together, replaces any and all prior agreements, whether written or oral, and can be added to or changed only by a subsequent written agreement.

8. Any provision in this agreement found to be invalid shall have no effect on the validity of the remaining provisions.

Dated: _____   Signature:_____
                                                    Aline Jones

Dated: _____   Signature:_____
                                                    Mary Wiebel

---

2. Contracts for Jointly-Acquired Items

Most couples we know adopt the basic keep-things-separate approach. Often, however, they want to own some major items together. The basic keep-things-separate contract in the previous section provides a structure for joint ownership of some property. You prepare a separate written contract covering each jointly-owned item. The following contracts accomplish this task. Modify one or the other to meet your needs, sign it and staple or clip it to your basic keep-things-separate contract.

If you completed a combine-income-and-accumulations contract, you don't need this joint-ownership agreement. You already provide for equal ownership.

JOINT OUTRIGHT PURCHASE

Carol Takahashi and Louise Orlean agree as follows:

1. We will jointly purchase and own a carved oak table costing $1,000.

2. If we separate and both want to keep the table, we will agree on its fair market price and flip a coin. **[For a very expensive item, you may want to add a mediation-arbitration clause.] T**he winner keeps the table after paying the loser one-half of the agreed-upon price.

3. If we decide to separate and neither wants the table, or if we both want it but can't arrive at a price we agree is fair, we will sell the table at the best available price and divide the proceeds equally.

4. Any provision in this agreement found to be invalid shall have no effect on the validity of the remaining provisions.

Dated: _____   Signature:_____
                                        Carol Takahashi

Dated: _____   Signature:_____
                                        Louise Orlean

Sometimes, only one partner can make a purchase. This commonly occurs when the purchase is made with a credit card in only one person's name. Here's a contract to make sure that the item bought on credit is jointly-owned.

JOINTLY-OWNED ITEM PURCHASED ON CREDIT IN ONE PARTNER'S NAME

James O'Brien and Brian Joyce make the following agreement:

1. James has a credit card with Sears. James and Brian purchased a washer-dryer for $1,000 from Sears using James' credit card.

2. James and Brian intend that the washer-dryer be owned equally and that each pay one-half of the $1,000, plus interest accrued on the credit card bill.

3. Neither James nor Brian want to incur a lot of interest on the purchase. Therefore, they agree to pay $250 per month for four months to pay it off. They acknowledge that the final payment will be more than $250, as it will include interest accumulated on the bill for the previous three months.

4. Each month, Brian will give James $125. James will then directly pay Sears the entire $250 on or before the date it's due.

5. If one person fails to pay his share, the other has the right to make the entire payment and will proportionally own more of the washer-dryer. Thus, if James ends up paying $750 and Brian $250, Brian will own three-fourths and James, one-fourth.

6. If James or Brian dies, the financial interest in the washer-dryer belonging to the deceased person will go to the survivor, who will be obligated to pay the entire amount still due. [**For an expensive item, such as a car, consider adding: "This provision shall be incorporated into James' will and Brian's will."**]

7. If James and Brian separate, either may buy out the other's interest in the washer-dryer by paying one-half the fair market value, less any money still owing.

8. If James or Brian can't agree on who will buy the other out or the amount to be paid, the washer-dryer will be sold. Each will receive one-half of the net proceeds from the sale, unless one has paid more than the other, as provided in Clause 5. In that case, each will receive the percentage of the net proceeds corresponding to the percentage of the payments he's made.

9. Any provision in this agreement found to be invalid shall have no effect on the validity of the remaining provisions.

Dated: _____   Signature:_____
                                          James O'Brien

Dated: _____   Signature:_____
                                          Brian Joyce

⚠ Only the partner whose name is on the credit card is legally obligated to pay, even if you have an agreement splitting the cost. Thus, Brian doesn't have to pay Sears if James stops. Brian has a legal contract with James, but not with Sears. Of course, the store doesn't care who pays the bill. Brian can send the money and the store will credit James's account.

3. Contracts for Long-Term Couples

Not long ago, we got a letter from a woman asking the following:

My partner and I have been living together, with commingled finances, for some time

and only now are drawing up a contract. When we moved in together, right out of college, we couldn't afford the fees for two bank accounts; we could barely afford the relationship, and pooling our resources was the only way to go. I suspect this configuration is fairly common for people our age (early 30s). So how do we draw up a contract when we've gone from no income and quite a few debts to two stable incomes, few or no debts, and some jointly-owned property?

Long-term couples who want to draw up a contract must decide one important issue: Do we keep things as is or start all over? In either case, you must acknowledge how it's been—that is, what you've orally or implicitly agreed to over the years—and how you want it to be in the future.

LONG-TERM COUPLES

Ralph Palme and Hinton Wayne agree as follows:

1. We have been living together for 14 years. We moved in together as college juniors. It has been a continuous relationship since then.

2. We each had very little money and property when we first got together. Ralph had moved here from Sweden and left his belongings behind. He had his clothes and some Swedish albums and books. Hinton furnished the apartment with hand-me-down furniture from his parents. The art that decorated our apartment was movie posters from our friend Cynthia who worked at a retro movie house.

3. Since we have been together, we have pooled all our money and jointly paid all our expenses. Over the years, one of us may have been out of work or in school while the other worked full-time. When we've both been working, our salaries have varied a lot. Sometimes Ralph earns more; sometimes Hinton does.

4. We agree that our financial life is so intertwined that everything we have is jointly owned, and all debts are jointly owed. We agree to review all title documents (for the two cars and deposit accounts) and change all title slips to include both names.

5. We recognize that one or the other of us may have a preference for certain things we own. Therefore, we attach three lists to this agreement. List 1 is the property we agree Ralph gets if we split up. List 2 is the same for Hinton. List 3 is the rest of our property.

6. We agree to continue living as we have. Once a year, during the week of our anniversary, we will pull out our lists and add purchases made during the past year to List 1, 2 or 3.

7. We each agree to make a valid will, revocable upon the termination of this agreement, leaving all his property to the other upon death.

8. If we separate, Ralph gets the items on List 1 and Hinton the items on List 2. We will equally divide the items on List 3 in a way to even things up in the event the items on List 1 and List 2 are of unequal value.

9. Any provision in this agreement found to be invalid shall have no effect on the validity of the remaining provisions.

Dated: _____   Signature:_____
                                        Ralph Palme

Dated: _____   Signature:_____
                                        Hinton Wayne

P.S. One couple we know sat down to draft this very agreement the summer before their eighth anniversary. They got so depressed at the thought of dividing their property if they split up that they tossed the agreement into the recycling bin before they could complete lists 1 and 2. That was eight years ago and they're still very happy and very together. Moral of the story: Sometimes, history and trust is enough. If the thought of writing a contract after years of not having one makes you depressed, throw out the paper and go have dinner.

4. Contracts for Sharing Household Expenses and Chores

Thousands of gay and lesbian couples find themselves in the same situation as Lynne and Sarah. They are both professionals—Lynne's an ad executive and Sarah works as a designer—who make about the same amount of money. They want to keep their property separate, but want to share household expenses.

SHARING HOUSEHOLD EXPENSES

Lynne Jacobs and Sarah Elderberry agree as follows:

1. We plan to live together indefinitely.

2. We will maintain separate bank and credit accounts.

3. Our earnings and property will be kept separate.

4. Any item of separate property can become joint property or the separate property of the other only by a written agreement signed by the person whose property is to be reclassified.

5. We will each be responsible for our own personal expenses. This includes clothing, medical/dental bills, and long-distance telephone calls. We will pay household expenses, including rent, food, utilities and cleaning, jointly. We agree to keep receipts for all expenses, and to do an accounting each month. The person who spends less will pay the other whatever sum is necessary to arrive at a 50-50 split.

6. Lynne, because she's a gourmet, will food shop and cook. Sarah will wash dishes and do general cleaning. We will both maintain the plants and pets.

7. We each agree to make a valid will, revocable upon the termination of this agreement, leaving all her property to the other upon death.

8. Either of us can end this agreement at any time. If we separate, we will equally divide jointly purchased property. Neither, however, will be obligated to support the other.

9. Any provision in this agreement found to be invalid shall have no effect on the validity of the remaining provisions.

Dated: _____   Signature: _____
                                        Lynne Jacobs

Dated: _____   Signature: _____
                                        Sarah Elderberry

5. Contracts for Joint Projects

A joint project agreement can cover building a cabin, refurbishing a boat or any other major project. We include two contracts, although, of course, we don't cover every contingency. What happens, for example, if the project costs more than originally estimated? What arrangements should be made for operating the greenhouse, once it's finished?

Example: Tony and Ray live together. Both are landscape gardeners and share a dream of building a greenhouse and raising orchids on a piece of land they jointly own. They know it's a big job and want to anchor their dream on a strong foundation of good business practice, so they make an agreement reflecting that.

JOINT PROJECT AGREEMENT

Tony Freeling and Ray Vivaldi agree as follows:

1. They both want to build a glass and wood greenhouse to house tropical orchids.

2. Each will contribute $9,000 towards the purchase of construction materials. The money will be kept in a joint bank account and both Tony and Ray's signatures will be required on checks.

3. Each will work at least 40 hours per month on building the greenhouse.

4. They will keep neat records, recording all hours worked and money spent for materials.

5. If they separate, Ray will have the opportunity to buy Tony's share for an amount equal to Tony's actual cash investment plus $15 per hour for the time he has worked on building the greenhouse. [If Tony was a professional carpenter and Ray was not, it may be fairer for Ray to contribute more money (Clause 2) or for Tony's hourly salary to be greater.]

6. At separation, if Ray decides not to buy Tony's share under the terms of Clause 5, Tony will have the opportunity to buy Ray's share on the same terms.

7. If neither Ray nor Tony elect to purchase the other's share of the greenhouse, they will sell it and equally divide the proceeds.

8. If either Tony or Ray fails to work on the greenhouse 40 hours per month for three consecutive months, the other may buy out his share under the terms set out in Clauses 5 and 6.

9. If either Tony or Ray dies, the other becomes sole owner of the greenhouse. If either Ray or Tony makes a will, this provision will be incorporated into that will.

10. Any provision in this agreement found to be invalid shall have no effect on the validity of the remaining provisions.

Dated: _____ Signature: _____
                                        Tony Freeling

Dated: _____ Signature: _____
                                        Ray Vivaldi

Tony and Ray's joint project augmented their home. Other couples use a joint project agreement to cover professional endeavors.

Example: Patti and Maria's shared dream is to own and run a bakery—supporting themselves through their mutual love of scones and croissants. They know the odds are against any small business succeeding and that they'll have to work extremely hard to make their dream a reality. They want to protect their enterprise if they separate, or if one loses interest but the other wants to continue. They face another challenge—Patti has more cash to invest initially, but they eventually want to own the business equally.

JOINT PROJECT AGREEMENT

Patti Valdez and Maria Ness agree as follows:

1. We desire and intend to jointly own and operate a bakery in San Francisco, California (at a rented location not yet ascertained).

2. Patti will contribute $75,000 and Maria $25,000 toward the working capital of the business.

3. We both will work diligently in our bakery business, and it will be the principal business endeavor of each.

4. Initially, Patti will own 3/4 of the business and Maria 1/4. Each of us will receive pay of $700 a week for her work in the bakery. Any profits beyond salaries and operating expenses will be paid to Patti, until she receives $50,000 plus interest at 10% per year on the unpaid balance of the $50,000. Once Patti receives the $50,000 plus interest, we will co-own the business equally, and divide equally all profits beyond salaries and operating expenses.

5. If either of us decides she no longer wants to operate the bakery, the person wishing to continue may purchase the other's interest in the bakery as set out under Paragraph 7.

6. If we separate and are unable to work together, but both want to continue the bakery under sole ownership, we will ask someone to flip a coin; the winner will have the right to purchase the loser's interest as provided in Paragraph 7. Likewise, if we separate and only one of us wishes to maintain the bakery, that person has the right to purchase the other's interest as provided in Paragraph 7.

7. If for any reason one of us wants to purchase the other's interest in the business, she will pay the fair market value of the other's share. If we cannot agree on the fair market value, we agree to accept the fair market value as determined by Bill's Commercial Real Estate Appraisers.

8. If either of us dies, the other will become the sole owner of the bakery. We agree to each make a will containing this provision.

9. Any provision in this agreement found to be invalid shall have no effect on the validity of the remaining provisions.

Dated: _____   Signature:_____
                                        Patti Valdez

Dated: _____   Signature:_____
                                        Maria Ness

Do you need to see a lawyer? As you know, we don't advise seeing a lawyer for every little problem. If you and your lover are opening a business together, however, you will be investing a great deal of your time—and probably money. To begin with, you need a formal partnership agreement, and we recommend *The Partnership Book*, by Denis Clifford and Ralph Warner (Nolo Press) or *Nolo's Partnership Maker* software for IBM-compatible computers. You should also have your agreement checked by a lawyer with small business experience. (See Chapter 10.)

6. Contracts to Give a Partner "Time Off"

Oftentimes, when both lovers work outside the home, one wants to take time off to study art, travel, have a child or just stay home. The challenge is working out the details so that the person who continues to earn a living doesn't get resentful and the person taking time off doesn't start feeling guilty. One option is to alternate earning an income and taking time off; that way, each partner takes time to financially support the couple. Another possibility is for the person working to loan money to the one taking time off. Or, if the person taking time off will be raising a child, clearly both partners are contributing to the relationship and no "equal time off" or loan is needed. No matter what you arrange, you must specify how much time equals how much money, and, if appropriate, set a method of repayment.

Below is a "time-off" agreement for a couple who are both artists, but need to hold regular jobs to pay the bills.

Example: Martha and Lianne have lived together on and off for three years. Martha is a poet and Lianne an illustrator, but both have other part-time jobs to make ends meet. They recently moved in together, and decided to "trade" working. Each will work full time at her art, as they take turns supporting each other. Not only can they be creative, but they can also pay their rent and groceries.

ALLOWING ONE PERSON TIME OFF

Martha Rutherford and Lianne Wu agree as follows:

1. Each of us will retain whatever property we currently own as our separate property (lists are attached to this contract). All income stemming from the earnings of either of us while we live together, including income from our artistic pursuits, will be jointly owned and kept in joint bank accounts. Any property purchased with this income will be jointly-owned.

2. We will each work at full-time jobs for alternating six-month periods for the duration of this agreement. Lianne will work the first six-month period and then it will be Martha's turn.

3. The person employed will be responsible for all personal and household expenses for both of us.

4. If we separate during a year—that is, before each person has supported the other for six months—the support obligation will continue for the remainder of the year in an amount roughly equal to that previously contributed.

5. If one of us wants to end the living arrangement, we agree to participate in mediation sessions with a mutually acceptable third person. If, after a minimum of three sessions, one of us still wants to separate, we will. Each will take her separate property (property owned prior to living together), and all joint property (property acquired while living together) will be equally divided. No financial or other responsibilities will continue between us after we separate, except as set out in Clause 4.

6. Any provision in this agreement found to be invalid shall have no effect on the validity of the remaining provisions.

Dated: _____   Signature:_____
                                        Martha Rutherford

Dated: _____   Signature:_____
                                        Lianne Wu

7. Contracts for People in School

It's common for one partner to help the other with educational expenses or support while he or she's in school. This is a situation for a written agreement.

Example: Sam supports George while he's in plumber's school. Sam expects their financial lives to improve once George graduates. If George leaves Sam just after graduating, Sam is likely to feel that George owes him something. A court might agree, but the couple shouldn't leave it to a court to decide. So they define their expectations in a written agreement.

EDUCATIONAL SUPPORT

Sam Adaba and George Fujimoto make the following agreement:

1. Each wants to further his education, and so they will take turns going to school. Sam has already started school to learn plumbing, and his schooling is shorter than George's, so he will go first. George will pay Sam's educational expenses and support for them both for the next 18 months. After 18 months, Sam will assume these responsibilities for two years while George finishes his accountant's training. If their relationship dissolves during the first three and one-half years, the financial responsibilities won't be affected.

Specifically, if Sam and George separate during the first 18 months, George will continue to pay Sam's tuition and will pay Sam $5,000 per year for living expenses. At the end of the 18 months, Sam will pay George's tuition, and his living expenses at $5,000 per year, for two years. If they separate after George starts school, Sam will pay George's remaining tuition up to two full years in accounting school and pay him $5,000 a year for living expenses. Expenses will be paid in 12 equal monthly installments on the first day of each month.

2. All property owned by Sam or George before the date of this contract remains his separate property and can't be transferred to the other except by a written agreement.

3. During the first three and one-half years, all income and property accumulated with that income, except gifts and inheritances, will be jointly-owned. When both Sam and George finish school, they will make a list of all jointly-accumulated property. That property will be divided equally if they separate. Thereafter, each person's earnings will be his separate property and neither will have any right in the property of the other. If they separate before the end of three and one-half years, all property accumulated since the beginning of this agreement will be divided according to the fraction of the time each provided support. [For example, if Sam supports George for 18 months and George supports Sam for 12, Sam is entitled to three-fifths of the property.]

4. Any provision in this agreement found to be invalid shall have no effect on the validity of the remaining provisions.

Dated: _____   Signature:_____
                                              Sam Adaba

Dated: _____   Signature:_____
                                              George Fujimoto

8. Contracts for Work Done Around the House

In some relationships, one person works outside the home while the other cooks, cleans, shops and otherwise takes care of the place. This sort of labor division can raise questions, such as whether the homemaker should be compensated.

More frequently, both partners work outside the home, but one also makes significant improvements to the home, while the other idles in the sauna. Is it fair that the person who does the extra work should receive nothing for her labor? Only you can answer these questions, and no two answers will be the same. But remember one thing—these situations are likely to lead to misunderstandings unless you discuss them, and write down your agreement.

The worst thing you can do if one person contributes all the money or does all the work around the house is ignore it. First, a person with money also has power, and relationships rarely prosper when one person has too much of anything. Second, a person who does all the work around the house tends to feel resentful toward the other.

So here are some solutions. A person who spends all weekend fixing up a jointly-owned house can be paid an agreed-upon hourly rate, with the compensation either paid in cash by the other or added to the carpenter's equity in the house.[7] A stay-at-home mate can be given a weekly salary or can trade services (you fix the car while your lover does the laundry). You should also think about the homemaker's future if you split up. You can agree on a period of support payments for the homemaker, thereby creating your own alimony-like arrangement by contract.

COMPENSATING A HOMEMAKER

Sandi Potter and Carole Samworthe agree that as long as they live together:

1. Sandi will work full-time (at least 40 hours a week).

2. Carole will work in the home, taking care of her daughter, Judy, and performing the domestic chores, including cleaning, laundry, cooking and yard work. Sandi will pay Carole $200 a week for her services. This payment will be adjusted from time to time to reflect changes in the cost of living.

3. Sandi will also provide reasonable amounts of money each month for food, clothing, shelter and recreation for the entire family as long as they live together. This payment will be adjusted from time to time to reflect changes in the cost of living. Sandi, however, assumes no obligation to support Carole or Judy upon termination of this agreement.

4. Sandi, as Carole's "employer," will make Social Security payments for her and will obtain medical insurance for her and Judy.

5. All property purchased or accumulated by either Carole or Sandi will be owned by the person purchasing or accumulating it. The property cannot be transferred from one person to the other except by a written agreement. The house will be provided by Sandi and will be owned solely by her.

6. Either Sandi or Carole can end this agreement by giving the other two months' written notice. If Sandi and Carole separate, Sandi will pay Carole severance pay at the rate of two months for every year the agreement has been in effect. Sandi's agreement to pay this money is part of the consideration necessary to get Carole to agree to this contract. This money will be paid in a lump sum at the time of separation. Neither Carole nor Sandi will have any other financial obligation to the other upon separation.

7. Any provision in this agreement found to be invalid shall have no effect on the validity of the remaining provisions.

Dated: _____   Signature:_____
                                                  Sandi Potter

Dated: _____   Signature:_____
                                                  Carole Samworthe

E. Modifying Your Agreement

Modifications of a written living together contract should always be in writing. This is because ancient, but still applicable, legal doctrines usually make oral modifications of a written contract invalid. In addition, our contracts expressly state that any modifications must be in writing. A modification can simply state that you agree to change your contract, and then set out the change. Date and sign all modifications. But if you're making really major changes, tear up the old agreement and start over.

Endnotes

[1] 18 Cal.3d 660 (1976).

[2] This is the wonderful legal term for what goes on between people who make love without a marriage license. (It sounds like a great business. Can't you hear the phone receptionist, "Hello, Meretricious Sexual Services ..."). If you put in your contract that it is based on the performance of sexual acts, the contact is invalid.

[3] *Crooke v. Gilden,* 414 S.E.2d 645 (Georgia, 1992).

[4] *Jones v. Estate of Daly,* 122 Cal.App.3d 500 (1981). But in *Whorton v. Dillingham,* 202 Cal.App.3d 447 (1988), the court ruled that the inference to sex (using the term lover) could be cut off and the rest of the contract enforced.

[5] No Income, No Kids.

[6] This is called making a gift. Normally, it's not a problem. But if one person gives another property worth over $10,000 a year, gift taxes may be assessed against the gift giver's estate after she dies. (See Chapter 5.)

[7] See Chapter 7 for contracts related to buying or fixing up a house. ■

Buying a Home Together (and Other Real Estate Ventures)

Your Home As Investment and Tax Shelter

There are many financial benefits to owning a home, especially in times of rapid inflation. With any luck your investment will go up in value. You can deduct from your taxable income all interest you pay on your mortgage, and all your property taxes. By comparison, renters get no such deductions, even if, as is usual, their rent helps pay the landlord's taxes and mortgage interest payments.

Homeowners qualify for another tax advantage. If you sell your home and use the proceeds to buy another of greater value within 24 months, you're allowed to postpone paying taxes on the profit made in the first sale until you sell your second home. And, if you sell the second and buy a third, you get the same postponement. This means you can keep buying up more expensive properties and postpone paying taxes on your accumulated profits while you're doing it. Or to say it another way, you can use money you would have had to pay taxes on for a larger investment.

Another tax rule helps older folks whose homes have skyrocketed in value. It works like this: Any time after you reach age 55, you can sell your home without paying taxes on the first $125,000 profit. You can do it only once. As with all rules we discuss here, however, be sure to check the current status of the tax laws before acting.

To Freud, a home symbolized motherhood. For E. M. Forster, in *Howard's End,* it was a sign of stability and the best of the old order. Others have likened a home to a castle and valued it as a haven of peace and refuge. One way or another, home ownership has long been an important part of our culture. Indeed, it's probably fair to say that if you dream of purchasing a home, you dream along with much of America.

Beyond the emotional urges, there are many practical reasons to own a home—a hedge against rent increases and an unstable economy, avoiding the powerlessness of being a tenant and the tax deductibility of mortgage interest. In addition, owning a home offers a lesbian or gay couple some privacy from the sometimes hostile intrusions of the world.

At the same time, home ownership has drawbacks. When the boiler explodes, you may pine for the days when you could just call your landlord. You might recall Thoreau, who noted that most people didn't own their houses; their houses owned them. Still, despite the drawbacks, it *is* your home. It can be fun to tear down walls, plant your own trees, paint an ivy decoration across the dining room walls or even fix the boiler. Most Americans agree with Mark Twain, who advised, "Buy land. They aren't making any more of it."

Buying and fixing up a home with a lover can be a wonderful foundation for a relationship, both spiritually and economically. Of course, it can be damn scary too. The bulk of this chapter suggests ways to handle the practical aspects of buying a home. Even if you skipped Chapter 6 on living together contracts, you will need a contract regarding the ownership of a house. And recognizing what continues to be a trend in the lesbian and gay community, some of these contracts are for friends, with or without lovers, who buy together.

Before you can pin down your agreement, you have to find the house, arrange for financing and understand the ways in which you can hold title to the property. Let's begin with these first steps.

A. Finding a House

Given your needs, tastes and finances, you probably already have a good idea of the type of house you want to buy. Indeed, if you sit quietly for a few moments, shut your eyes and let your imagination do the walking, you can probably conjure up an image of the house, or perhaps if you're a flexible sort, several houses that you would dearly love to call home.

We have no advice to give you on what type of home to look for. Some folks love living on a dusty road in outer suburbia; others want the convenience of living in a townhouse in a major city. Many people enjoy fixing a place up while others insist on move-in condition. Some crave a view, while others can live with almost no light.

But we do have something to say about buying a house you'll be happy with. You need an organized house-buying method to translate your dream into reality. This is particularly true in high-priced markets (often urban areas) where most buyers face an affordability gap between the house they'd like to buy and the one they can afford. Without an organized approach, there is a good chance you'll be talked into compromising on the wrong house by friends, relatives, a real estate agent or even yourself.

"Not me, I know my own mind," you say. "Nonsense," we reply. In today's market, almost everyone must trim their desires to fit their pocketbook and it's easy to buy the wrong house in the wrong location. So easy, in fact, that every day many confident and knowledgeable people become so anxious and disoriented in the process of searching for a house that they purchase one they later come to regret buying, sometimes bitterly.

Here is our method to all but insure that you buy a house you'll enjoy living in, even if it's substantially more modest than your dream house:

- Firmly establish your priorities before you look at a house.
- Insist that any house you offer to buy meets at least your most important priorities.
- Do this even if, in buying a house which meets your priorities, you must compromise in other areas and purchase a house less desirable than you really want.

The reason this method works well should be obvious. If your priorities are clearly set in advance, you're likely to compromise on less important features. If they aren't, you may become so disoriented by the house purchase process that you buy a house without the basic features that motivated you to buy in the first place.

Lesbian and gay couples usually have no special problems in finding a house to buy. Be aware, however, that some communities (or neighborhoods) have adopted zoning ordinances prohibiting unrelated people from living together.[1] Most of these laws are aimed at barring groups, foster families, shelters or boarding houses, and few prohibit two unrelated adults from living together. But the most restrictive of these laws have been used to harass lesbians and gays who lived together, just as they have been used to discriminate against unmarried heterosexual couples. Before you buy, make sure the town—or neighborhood—isn't zoned only for people related by "blood, marriage or adoption."[2]

Also, some sellers may hesitate to sell to you because they think you are immoral or even criminal. We've never heard of anyone ultimately refusing to sell to a lesbian or gay couple, however; the god Mammon appears to be stronger than the god Discrimination.

The most common way to find a home is to use an agent, broker or realtor. (We use the term realtor for simplicity.) Again, you may encounter a realtor who refuses to work with a lesbian or gay couple, although we're not aware of anyone this has happened to. To avoid it, you have two choices: Look for a gay or gay-friendly realtor. (Ask your gay home-owning friends who they used.) Or buy on your own, without a realtor. (Lots of people do this; it saves on the fees you pay.)

Indeed, you may well be tempted to proceed on your own. But bear in mind that buying real estate takes a lot of work and patience, and involves understanding much strange jargon. It's often easier to let someone knowledgeable do the work. If you decide to use a realtor, keep in mind that you are not obligated to work with just one. Shop around. Eventually, you may select one to work with. The advantage is that, at least in theory, you get a chance at the "hottest" deals—the ones the realtor would otherwise save for his close relatives. If a dozen agents are looking for you, chances are none of them are looking very hard.

Just as you (the buyers) don't have to hire a realtor, neither does the seller. A small but significant number of people sell their homes this way. You can find homes sold by owners by checking newspaper ads or driving around and looking for "for sale by owner" or "FSBO" (pronounced fizzbo) signs. There are several books explaining the ins and outs of buying or selling a home yourself.[3]

Working With a Realtor

In most states, realtors assist with all aspects of the purchase. In addition to finding homes, they can give you advice on prices, school districts, transportation, demographics and economic trends in the area (whether property values going up or down). A realtor should also help you find the experts you need—such as a termite inspector, a roofer or a soil engineer—and assist with arranging financing and the closing.

A realtor's commission is a percentage of the price of the home, and is paid by the seller. Because the realtor isn't being paid on an hourly basis, take your time and ask all the questions you want. A common commission is 6%, but it's supposedly negotiable. You may find commission competition in some urban areas, and a seller may find someone who'll do a good job and charge less. After all, 6% can be a large chunk of money. Because the seller pays the commission, however, the buyer won't save much unless the seller's willing to pass along some of the savings.

Legally, realtors who share in the commission paid by the seller represent the seller. This is true even if the realtor has actively showed you houses and has never met the seller. When it comes to the negotiations, however, quite a gap can develop between this legal truth and the marketplace reality. A realtor doesn't get a commission until a sale is consummated; it's therefore in her interest to consummate the deal. This may not be in your interest at all. So be careful you're not talked into a house you don't want.

B. How Much House Can You Afford?

Many prospective home buyers face an affordability problem when it comes to buying the house they'd really like to live in. This is still true, even though most house prices are slightly more affordable than they were a few years ago and mortgage interest rates are at comparatively reasonable levels.

Against this somber background, it's essential to determine how much you can afford to pay before you look for a house. Sounds basic, but apparently it isn't, as many people never take the time to understand how institutional lenders (banks, savings and loans, credit unions) calculate a buyer's affordability amount until they make an offer on a house and apply for financing. Then reality hits. Often they can't qualify for the necessary loan.

Let's start with the basics. As a broad generalization, most people can afford to purchase a house worth about three times their total (gross) annual income, assuming a 20% down payment and a moderate amount of other long-term debts. With no other debts, they can afford a house worth up to four times their annual income.

A much more accurate way to determine how much house you can afford is to compare your monthly carrying costs[4] plus your monthly payments on other long-term debts, to your gross (total) monthly income. This is called the "debt-to-income ratio." Lenders normally want you to make all monthly payments with 28%-38% of your monthly income. You can qualify near the bottom or the top of this range depending on the amount of your down payment, the interest rate on the type of mortgage you want, your credit history, the level of your other long-term debts, your employment stability and prospects, the lender's philosophy and the money supply in the general economy.

Generally, the greater your other debts, the lower the percentage of your income lenders will assume you have available to spend each month on housing. Conversely, if you have no long-term debts, a great credit history and will make a larger than normal down payment, a lender may approve carrying costs that exceed 38% of your monthly income—sometimes as high as 40% or 42%. In either case, these rules aren't absolute.

Given this, determining in advance the percentage of your income you'll need to make monthly costs on a mortgage of a particular amount is key.

1.   Prepare a Financial Statement

The first step to determine the purchase price you can afford is to thoroughly prepare a list of your monthly incomes and your monthly expenses.

Total monthly gross income. List your gross monthly income from all sources. Gross income is total income before withholdings are deducted. Include income from:

• employment—your base salary or wages plus any bonuses, tips, commissions or overtime you regularly receive
• public benefits

• dividends from stocks, bonds and similar investments
• freelance income, self-employment and hobbies, and
• royalties and rents.

Total monthly deductions. Total up all required monthly deductions from your income (such as taxes and Social Security deducted from your paycheck). Don't include money deducted to pay credit unions, child support or other debts. If you deliberately have more money than necessary subtracted from federal or state income tax by underclaiming deductions, ask your employer what amount you are obligated to pay.

Total monthly net income. Subtract your total monthly deductions from your total monthly gross income to arrive at your net income.

Total monthly expenses. List and total up what you spend each month on the following:

• child care
• clothing
• current educational costs
• food—include eating at restaurants, as well as at home
• insurance—auto, life, medical, disability
• medical expenses not covered by insurance
• personal expenses—include costs for personal care (hair cuts, shoe repairs and toiletries) and fun (attending movies and theater, renting videos, buying CDs, books and lottery tickets, subscribing to newspapers and magazines)

- installment payments—student loans, car payments, child support, alimony, personal loans, credit cards and any others
- taxes
- transportation
- utilities
- other—such as regular charitable or religious donations and savings deposits.

2. How Much Down Payment Will You Make?

Unless you're eligible for a government-subsidized mortgage that has low or—in the case of the Veterans Administration—no down payment, you'll probably need to put down 10%-25% of the cost of the house to qualify for a loan. Also, you'll have to pay the closing costs, an additional 2%-5% of the cost of the home.

Generally speaking, the larger the percentage of the total price of a house you can put down, the easier it will be for you to qualify for a mortgage. This is because larger down payments mean less money due each month to pay off your mortgage. The monthly mortgage payment (plus taxes and insurance) is the major factor in determining the purchase price of the house you can afford.

Total up the money you have for a down payment and then multiply this number first by five and then by ten. These figures represent the very broad price range of house prices you can likely afford, based on your ability to make a down payment. Of course, you must be able to afford the monthly mortgage, interest and property tax payments too. If your income is relatively low, you'll have to increase your down payment to 25%-30% or even more of the price of a house to bring down the monthly payments.

3. Estimate the Mortgage Interest Rate You'll Likely Pay

Because different mortgage types carry different interest rates, start by deciding the mortgage type you want. For a reading of the market's direction, check the mortgage interest rate round-up published in the real estate sections of many Sunday newspapers.

In general, adjustable rate mortgages (ARMs) have slightly lower initial interest rates and payment requirements than do fixed rate loans, and are therefore more affordable than fixed rate loans. This isn't saying they're better, however, and before selecting an ARM, compare interest rates by looking at the ARM's annual percentage rate (APR), not just its introductory rate. (APR is an estimate of the credit cost over the entire life of the loan. APR comparisons can sometimes be deceptive.)

4. Calculate How Much House You Can Afford

Now that you have a pretty good idea of the size of your down payment and the interest rate you expect to pay, you can calculate how much house you can afford.

Step 1. Estimate the price you think a house with your priorities will cost.

Step 2. Estimate the likely mortgage interest rate you'll end up paying. If you're eligible for a government-subsidized mortgage, be sure to use those rates.

Step 3. Find your mortgage interest and principal payment factors per $1,000 over the length of the loan (30 years is most common) on the chart on page 7-12.

Step 4. Subtract the down payment you want to make from your estimated purchase price. The result is the amount you'll need to borrow.

Step 5. Multiply the factor from the chart ahead by the number of thousands you'll need to borrow. The result is your monthly principal and interest payment.

Monthly payments on a $100,000 fixed rate mortgage

Interest rate (%)	15-year period monthly payment ($)	Total payments ($)	30-year period monthly payment ($)	Total payments ($)
6.5	871.11	156,799	632.07	227,544
7.0	898.83	161,789	665.30	239,509
7.5	927.01	166,862	699.21	251,717
8.0	955.65	172,017	733.76	264,155
8.5	984.74	177,253	768.91	276,809
9.0	1,014.27	182,569	804.62	298,664
9.5	1,044.22	187,960	840.85	302,708
10.0	1,074.61	193,430	877.57	315,926
10.5	1,105.40	198,972	914.74	329,306
11.0	1,136.60	204,588	952.32	342,836
11.5	1,168.19	210,274	990.29	356,505
12.0	1,200.17	216,031	1,028.61	370,301
12.5	1,232.52	221,854	1,067.26	384,214
13.0	1,265.24	227,743	1,106.20	398,232
14.0	1,331.74	239,713	1,184.87	426,554

Here's how to put the first five steps together.

Example: Bill and Mark estimate the house they want to buy will cost $200,000. A 20% down payment of $40,000 leaves them with a $160,000 mortgage loan. They plan to finance with an adjustable rate mortgage (ARM), which they believe they can get at an interest rate of 6%. The monthly factor per $1,000 for a 30-year loan at 6% rate is 6. So their monthly payments will begin at (because it's adjustable) 160 x 6, or $960.

Step 6. To get the total carrying costs for the mortgage loan, you must add the estimated monthly costs of homeowner's insurance and property taxes. Very roughly, homeowner's insurance costs about $400 per $100,000 of house value. On a $200,000 house, expect to pay $800 per year or $67 per month.

Step 7. Property taxes are initially based on the new assessed value (market price) of the house as of the date of transfer of title. They vary state to state and even county to county, so use 1% of the market value as an estimated annual tax. (For an exact number, call the tax assessor in the county in which you're looking to buy.) On a $200,000 house, taxes would be about $2,000 per year or $167 per month.

Mortgage Principal & Interest Payment Factors (Per $1,000)

Interest rates	15-year mortgage	20-year mortgage	25-year mortgage	30-year mortgage
5.00	7.91	6.60	5.85	5.37
5.25	8.04	6.74	5.99	5.52
5.50	8.17	6.88	6.14	5.68
5.75	8.30	7.02	6.29	5.84
6.00	8.44	7.16	6.44	6.00
6.25	8.57	7.31	6.60	6.16
6.50	8.71	7.46	6.75	6.32
6.75	8.85	7.60	6.91	6.49
7.00	8.99	7.75	7.07	6.65
7.25	9.13	7.90	7.23	6.82
7.50	9.27	8.06	7.39	6.99
7.75	9.41	8.21	7.55	7.16
8.00	9.56	8.36	7.72	7.34
8.25	9.70	8.52	7.88	7.51
8.50	9.85	8.68	8.05	7.69
8.75	9.99	8.84	8.22	7.87
9.00	10.14	9.00	8.39	8.05
9.25	10.29	9.16	8.56	8.23
9.50	10.44	9.32	8.74	8.41
9.75	10.59	9.49	8.91	8.59
10.00	10.75	9.65	9.09	8.78
10.25	10.90	9.82	9.26	8.96
10.50	11.05	9.98	9.44	9.15
10.75	11.21	10.15	9.62	9.33
11.00	11.37	10.32	9.80	9.52
11.25	11.52	10.49	9.98	9.71
11.50	11.68	10.66	10.16	9.90
11.75	11.84	10.84	10.35	10.09
12.00	12.00	11.01	10.53	10.29

Step 8. Now total up your mortgage/ interest payment, insurance and taxes. This is your monthly carrying costs.

Step 9. Total up the monthly payments on your long-term debts and add this number to the monthly carrying costs you arrived at in Step 8. Then, divide that total by a number between .28 and .38, depending on your debt level (the fewer your debts, the higher number to divide by), to determine the monthly income needed to qualify.

C. Proceeding With Your Purchase

Once you find the house you want to buy, you need to take care of a few details before you actually buy it.

1. Inspections

Any contract to purchase a home should allow you time to make all necessary inspections. A buyer often pays for inspections, but it is possible to negotiate with the seller and have her pay a portion. These routinely include termite, electrical and plumbing, and a roof inspection. In addition, you may want a soil engineer to check the foundation, or a general contractor to do a full inspection. Your purchase contract should be contingent upon these experts reporting that the house either is in good condition or can be repaired for a reasonable price.

2. Financing That White Picket Fence

After you've conducted the inspections and reached a firm agreement on price and terms, you will have to come up with money. Usually, your obligation to buy is contingent on your finding financing for a specific amount at a specific interest rate. Obviously you don't want to sign a contract to purchase a home, and then not be able to find a loan you can afford.

Few of us can pay all cash for a house. We borrow money from a lending institution, family member, the seller or a loan shark, and accept whatever conditions the lenders impose. Most often, you'll borrow from a bank. In exchange, the bank will require you to sign a note promising to repay the money plus a healthy interest. Your promise to pay, standing alone, however, won't be sufficient security for the bank; it will also require you to sign a document giving it the power to foreclose on the house if you default on your payments. This document is normally called a mortgage, or a deed of trust.

Discrimination Against Lesbian and Gay Couples. In the distant past, many lenders refused to loan to lesbian and gay couples. Same-sex couples were considered immoral or unstable, no matter what their financial worth. Throughout the 1970s and easy-credit 1980s, times changed. Banks just looked at both persons' incomes. If the money was there, so came the loan, regardless of your sleeping arrangement.

Today, that's still the norm, though an article entitled "Home Sweet Homo" in the Fall 1992 issue of *Out* magazine reported a disturbing occurence by lenders of looking beyond financial qualifications when considering making mortgage loans. The lenders interviewed for the article denied the practices, but the author reported the following:

- A lender asking a lesbian couple to sign a statement stating that they were normal human beings.

- A lender asking a mortgage broker to supply a letter explaining the nature of the relationship of two gay men he was trying to secure a loan for.

- Rejections for seemingly non-prejudicial reasons ("you haven't been on the job long enough to qualify") when it's really based on the homophobia of the lender.

Some lenders admit that they view lesbian and gay relationships as inherently unstable and therefore consider it too risky to lend to lesbian and gay couples. Unfortunately, this kind of discrimination is legal. You will need to present yourselves as sophisticated buyers. Do your homework. Know the interest rates from several other lenders before you walk in the door. Get familiar with fixed rate loans, adjustable rate mortgages, special 15-year mortgages, points, closing costs and the rest.[5] Provide information showing that you're both on your jobs for the long haul (get letters from your supervisors) and are up for a promotion or a raise. And then be persistent.

To the extent it's possible, try to be creative in your financing. You may be able to "assume" a seller's loan. Or, she may be willing to finance any portion of the purchase. If she doesn't need all the money at once, she might give you a second mortgage.

Example: Wendy and Alice love a home selling for $180,000. Their savings, borrowing from parents and friends total $36,000. They need $144,000 more (plus $9,000 for closing costs). The seller has owned the home for a few years and has a $90,000 mortgage at 8% interest. Here are several possible methods of financing their purchase:

Plan A

- *$36,000 down payment*

- *$144,000 at current bank interest rates.*

Plan B

- *$36,000 down payment*

- *$90,000 by assuming the seller's old mortgage at 8%*

- *$54,000 loan from the seller including interest at 10%, with a final (balloon) payment for whatever balance is due in seven years. (The monthly interest payment rate and the time of the balloon payment will be negotiable.)*

Plan C

- *To make it more attractive to the seller, they offer $2,000 above the sales price*

- *$36,000 cash down*

- *$90,000 by assuming the seller's old mortgage at 8%*

- *$56,000 loan from seller including interest at 10%, with a final (balloon) payment for whatever balance is due in seven years.*

3. Escrow and Closing Costs

In buying and selling a house, paperwork and money must eventually change hands. The practice is for the buyers to deliver their money and the sellers to deliver the house deed to a third person, called an escrow holder. The escrow holder hangs on to everything until all inspections are complete, the papers are signed and financing is arranged. Then, "escrow closes," the deed is recorded with the county, the buyers receive the deed establishing that they now own the house and the seller gets the money. And the buyers pay their closing costs.

Closing Costs and Loan Fees

Closing costs and loan fees can add up to 5% to your mortgage. Some fees are paid when you take out the loan, but most are paid the day you close escrow. Not all lenders and escrow holders require all the fees (some are waived as part of special offers). When escrow closes, you'll receive a statement with an itemized list of the closing costs.

Typical closing costs and loan fees are:

Application fee: Loan application fees (typically $350-$400) cover the lender's cost of processing your loan.

Appraisal fees: Charged by an appraiser hired by the lender to appraise the property to be sure it's worth what you've agreed to pay. They usually run between $275 and $300 for a regular-sized single-family home, and somewhat more for a very large, or multiple-unit building.

Assumption fee: Typically 1% of the loan balance to assume the seller's existing ARM; to assume an FHA or VA loan, the fee will range from $50 to $100.

Credit report: Can cost up to $75 to check each partner's credit. While standard credit checks cost $5-$15, for home loans lenders check two credit reporting agencies' files and the county records for judgment and tax liens.

Escrow company fees: An escrow company that is not a title insurance company may charge a nominal fee for doing the escrow work.

Garbage fees: Real estate business slang for a number of small fees, including notary, courier and filing fees, which typically run from $150 to $250.

Loan fees: This includes points (one point is 1% of the loan principal) and an additional fee, usually between $100 and $450. Lenders also often charge $150 to $250 to complete the loan paperwork.

Physical inspection reports: May add several hundred dollars or more, depending on how many are requested.

Prepaid homeowner's insurance: Amount as required by lender; depends on the house's value, level of coverage and location of the house.

Prepaid interest on the loan: You'll be asked to pay per diem interest in advance, from the date your loan is funded to the end of that month. The maximum you'll be charged is 30 days of interest.

Prepaid property taxes: Depends on tax assessment; covers the time period between closing and your first monthly mortgage payment.

Private mortgage insurance: For a loan with 10% down, the total PMI you will pay is about 1.6%-2% of the loan. In the first year, you'll pay approximately .5% of the total loan. For each year you renew your PMI policy, you'll pay about .35% of the outstanding loan. PMI on FHA loans costs 3.8% of the loan. Most lenders require the first few payments to be made up front.

Recording and filing fees: The escrow holder will charge about $100 for drawing up, reviewing and recording the deed of trust and other legal documents. The total escrow and title fees can amount to 0.5% of the loan.

Survey fee: May be needed to show plot measurements if house has easements; will run about $150.

Tax service fee: Issued to notify the lender if you default on your property taxes; usually costs about $75 to $80.

Title search and title insurance: Not all buyers must pay the title costs. Most lenders require title insurance for the face amount of their mortgage or for the value of their loan. Title insurance is a one-time premium which costs about .075% of the cost of your house.

Transfer tax: Tax assessed by the county when the property changes hands. May be split with seller, and costs about $.55 per $1,000. Many cities also charge transfer tax; it varies city to city, but usually is not more than 1.5% of the purchase price.

In some states, such as Florida and New York, lawyers have a monopoly over real estate closings. Realtors cannot conduct closings, or even give their clients advice about them, as that would be practicing law without a license. You must waste time and money by hiring a lawyer, or do it yourself. Most people hire the lawyer. If you do, you will need to add the lawyer's fee to your total closing costs.

D. Taking Title to Your New Home

When you buy your home, you have to decide how you want the recorded deed to read, or as they say, how to "take title." This has lasting importance. You have three choices:

- one person only holds title
- both of you hold title as "joint tenants"
- both of you hold title as "tenants in common."

Here's what each means:

1. In One Person's Name

This means that absent a contract to the contrary, only the person named in the deed owns the house.[6] It isn't wise to put only one name on the deed unless in truth only one of you owns the house. Sometimes, a couple who jointly owns a home is tempted to put only one name on the deed to save on taxes or avoid creditors. The tax savings is attractive if one of your incomes is very high and the other's is very low; the high-income person takes all the house tax deductions. But in general, this is a bad strategy. Although you might fool a few creditors, there are real risks to this.

If the person on the deed (and the therefore presumed sole owner) sells the house and pockets the money, or dies without making provisions, the other person may be out of luck. Sure, she can sue to recover her portion of the property. But a lawsuit to recover your share might be difficult, or even impossible. In any case, it's absurd to risk a lawsuit. If more than one person is buying the property, all owners should normally be named on the deed. If you are not planning to do this, have a lawyer draft a contract clearly spelling out the interests and rights of both owners.

2. Joint Tenancy

Joint tenancy means you share property ownership equally, and that each of you has the right to use the entire property. Joint tenancy also comes with something called the "right of survivorship." In fact, the deed sometimes reads "joint tenancy with right of survivorship." This means that if one joint tenant dies, the other automatically takes the deceased person's share, even if there's a will to the contrary. And when joint tenancy property passes to the other joint tenant at death, there's no necessity of any probate proceedings.

Another feature of joint tenancy is that if one joint tenant sells his or her share, the sale ends the joint tenancy. The new owner and the other original owner become tenants-in-common (see below). Each joint tenant has the right to sell his or her interest, regardless of whether the other joint tenants agree with, or are even aware of, the sale.

Joint tenancy can't be used if a house is owned in unequal shares. It's appropriate only when each joint tenant owns the same portion. This means that you and your lover could put a house you owned 50-50 in joint tenancy or that three people could have joint tenancy with each owning one-third of a property. If you own 65% of a house, however, and your lover owns 35%, joint tenancy won't work.

3. Tenants in Common

Tenancy in common is another way to hold title when there's more than one owner. The major difference between joint tenancy and tenancy in common is that tenancy in common has no right of survivorship. This means that when a tenant in common dies, her share of property is left to whomever she specified in a will, or if there's no will, by the process of "intestate succession." (See Chapter 5.)

Also, and of particular importance in many lesbian or gay real estate ventures, tenants in common can own property in unequal shares—one person can own 80% of the property, another 15% and a third 5%. All are listed on the deed as tenants in common. You can specify the precise percentages on the deed, for example, "the owners named are tenants in common; Sappho has a one-third interest and Joan of Arc two-thirds." Or you can simply list all owners' names on the deed and set out the shares in a separate written agreement. Especially if shares are unequal, it's important to prepare a contract.

You can change title after the purchase; you need only record a new deed. For instance, if you want to start as tenants in common and later change to joint tenants, make and record a deed granting the property "from Sappho and Joan of Arc as Tenants in Common, to Sappho and Joan of Arc as Joint Tenants." If you add a new person, the IRS will call it either a sale or a gift and tax you accordingly, which can be expensive.

E. Contracts for People Buying or Owning Homes Together

A house is a major economic asset. It's foolish to avoid or postpone clearly defining your mutual expectations and obligations. In this section, we discuss ways to handle joint ownership problems and give sample contracts to cover the most common.

In the previous chapter of this book, we suggested that you prepare a living together contract. Even if you don't take that advice, you absolutely should prepare a contract if you plan to jointly own a home. As you'll see, most of the samples we give are simple and uncomplicated. We have found that the people who most often resist contracts are those who don't have a solid agreement in the first place. If this is your situation, sit down immediately and have a long, honest talk.

Although we recommend simple, uncomplicated contracts, some complicated home ownership arrangements will require complicated contracts. If this is your situation, you may want to have your agreement checked by a lawyer familiar with real estate, and sympathetic to lesbian and gay couples. This doesn't mean you should take a full wallet and a basketful of problems to the lawyer. Do as much work as possible yourself and use the lawyer to help you with particular problem areas or to check the entire agreement when you're finished.

1. Agreement for Equal Ownership

Let's start with a sample agreement between two people who contribute equal amounts of money for the down payment and intend to share all costs (and eventual profits) equally.

In this contract, Michael and Hadrian take title as joint tenants. As we discussed above, this means that if either dies, the survivor would automatically get the other's share. If Michael and Hadrian took title as tenants in common and one died, his heirs, or whomever he has designated in his will, would inherit his half of the property. Taking title in joint tenancy is common with long-term couples who don't want to hassle with probate, or with setting up a living trust.

Michael and Hadrian also wanted to make sure Michael's mother received the $20,000 she gave him for the down payment if he died while she was still alive. So they had to work that into their agreement.

CONTRACT FOR EQUAL OWNERSHIP

Michael Angelo and Hadrian Rifkin make the following agreement to jointly purchase a house that they will live in. They agree that:

1. They will buy a house at 423 Bliss Street, Chicago, Illinois, for $180,000.

2. They will take title as joint tenants.

3. They will each contribute $20,000 to the down payment and closing costs and will each pay one-half of the monthly mortgage and insurance costs, as well as one-half of the property taxes and costs for repairs that both agree are needed.

4. If either Michael or Hadrian want to end the relationship and living arrangement, and if both men want to keep the house, a friend will be asked to flip a coin within 60 days of the decision to separate.[7]

The winner of the coin toss will be entitled to purchase the house from the loser, provided that the winner pays the loser the fair market value (see Clause 5) of his share within 90 days. When payment is made, Michael and Hadrian will deed the house to the person retaining it in his name alone. If payment isn't made within 90 days, or if neither person wants to buy the house, it will be sold and the profits divided.

5. If Michael and Hadrian cannot agree on the fair market value of the house, this value will be determined by an appraisal conducted by Sheila Lim, the real estate agent they used when they bought the house.

6. Michael and Hadrian agree to maintain life insurance policies for at least $100,000, naming the other as beneficiary. If Michael dies while his mother is alive, Hadrian agrees to pay her $20,000 out of the proceeds of Michael's life insurance policy.

7. If either Michael or Hadrian must make a payment of mortgage, taxes or insurance for the other, who is either unable or unwilling to make the payment, that payment will be treated as a loan to be paid back within six months, including 10% interest per year.

8. This contract is binding on our heirs and our estates.

Dated: _____   Signature: _____
                                                   Michael Angelo

Dated: _____   Signature: _____
                                                   Hadrian Rifkin

2. Owning a House in Unequal Shares

If each person puts up the same amount for the down payment, pays equal shares of the mortgage and other expenses and contributes equally to fix up fees, each person would have an equal share of the ownership. It's common, however, for joint purchasers to contribute unequally. One person may have more money for the down payment. Another person may be able to afford larger monthly payments than the other, or has skills (such as carpentry) and can renovate the house while the other sits by, beer in hand, and kibbitzes.

Below are sample contracts for unequal ownership. Some factors to consider are easily expressed in cash (making comparisons simple), while other factors are almost impossible to evaluate financially. For example, work on the house can be given a cash value by establishing an hourly wage and multiplying it by the number of hours worked. But what value do you assign to someone's ability to borrow the down payment from his parents—especially in a society structured to reward the owners of capital? We don't mean to suggest that you must arrive at a mathematically exact determination—as you'll see, we suggest that it's enough to decide on rough values that satisfy you both.

a. Two-Thirds/One-Third Ownership

Tina and Barb purchased a home. Tina had more capital, so she made two-thirds of the down payment and owns two-thirds of the house. To keep things simple, Tina will pay two-thirds of the mortgage, taxes and insurance.

Here's their contract:

CONTRACT FOR OWNERSHIP AND PAYMENTS SPLIT 2/3 - 1/3

We, Tina Foote and Barb Bibbige, enter into this contract and agree as follows:

1. Property: We will purchase the house at 451 Morton Street, in Upper Montclair, New Jersey.

2. Contributions: We will contribute the following money to the down payment:

Tina $20,000
Barb $10,000

3. Ownership: We will own the property as tenants in common with the following shares:

Tina 2/3
Barb 1/3

4. Expenses and Mortgage: All expenses, including mortgage, taxes, insurance and repairs on the house, will be paid as follows:

Tina 2/3
Barb 1/3

5. Division Upon Sale: In the event the house is sold, the initial contributions ($20,000 to Tina and $10,000 to Barb) will be paid back first; the remainder of the proceeds will be divided two-thirds to Tina and one-third to Barb.

6. Contingencies:

a. We agree to hold the house for three years unless we mutually agree otherwise. After three years, either person may request the house be sold. The person who doesn't want to sell has the right of first refusal; that is, she has the right to purchase the house at the agreed-upon price, and must state in writing that she will exercise this right within two weeks of the setting of the price. She has 60 days to complete the purchase, or the right lapses.

b. If one owner moves out of the house before it's sold, she will remain responsible for her share of the mortgage, taxes, insurance and repairs. She may rent her quarters with the approval (which won't be unreasonably withheld) of the other. The person who stays in the house has the first right to rent the quarters herself or assume the cost if she so chooses.

c. If Tina and Barb decide to separate and both want to keep the house, they will try to reach a satisfactory arrangement. If by the end of two weeks they can't, they will ask a friend to flip a coin. The winner has the right to purchase the loser's share provided the winner pays the loser her fair market value within 90 days of the toss.

d. If either Tina or Barb dies, the other, if she hasn't been left the deceased person's share, has the right to purchase that share from the deceased's estate within six months. The value of the share will be determined as set out above.

7. Binding: This agreement is binding on us and our heirs, executors, administrators, successors and assigns.

Signed in: _____
              (City)   (State)

Dated: _____   Signature: _____
                                     Tina Foote

Dated: _____   Signature: _____
                                   Barb Bibbige

b. Unequal Ownership Turns Into Equal Ownership

For the next example, let's fantasize that we're drawing up a contract for Gertrude and Alice. Gertrude can sell some valuable antiques and come up with the full $50,000 down payment for a little cottage with a mansard roof. Alice can pay one-half the monthly mortgage, insurance and maintenance costs, but has no money for the down payment. They eventually want to equally own the home, but also want to fairly account for Gertrude's down payment.

Gertrude could make a gift of one-half of the down payment to Alice, but she'd be liable for a gift tax and doesn't feel quite that generous. We suggest that Gertrude call one-half of the down payment a *loan* to Alice that can either be paid back in monthly installments or deferred until the house is sold. If this is done, they should write a contract similar to Michael and Hadrian's, indicating a 50-50 ownership. They should also execute a promissory note providing a record of the loan.

PROMISSORY NOTE FOR DOWN PAYMENT MONEY

I, Alice B. Toklas, acknowledge receipt of a loan of $25,000 from Gertrude Stein, to be used as my share of the down payment for our house located at 10 Rue de There, Oakland, California. I agree to pay this sum back, plus interest, at the rate of 10% per year, by making monthly payments of $_____, all due in seven years. [*Or:* I agree to pay the entire loan and interest at 10% per year when and if the house is sold.][8]

I agree that if the loan and all interest due hasn't been repaid when the house is sold, the remaining balance owed will be paid to Gertrude before I receive any proceeds from that sale.

Dated: _____   Signature: _____
                                                    Alice B. Toklas

---

c. *One Person Buys the House and the Other Fixes It Up*

It's sometimes common for one person to contribute a greater portion, or even all, of the down payment, and the other to contribute labor and/or materials to fix a place up. When this occurs, we have a strong bias for a simple contract. If special circumstances require more complex details, have a lawyer look at your agreement.

Stephan, Bob and Lyn decide to purchase a graceful but dilapidated Victorian.

Stephan and Bob can put up the cash for the down payment and Lyn the expertise and time to fix it up. They can each afford to pay one-third of the monthly expenses. Like Gertrude and Alice, they want to own the place in equal shares and need guidance *only* on how to do it. Because Stephan and Bob are each going to contribute $17,000 to the down payment, they agree that Lyn should contribute $17,000 worth of materials and labor (at $10 an hour) to fix up the house.

AGREEMENT TO CONTRIBUTE CASH AND LABOR

We, Stephan, Bob and Lyn, agree as follows:

1. We will purchase the house at 225 Peaches Street, Atlanta, Georgia, for $200,000 and will own the house equally as tenants in common.

2. Stephan and Bob will each contribute $17,000 to be used as the down payment.

3. Lyn will contribute $11,000 for materials over the next seven months and 600 hours of labor (valued at $10 per hour) making a total contribution of $17,000, toward fixing up the house.

4. If we all agree that more labor or materials are needed to fix up the house, the materials will be paid equally by Lyn, Bob and Stephan, and Lyn (or Bob or Stephan if they work) will be credited $10 an hour unless all three work an equal number of hours.

5. All monthly expenses will be shared equally.

6. This contract may be amended in writing at any time by unanimous consent.

Dated: _____   Signature: _____
                                                     Stephan Valery

Dated: _____   Signature: _____
                                                     Bob Bisell

Dated: _____   Signature: _____
                                                     Lyn Rosenthal

---

It's easiest to determine ownership interests based on the contributions made (or promised) at the time the contact is drafted. It's possible, however, to provide for ownership shares that will fluctuate over time. Obviously, doing this can get complicated. If Stephan, Bob and Lyn want to vary their shares, with Stephan and Bob owning the place to start with and Lyn's share growing as he contributes labor and materials, they could append to their contract a sheet showing all contributions. Such a sheet might look like this when Lyn finished his work:

SHEET 1—CAPITAL CONTRIBUTIONS

Nature of Contribution	Date	Value	Contributed by: Stephan	Bob	Lyn
Cash	1/29	$34,000	$17,000	$17,000	
Paint, Roof Supplies	3/10	4,000			4,000
Wood	3/12	3,500			$3,500
Floor Supplies	3/12	3,500			3,500
Labor	3/13-6/15	6,000			6,000
Cash: Hot Tub	7/20	1,500	500	500	500
Totals		$52,500	$17,500	$17,500	$17,500

We cannot overemphasize that the best contracts are simple contracts. For example, round ownership interests off (e.g., 25% and 75%, not 26.328% and 73.672%). Why? Because trying to achieve absolute accuracy—even if such a thing were possible—is usually more trouble than it's worth. If one person puts up a little extra cash or labor, or forks out more money in an emergency, consider the extra contribution a loan to be paid back, either when the house is sold or by the other owner making a similar extra contribution, rather than redrafting the basic agreement. As long as any promissory notes are paid off before the house is sold, this approach is safe and simple.

d. Complicated Contribution Contracts

Our friends Rosemary and Glenna decided that a very detailed contract would be fairer than a rough, general division. Rosemary is a carpenter by trade, and she and Glenna agreed that her carpentry work should be valued at a higher hourly rate than the ordinary labor of either. Here's the contract they drew up. We believe it's more cumbersome than most people need, but for those of you with very tidy minds, we've seen it work very well in several instances.

DETAILED PROPERTY AGREEMENT

Glenna O'Brien and Rosemary Avila agree as follows:

1. That they will buy the house at 15 Snake Hill Road, Cold Springs Harbor, N.Y. The initial investment (down payment and closing costs) of $24,987.07, will be contributed by Rosemary. The title to the house will be recorded as Rosemary Avila and Glenna O'Brien as tenants in common.

2. They will each pay one-half of the monthly mortgage, tax and homeowner's insurance payments, and will each be responsible for one-half of any costs necessary for maintenance and repairs.

3. They will contribute labor and materials to improve the house. Rosemary's labor—doing carpentry—will be valued at $14 per hour and both Glenna and Rosemary's labor making other house repairs will be valued at $7 per hour; these rates may be raised in the future if both agree. Materials will be valued at their actual cost.

4. They will maintain a ledger marked "Exhibit I - 15 Snake Hill Road Home Owner's Record." This ledger is considered a part of this contract. They will record the following information in the Home Owner's Record:

a. The $24,987.07 initial contribution made to purchase the house by Rosemary.

b. Their monthly payments for the mortgage, property taxes and homeowner's insurance.

c. Rosemary's labor as a carpenter on home improvements valued as stated in clause 3.

d. Their labor on noncarpentry home improvements valued as stated in clause 3.

e. All money that they pay for supplies and materials necessary for home improvements.

f. Any other money that either spends for improvements as long as the expenditure has been approved in advance by the other.

5. Their ownership shares of the house are determined as follows:

a. The dollar value of all contributions made by either will be separately totaled, using the figures set out in the 15 Snake Hill Road Home Owner's Record.

b. They may add interest to their investment totals in the amount of 10% per year simple interest. Simple interest will be calculated twice a year (January 1 and July 1), with the interest being added to each person's total investment as of that date.

c. The total equity interest in the house will be computed by subtracting all mortgages and encumbrances outstanding from the fair market value as of the date of the computation. If they can't agree on the fair market value, each will have the house appraised by choosing a licensed realtor familiar with their neighborhood to do an appraisal. The average of the two appraisals will be the fair market value of the house.

d. A fraction will be created. The numerator will be the larger share (as computed in (5a) and (5b) above) and the denominator will be the total amount of both owner's shares. This fraction represents the total equity in the house of the person with the larger share. The person with the smaller share will compute her share by either subtracting the larger share from the number "1," or by also forming a fraction using the steps outlined above.

6. If either does not pay her share of the mortgage, taxes or insurance in a timely manner, the other person may make the payment, and that payment will be treated as a loan to be paid back as soon as possible, but not later than six months, plus interest at the rate of 10% per annum.

7. Either person can terminate this agreement at any time. If this occurs, and both women want to remain in the house and can afford to buy the other out in 90 days, a third party will flip a coin to determine who keeps the house. If only one person wants the house, she will pay the other her share within 90 days. If the person who wants to keep the house is unable to pay the other within 90 days, the house will be sold and the proceeds divided according to the shares established under clause (5d).

Dated: _____   Signature: _____
                                         Glenna O'Brien

Dated: _____   Signature: _____
                                         Rosemary Avila

3. When Not All Owners Live in the House

If only some owners live in the house (as often happens when a group invests), those living in the house usually pay a fair rental value to the "partnership,"—the group of owners. If this rent doesn't cover the monthly expenses, then each owner (including those living in the house) must pay his or her share of the difference. If the rent exceeds the monthly expenses, deposit the profits into a "partnership" bank account and divide it among the owners, in proportion to ownership shares, once a year. The fair rental value should be adjusted every year or two.

There are other considerations. Those living in the home want low rent and will resist sale of the house. It is their home, not just an investment. The outside investors might want high rent, low maintenance and sale for peak profit. Expectations can differ considerably concerning the quality of maintenance and improvement, or what happens when the occupants want to put in a hot tub costing $1,500, of no immediate benefit (but perhaps an expense) to the investors? The potential conflict should be addressed in advance in a contract.

Other issues to put in the contract include:

- The set period of time after the purchase in which the house will be sold or the non-occupant investors may withdraw their money and profit.
- The fair rental value to be paid by the occupants. Rental value often (but by no means always) equals the total of all ordinary monthly payments for mortgages, insurance and taxes, plus something extra for minor repairs. The rental value ought to be adjusted every year or two.
- An understanding that the occupants may improve the premises, but that purely decorative improvements are at their own expense. Necessary improvements and major repairs are usually charged to the entire "partnership."
- The right of the occupant-owners to buy out the nonoccupant-owners at a specific time for the net fair market value. Net fair market value means that expenses such as termite clearances, a broker's fee and loan prepayment penalties are subtracted from the appraised value.

Let's assume that Violet Clarke and Teresa Conroy are lovers who want to buy a little island of peace. Their friend Melanie Stuart has some money, is looking for an investment and wants to help. Their contract is simple and to the point. If Melanie's lover, Janet, wanted to help out too, this contract could easily be modified to provide for four owners.

CONTRACT WHEN ONE OWNER DOES NOT LIVE ON THE PREMISES

We, Violet Clarke, Teresa Conroy and Melanie Stuart agree as follows:

1. We agree to purchase the home known as 21 Island Retreat.

2. We will contribute the following money for the down payment:

Melanie	$10,000
Violet	$5,000
Teresa	$5,000

3. We will own the property in the following proportions: Melanie—50%, Violet—25% and Teresa—25%. If we sell the house, each person will be repaid her initial contribution; then the remaining profit or loss will be divided: Melanie—50%, Violet—25% and Teresa—25%.

4. Violet and Teresa will live on the property and will pay rent of $750 per month for the first two years. At the end of two years, we will decide what is a fair rent, taking into consideration that Violet and Teresa do all the work necessary to maintain and manage the property.

5. Mortgage payments, insurance and taxes total $695 per month. These expenses will be paid from Violet and Teresa's rent. Violet and Teresa will be responsible for all maintenance and repair.

6. We will sell the house within five years unless we unanimously agree in writing to keep it longer. If at any time after two years and before five years Violet and Teresa desire to purchase Melanie's share, they may do so at the fair market value of Melanie's interest.

7. Mediation—Arbitration clause. **(See Chapter 6, Section C.3.)**

8. Moving-on clause. **(See Section E.5, below.)**

9. If one of us isn't able to make a timely payment, then either one or both of the other women may make the payment, and the payment will be considered a loan at 10% interest to be paid back within six months.

10. If any one of us dies and doesn't leave her share to the other owners, the survivors have the right to purchase that share from her estate. The value of that share will be the initial down payment plus an increase of 3% per year (simple interest). The surviving owners may buy this share with no down payment and pay the estate over a ten-year period, including interest of 10% per year on the share.

11. This agreement is binding on our heirs, executors, administrators, successors and assigns.

Dated:_____   Signature: _____
                                            Violet Clarke

Dated:_____   Signature: _____
                                            Teresa Conroy

Dated:_____   Signature: _____
                                            Melanie Stuart

Another example of group ownership is provided by Sarah, Guy and Millet. They bought a duplex together with the understanding that Sarah and her children would live in one half and Guy would live in the other half. Millet joined the venture to invest some money and aid her friends. Here's their contract:

ANOTHER CONTRACT (WHEN NOT EVERYONE LIVES ON THE PREMISES)

We, Sarah Wren, Guy Wright and Millet Victor, on _____, 19__, agree to enter into a joint venture as follows:

1. <u>Purpose:</u> The purpose of the joint venture is to purchase the property known as 1 Lake Front, Jefferson, Iowa.

2. <u>Duration:</u> The joint venture will commence this day and will continue until dissolved by mutual agreement or sale of the property.

3. <u>Contributions:</u> The parties will make the following contributions, which will be known as their Capital Contribution:

Guy Wright	$20,000
Sarah Wren	$12,000
Millet Victor	$8,000

4. <u>Responsibility for Loans:</u> In addition to the Capital Contribution, the parties agree to be responsible for the loans and mortgages as follows:

a. Sarah will be responsible for 50% of all payments due to The Jean Mortgage Company.

b. Guy will be responsible for 50% of all mortgage payments due to The Jean Mortgage Company.

c. Millet will have no additional responsibility beyond her initial capital contribution.

5. <u>Mortgages:</u> If at any time Sarah or Guy cannot make her or his half of a mortgage payment in a timely manner, one or both of the other parties, at their option, may make the payment in order to keep the property from being foreclosed. The person(s) making the payment will be repaid within six months, with 10% annual interest.

6. <u>Rights and Duties of the Parties:</u> Guy has the right to live in the upper unit of the building or to rent it out at whatever rate he may choose. If he rents it out, he remains responsible for 50% of the Jean Mortgage Company payment, and, in either case, he's responsible for all repairs and maintenance of the upper unit.

Sarah has the right to live in the lower unit of the building or to rent it out in whole or part at whatever rate she may choose. If she rents it out, she remains responsible for 50% of the Jean Mortgage Company payment, and, in either case, she's responsible for all repairs and maintenance of the lower unit.

Millet isn't responsible for any payments beyond her initial Capital Contribution.

7. Repairs: Either Guy or Sarah may need to make extensive repairs to the building. The cost of major repairs (like the roof or boiler) will be divided evenly between them. If either wants to improve her or his unit, either may do so under the following rule:

• Any repairs or additions costing more than one thousand dollars ($1,000) will be considered a capital investment, credited to the party's Capital Account and paid back upon sale of the building.

• Repairs or additions above $1,000 must be approved by Sarah, Guy and Millet in writing if they want to be paid back.

8. Forced Payments: If Guy or Sarah can't make a payment in a timely manner, then the other may make that payment for them, and the payment will be considered a loan at the highest interest rate allowed by law, to be paid back in six months.

9. Shares: Sarah will own 30% of the property, Guy will own 50% and Millet will own 20%.

10. Profit and Loss: Upon the sale of the building, the respective capital investments, reflected by the Capital Account, will first be returned to the parties. The remaining profit or loss will be distributed as follows: Sarah 30%; Guy 50%; Millet 20%.

11. Regular books will be kept that are open to inspection by all parties upon reasonable notice.

12. Time: Sarah, Guy and Millet agree to hold the property for five years; no sale or encumbrance will be made without unanimous consent. At the end of five years, any one of the parties may request a sale of her or his share by giving four months written notice.

13. Election to Keep Building or Sell: If the venture is dissolved due to the death, withdrawal or other act of any party before the expiration of the five years, the remaining parties may continue to own the building. If the remaining owners so elect, they will have the right to purchase the interest of the other person in the building by paying to such person, or the legal representatives of such person, the value of such interest as follows:

Appointment of Appraisers. The parties desiring to continue ownership will appoint one appraiser; the withdrawing person or the legal representative of a deceased or incapacitated person will appoint a second appraiser. The appraisers will determine the value of the assets and liabilities of the venture, and the parties desiring to continue ownership will pay to the other, or the representative, his or her capital investment plus the share (as set out in clause 9 above) of the gain or loss of the venture. The withdrawing person or the legal representative will execute the documents necessary to convey such person's interest in the venture to the other parties.

Additional Appraiser in Event of Disagreement. In the event the appraisers cannot agree on the value of the venture within 15 days after their appointment, they will designate an additional appraiser whose appraisal will be binding on all parties. If any selected appraiser becomes unable or unwilling to serve, the person(s) originally selecting him or her shall appoint a substitute. In the event the two appraisers first appointed cannot agree on a third appraiser, such appraiser will be appointed by the director of the _____ (e.g., **local gay rights organization**).

Rights and Obligations of Continuing Parties. The parties continuing the venture will assume all of the existing obligations and will indemnify the withdrawing party against all liability.

14. Dissolution: In the event that all parties agree to dissolve the venture, the building will be sold, the debts paid and the surplus divided among the parties in accordance with their interests as set out in clause 9.

15. Amendments: This agreement may be amended at any time in writing by unanimous agreement.

Executed at _____ on _____
                          (City, State)   (Date)

_____
            Sarah Wren

_____
            Guy Wright

_____
            Millet Victor

When the buyers are partners. In the last two contracts, the owners agreed that the persons not living in the house shouldn't be responsible for maintenance and repairs. Often, the nonoccupant wants to limit her or his liability. A simple method for this is clause 4c, above, in Sarah, Guy and Millet's contract, where Millet isn't obligated to make any payments beyond her initial capital contribution.

Although this is binding between the three partners, if a new roof is added, and Sarah and Guy fail to pay the roofer, the roofer could sue Millet. To insure that Millet wouldn't have to pay the roofer, or face any other liability on the basis of another partner's acts, they could form a limited partnership.

A limited partnership is a special type of legal animal. Specific state laws and registration procedures must be followed to create a valid limited partnership. Each investor is called a "partner." The ones with limited liability are called "limited partners." The partners fully liable are called "general partners." A disadvantage is that a limited partnership is a legal entity of its own, and, requires a tax number and a tax accounting each year. Another disadvantage is that limited partners cannot claim some of the tax deductions general partners can claim. This may be reason enough not to form a limited partnership. But a limited partnership is an excellent idea if one investor (who cannot have a management role) wants to fully protect herself or himself. The limited partner is liable only for the money she has invested; she's not liable for anything beyond that. To learn more about limited partnerships, see *The Partnership Book*, by Ralph Warner and Denis Clifford (Nolo Press).

4. When You Move Into Your Lover's Owned Home

Nate fell in love with Alan and wanted to move in with him. Alan agreed, asking Nate to share the monthly house payments, property taxes, fire insurance and utilities. Nate agreed, "but only if I somehow get to own part of the house." Alan, in the rush of first love, murmured he'd be willing to give Nate half of everything.

Should You Just Add Your Lover's Name to the Deed?

Like Alan, some lesbians and gay men who own their own houses are tempted to put the deed into joint tenancy with their lovers when their lovers move in. This assures that the lover will get the house if the original owner dies.

But it's not wise. By putting the house in joint tenancy, you make a gift of one-half of it to your lover. Not only might you owe gift taxes, but if you later split up, you have no right to have the house deeded back to you. It makes more sense for you to keep the house in your name and make a will or living trust leaving the house to your lover. If you split up, you can change the will or trust.

The other option is for the lover to buy into the house by paying a share of the mortgage payments. See Nate and Alan's agreement.

Alan's house is worth $220,000; his existing mortgage is $120,000, and so his equity is $100,000. After careful thought, Alan told Nate that if he paid one-half of all the monthly payments, it would be fair to give him some of the equity in the house. But Alan still had two serious questions.

- "I already have a $100,000 equity in the house; how can Nate ever hope to accumulate anything more than a negligible share?"

- "I agree it's fair for Nate to have some equity in the house, but how can we work out the details?"

We offered four solutions.

1. The simplest was for Nate to forget buying part of the house and instead pay Alan monthly rent. With this alternative, Nate's rent should be considerably less than one-half the mortgage, tax and insurance because Nate would be getting no equity. A fair rent could be determined by ascertaining the rent for a portion of similar homes in the neighborhood.

2. Another easy solution would be for Nate to pay Alan $50,000. This is one-half of Alan's equity in the house and Alan could then deed the house to himself and Nate as either "joint tenants" or "tenants in common." Nate stood up and emptied his pockets. He had $68, some change and a Swiss army knife, which he said was a significant part of his net worth.

3. Next we offered a less simple suggestion. The two men could sign a contract where Nate agreed to pay one-half (or all, or any other fraction) of the monthly mortgage, tax and insurance in exchange for a share of the equity in the house equal to the percentage his total principal payments bear to the total amount of money invested in the house by both men. Sounds complicated? Well, it's really not that difficult to understand.[9]

After one year of payments of $7,000 each, Alan would own ($107,000/$114,000) x 100 or 94% and Nate, ($7,000/$114,000) x 100 or 6%.

4. Our final suggestion was that Alan sell Nate one-half of the house at present fair market value, and take a promissory note for the payment. The note would be paid in full if the house was sold or refinanced. This method is generous to Nate because he'd be get the advantage of ownership (tax advantages and market-caused value increases) with no money down. But the simplicity appealed to both, and that's what they did. Here's the agreement they prepared.

SELLING A SHARE OF YOUR HOUSE TO YOUR LOVER

We, Alan Zoloff and Nate Nichols, agree as follows:

1. Alan now owns the house at 1919 Church Street, Seattle, Washington, subject to a mortgage for $120,000.

2. The present value of the home is $220,000.

3. Alan hereby sells one-half of the home to Nate for $110,000 and retains a one-half interest in the house, also valued at $110,000.

4. The $110,000 will be paid by Nate as follows:

$60,000: Nate agrees to assume responsibility for one-half of the $120,000 mortgage and to pay one-half of the monthly mortgage payments.

$50,000: Nate will sign a note to Alan for $50,000 plus 10% (simple) interest per year to be paid in full when the house is sold.

5. All other costs for the home, including taxes, insurance, utilities, repairs and maintenance will be divided evenly.

6. When the house is sold, after all other costs are paid, Alan will first receive the payment on Nate's note plus the interest due, and the remaining profit (or loss) will be divided evenly between Nate and Alan.

(Other clauses, such as including separation provisions, arbitration clauses, and the like should be included.)

Dated:_____   Signature: _____
                                            Alan Zoloff

Dated:_____   Signature: _____
                                            Nate Nichols

Alan needs to understand the tax consequences of the sale. If he receives no money for the sale, there's no immediate taxable gain (and, nothing to tax) from the sale. If he receives money from the sale, he must determine what percentage was a return on his capital investment or capital improvement (not taxed), and what percentage was interest on the note or profit on the sale (taxed). The IRS keeps changing the rules on "installment sales." Alan needs to spend an hour with his accountant.

5. Moving On

Relationships can end. Planning for this in advance is always wise. If you don't, and a person wants to move and sell her share, the household could be forced to sell and move out. Problems can also develop for the person wanting to move. If she's required by the agreement to continue to pay some expenses after moving out because she can't find a buyer, she may become a prisoner in the house and quite bitter.

a.   Clause to Add to Your Contract

Here's a clause to cover the contingency of one person moving on. Include it in the original contract, as an amendment to the original contract, or as its own "moving on" contract.

SAMPLE MOVING ON CLAUSE

If one owner moves out of the house, he remains responsible for his share of the mortgage, taxes and insurance. He may rent his quarters with the approval (which won't be unreasonably withheld) of the rest of the household. The remaining owners have the first right to rent the quarters themselves or assume the cost if they so choose at a fair market value. The remainder of the house owners must rent the quarters themselves or assume the cost if they reject at least three people the owner moving out proposes as renters.

At the end of two years following the owner's moving out, that owner will have the right to sell his share to the remaining owners or to a new person completely, subject to the approval (which won't be unreasonably withheld) of the remaining owners.

---

b.   When You Didn't Make a Contract

We hope you don't have to read this because you've already signed a home ownership contract carefully defining each person's rights and responsibilities if you separate. If you're in the process of separating and made no agreement in advance, be aware that you can make a contract now. It's harder than when you're on good terms, but it can be done. Here are your alternatives:

- Keep the property and run it as a joint venture (if one of you continues to live in it, that person should pay fair rental value of the home to the joint owners).

- Have one person buy the other out.

- Sell the property and divide the proceeds.

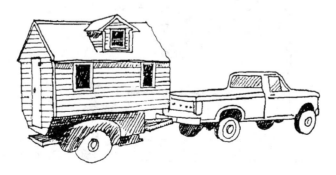

AGREEMENT TO SELL

This is an agreement between Art Phillips and Lee Aaronson to sell their house at 1618 Bestview Lane, Fort Lauderdale, Fla.

1. Art and Lee bought the house with each putting up one-half the money. As each has made one-half of the payments, they currently own the house 50-50.

2. They agree to sell the home and divide the profits (or losses) equally.

3. Art is moving out as of July 31, 19__. Lee will stay in the home, keep it presentable for showing to prospective buyers and pay Art a monthly rent of $600. All monthly expenses for repairs, mortgage, taxes and insurance will be paid equally until the house is sold. Lee will pay utilities and simple maintenance. He will keep track of all reasonable expenses incurred to prepare the house for sale, including his labor, valued at $12 an hour. He will be reimbursed from the proceeds of the sale.

Dated: _____   Signature: _____
                                           Art Phillips

Dated: _____   Signature: _____
                                           Lee Aaronson

Erna and Ann owned a house and decided to go separate ways. Erna paid 60% of the down payment, Ann 40%, and they agreed they owned the home according to those percentages. The difficulty was that Erna had a seven-year-old son and wanted to keep the home. But she didn't have the cash to buy out Ann. Their solution was to agree on an appraiser—who valued the home at $186,500. The couple then calculated the value of each person's share if the house was sold (the net fair market value) as follows:

DETERMINING NET EQUITY

Agreed upon fair market value:	$186,500
Balance of mortgages:	
First mortgage:	104,500
Second mortgage:	30,000
Expenses of sale:	
Prepayment penalty on first mortgage:	5,360
Realtor's commission of 6%	11,190
Other expenses necessary to get full price:	
Termite work necessary	2,000
New paint for kitchen	400
Total Mortgages and Expenses	153,450
Net Equity	33,050
Erna's interest: 60%	= $19,830
Ann's interest: 40%	= $13,220

Erna didn't have $13,220 to pay Ann. Their options are:

- Erna could try to get a loan to buy out Ann. This could be done by: refinancing the home and taking out a larger mortgage, say $150,000. She could pay off the existing mortgages of $104,500 and $30,000, leaving $15,500. If interest rates remain low, refinancing is wise, although it might cost her some money in points and other fees.

- Erna could write Ann a promissory note for her share, payable monthly, over enough years that Erna could afford the payments. This would work only if Ann had no pressing need for cash.

- Ann could move out, let Erna stay and pay rent or Ann's share, and have Erna either pay Ann her total share—or sell the house—in two years. This would let Ann remain an owner, receiving tax and investment advantages, while Erna got two years to either come up with the money or move. If the house went up in value in the meantime, it would be easier for Ann to refinance. Here's their agreement:

AGREEMENT FOR ONE OWNER TO RENT THE HOUSE FOR A PERIOD AND THEN SELL

1. This agreement is made between Erna Plank and Ann Cruz.

2. We own 637 Happy Hollow Road, Falmouth, Massachusetts, with Erna owning 60% and Ann owning 40%.

3. The monthly payments are:

Mortgage	$1,006
Taxes:	$50
Insurance:	$30
	$1,086 per month

4. Erna will rent the house for $1100 per month for two years (which we have determined is a fair market rent, giving Erna consideration for managing the property). Erna will be responsible for all maintenance and repairs. If a major repair (over $300) is required, we both must authorize the repair and will share costs in proportion to how much we own (Erna, 60%; Ann, 40%).

5. At the end of two years, we will sell the house and divide the profits (or losses); Erna will get 60% and Ann 40%. Erna has the right to purchase the house at any time during the two years for the fair market value by paying Ann her total net equity. **(Add the clause on determining value, found in the "Agreement for Equal Ownership," in Section E.1, above.)**

Dated:_____   Signature: _____
                                            Erna Plank

Dated:_____   Signature: _____
                                            Ann Cruz

If You Plan to Buy Out Your Lover

Before agreeing to buy out your lover, take a look at your contract with your lender. If it contains a "due-on-sale" clause, the lender *may* have the right to insist on immediate payment of the entire balance of the loan. But don't panic—this happens in very few situations.

If you see a due-on-sale clause, call your lender. Ask if the loan has been sold on the secondary mortgage market to either the Federal Home Loan Mortgage Corporation (FHLMC or Freddie Mac) or the Federal National Mortgage Association (FNMA or Fannie Mae). Lenders commonly sell loans to Freddie Mac or Fannie Mae to earn money to make more loans.

If your loan has been sold, rest easy. Freddie Mac and Fannie Mae guidelines prohibit the exercising of a due-on-sale clause when the sale is between co-borrowers as long as you took out the loan at least 12 months earlier and you intend to reside in the house.

Endnotes

[1] The United States Supreme Court upheld the constitutionality of a law prohibiting more than two unrelated adults from living together, against the charge that the law discriminated against unrelated people. *Village of Belle Terre v. Boraas,* 416 U.S. 1 (1974).

[2] Certain neighborhoods in Denver, Colorado, and White Plains, N.Y., restrict each household to people related by "blood, marriage or adoption." Unmarried heterosexuals have been forced to move out—or marry—a choice lesbian and gay couples don't have. Several states, however, including New Jersey and California, prohibit local communities from discriminating against unrelated people in housing.

[3] In California, see *How to Buy a House in California,* by Ralph Warner, Ira Serkes, & George Devine (Nolo Press) and *For Sale by Owner,* by George Devine (Nolo Press).

[4] Carrying costs are the money needed to make a monthly payment (both principal and interest) plus one-twelfth of the yearly bill for property taxes and homeowner's insurance. In real estate industry jargon, monthly carrying costs are often referred to as PITI (pronounced "pity"), which simply stands for principal, interest, taxes and insurance.

[5] *How to Buy a House in California,* by Ralph Warner, Ira Serkes and George Devine (Nolo Press) has been called "the most complete book for ... homebuyers." Although it's written for Californians, virtually all chapters, and especially the financing information (five chapters), apply everywhere.

[6] The deed often states the name of the buyer and adds "a single man/woman." Our friend Alice put down "a singular woman" but it never made it past the escrow officer.

[7] You might have the decision made by a mediator or arbitrator rather than the caprice of a coin. If so, see Chapter 3 on mediation and arbitration, to include a clause detailing the process. ∎

CHAPTER 8

Heterosexual Marriages —The Aftermath

Many lesbians and gay men have been married and become parents. These marriages often end dramatically—sometimes with bitterness, sometimes with real understanding. We have no statistics on the number of lesbians and gay men who have married and divorced, but the number is certainly large. The great variety of experiences makes it hard to generalize about lesbians, gay men and marriage.

The development of a lesbian or gay identity and the emotional consequence that "coming out" can have for spouses and children have been rich subjects for contemporary novelists. But, as is often the case, writers are hardly two exclamation points and a question mark ahead of lawyers, and many lesbians and gay men have watched their dreams of a new and free life unravel in courtrooms. Even people who have not been dragged into the legal arena realistically fear the possibility. We're regularly asked questions like these:

- Can my ex-husband get custody of the children if he learns I am a lesbian?

- My ex-wife says I can't have my lover with me when I take our boy for a weekend. Does she have that power?

- Is it okay to live with my new lover while I am getting divorced?

- My husband knows I am a lesbian. What should I tell my lawyer—and the judge?

- Will my being gay make a difference when it comes to dividing property or deciding on alimony?

- Can I just take the kids and move from this crazy place?

The purpose of this chapter is to discuss what happens legally when a marriage breaks up and one spouse is lesbian or gay. The rules governing divorce, child support, alimony, custody and property division are the same for gays and lesbians as for straights, but it is essential to examine them from a lesbian and gay perspective. Our goal is to help you to understand the legal risks and consequences of your actions so you can effectively enforce your rights.

A. Divorce—A Good Divorce Is As Precious As a Good Marriage

Egos are commonly bruised when a couple splits up, but when the split occurs because one partner has a new sexual identity, bruises can quickly turn into fractures. We don't have any magic formula to dispense with the pain and anger, but we do know three ingredients that are bound to help.

1. Be as sensitive as possible to the feelings and needs of your (ex) mate.

2. Avoid going to court if at all possible.

3. Even if you're sure that avoiding court is hopeless, try again, and keep trying.

Even if you're not in a mood to be sensitive, do your utmost to stay out of court. A court battle is almost certain to be emotionally draining, costly and unpredictable, even if you're lucky enough to appear before a non-homophobic judge—which, it doesn't take a genius to know, is no sure thing.

Arguing over the kids (who gets custody and who pays child support), the property and the debts is almost always part of ending a marriage. It is not, however, sufficient reason to hire an attorney and run off to court. Most people simply need to argue as they separate. Even if you have nothing major to argue about, you may still argue about who gets the waterbed or the antique lamp. When a lesbian or gay partner ends a marriage, there's obviously ready focus for the other spouse's pain.

If you have real disputes about money and property, fighting about them in court only decreases what's left to divide. A sign in one divorce courtroom reads "litigants should be aware that this court cannot resolve insoluble financial problems." Seeing a therapist, involving yourself with a gay, lesbian or bisexual support group, engaging in mediation or arbitration, or even moving ten miles away can be more effective ways of handling serious disputes than battling them out in court.

Compromise does not require capitulation. Leaving a marriage and giving up everything—especially custody of or visitation with your children—is rash and unwise, regardless of the reason. The joy of moving on, the fear of public disclosure of your sexual orientation or the desire to be rid of the past is no reason to stop parenting your children or give up your share of the property you accumulated while married. You don't want to spend months or years trying to obtain custody, support or property that you impulsively abandoned. Fortunately, getting out of a heterosexual relationship shouldn't require that much drama.

1. Getting a Divorce

The fact that you are lesbian or gay may not be significant in obtaining a divorce. In every state, a divorce based on either separation of the parties or "no fault" is available. In a no-fault divorce, a spouse simply alleges "an irretrievable breakdown of the marriage," "incompatibility" or "irreconcilable differences." A separation-based divorce requires that the spouses live apart for six months to a few years before divorcing.

States have adopted separation-based and no-fault divorces in recognition of the fact that a court is not suited to determine what truly (morally) happened in a marriage, and that it is both wasteful and degrading for spouses to allege and prove petty wrongs, unfulfilled expectations or betrayals. This isn't to deny that moral wrongs may have been committed—only that the courts have sensibly left them to be worked out by other forces. All that is legally important is that the marriage no longer works and at least one partner wants out. In a no-fault or separation-based divorce, no matter how much the other insists on staying married, he can't force it.

Although every state has either separation-based or no-fault divorce, 33 states still have divorces based on traditional fault grounds as well, such as adultery, mental cruelty or abandonment. For this reason, we can only state that your sexual orientation "may not" be significant in obtaining a divorce. If your spouse is in one of those states and so inclined, he or she could request a fault divorce—most likely asserting that you've treated him or her with mental cruelty or have committed adultery with a new lover.

Practically, this means that in some states, you could be awarded less than your share of the marital property or be awarded less (or ordered to pay more) alimony because you're gay or lesbian and have ended your marriage. But there is no general rule. Florida and Hawaii, for example, have done away with fault divorces, but still consider fault when dividing property and awarding alimony. Alaska and New Jersey, on the other hand, still have fault divorces but don't allow fault to influence property division or alimony. Yes, it's all illogical, but in law, illogic is routine.

One final note: No matter what type of divorce is obtained, "fault" (homosexuality or any other) may be raised in a child custody or visitation dispute.

Grounds for Divorce[1]

The grounds for divorce are the legal reasons a spouse (or the couple) must give to request a divorce. This chart sets them out state by state:

State	Fault Grounds	No-Fault Grounds	Separation	Length of Separation
Alabama	•	•	•	2 years
Alaska	•	•		
Arizona		•		
Arkansas	•		•	3 years
California		•		
Colorado		•		
Connecticut[2]	•	•	•	18 months
Delaware	•	•		
District of Columbia			•	6 months
Florida		•		
Georgia	•	•		
Hawaii		•	•	2 years
Idaho	•	•	•	5 years
Illinois[3]	•	•	•	2 years
Indiana	•	•		
Iowa		•		
Kansas	•	•		
Kentucky		•		
Louisiana	•		•	6 months
Maine	•	•		
Maryland	•		•	1-2 years
Massachusetts	•	•		
Michigan		•		
Minnesota		•	•	180 days

State	Fault Grounds	No-Fault Grounds	Separation	Length of Separation
Mississippi	•	•		
Missouri	•	•		
Montana		•	•	180 days
Nebraska		•		
Nevada		•	•	1 year
New Hampshire	•	•		
New Jersey	•		•	18 months
New Mexico	•	•		
New York	•		•	1 year
North Carolina	•		•	1 year
North Dakota	•	•		
Ohio	•		•	1 year
Oklahoma	•	•		
Oregon		•		
Pennsylvania	•	•	•	2 years
Rhode Island	•	•	•	3 years
South Carolina	•		•	1 year
South Dakota	•	•		
Tennessee[4]	•	•	•	3 years
Texas	•	•	•	3 years
Utah	•	•	•	3 years
Vermont	•		•	6 months
Virginia[5]	•		•	1 year
Washington		•		
West Virginia	•	•	•	1 year
Wisconsin		•		
Wyoming	•	•		

Fault Considerations in Distributing Marital Property [6]

Marital Fault Irrelevant to Property Division	Marital Fault May Reduce Share of Property
Alaska	Alabama
Arizona	Arkansas
California	Connecticut
Colorado	Florida
Delaware	Georgia
District of Columbia	Hawaii
Idaho	Maryland
Illinois	Massachusetts
Indiana	Michigan
Iowa	Mississippi
Kansas	Missouri
Louisiana	New Hampshire
Maine	North Dakota
Minnesota	Rhode Island
Montana	South Carolina
Nebraska	Texas
Nevada	Utah
New Jersey	Vermont
New Mexico	Virginia
New York	Wyoming
North Carolina	
Ohio	
Oklahoma	
Oregon	
Pennsylvania	
South Dakota	
Tennessee	
Washington	
West Virginia	
Wisconsin	

States in Which Fault May Bar or Limit Alimony

Alabama	Michigan	Pennsylvania
Arkansas	Mississippi	Rhode Island
Connecticut	Missouri	South Carolina
Florida	Nevada	South Dakota
Georgia	New Hampshire	Tennessee
Hawaii	New Mexico	Utah
Idaho	New York	Virginia
Louisiana	North Carolina	West Virginia
Maryland	North Dakota	Wyoming

2. Dividing Your Property and Debts

If your marriage has lasted long enough for the silver wedding presents to tarnish, you and your spouse have probably accumulated both property and debts. Property includes houses, furniture, cars, motorcycles, savings accounts, patents, invention royalties, stocks, bonds, income tax refunds, money owed to you by other persons, interests in retirement funds or pensions, some disability benefits, vacation pay, a business and everything else you can think of.

How a court would divide the property accumulated and allocate the debts incurred during your marriage depends on where you live. Arizona, California, Idaho, Louisiana, Nevada, New Mexico, Texas, Washington and Wisconsin follow community property rules. All other states except Mississippi follow equitable distribution principles. Under both systems, property acquired during marriage (except gifts and inheritances) is basically divided equally. Mississippi uses a "division by title" approach—that is, whoever's name is on an item, or whoever earned the money used to buy it, gets it.

Regardless of your state's laws, you and your spouse may divide your property however you want. For help in dividing your property fairly and without incurring substantial professional fees—lawyers, accountants, appraisers and the like—we highly recommend *Divorce and Money: How to Make the Best Financial Decisions During Divorce*, by Violet Woodhouse and Victoria F. Collins, with M.C. Blakeman (Nolo Press).

3. Paying or Receiving Alimony

Alimony is the money paid by one ex-spouse to the other for support following a divorce. Some states now call alimony "spousal support" or "maintenance." Fewer and fewer divorced spouses pay or receive alimony. This is largely because both men and women routinely work. Indeed, when younger couples break up, and both work outside the home, alimony is rarely granted or requested.

This doesn't mean that alimony is dead. Fading away slowly perhaps, but far from dead. For many couples where one spouse earned the money while the other raised the children, alimony is still necessary—at least until the children enter school full-time or the non-wage earner develops skills necessary to enter (or re-enter) the work force.

Just as some states allow fault to influence property division, several consider fault when awarding alimony. In addition, if you receive alimony, the law requires that it terminate if you remarry. But what if you move in with a lover? Can you lose it? Maybe. In a Minnesota case, an ex-wife's alimony was terminated when her ex-husband proved she had "entered into an apparently stable relationship with a woman." The state had no specific law on the subject.

The states with rules (Alabama, California, Georgia, Illinois, Louisiana, New York, Oklahoma, Pennsylvania, Tennessee and Utah) all apply to heterosexual cohabitation. In New York, for instance, cohabitation is ground for cutting off alimony only if the woman receiving the alimony holds herself out as the wife of the man she lives with. In California, the law states:

> Except as otherwise agreed to by the parties in writing, there shall be a reputable presumption ... of decreased need for support if the supported party is cohabiting with a **person of the opposite sex** [emphasis added]. Upon such a finding of changed circumstances, the court may modify the payment of support.

One California court did apply the "spirit" of this law to a case in which a woman receiving alimony moved in with her lesbian (wage-earning) lover. In another case, a woman was awarded alimony "until death or remarriage." When her ex-husband learned that she was a lesbian, he asked the court to set a date when the alimony would end. The court did so, finding a fixed time appropriate because there was no chance the wife would remarry.[7]

But the Georgia Supreme Court has ruled the opposite. In the case, the ex-husband petitioned the court for a modification of alimony based on the fact that his ex-wife was living with another woman. In rejecting his request, one justice wrote:

> It is unfair to expand the law [allowing a court to modify alimony when the recipient lives with a person of the opposite sex] by judicially imposing on homosexual couples a penalty placed on cohabitating heterosexual couples—who have the choice of marrying—without also according homosexual couples the benefits of marriage.[8]

4. Cooperating in Your Divorce

It's possible to cooperate with each other in obtaining divorce, even if your state still has fault divorces. Many people make decisions about children, support and property in a spirit of common sense and compromise rather than "who is more right." (As the saying goes, "Being right is the consolation prize of life.")

If your state considers "fault" in dividing property, and you've accumulated a lot of property and are having difficulty dividing it, reconcile yourself to a long court struggle and start saving money for lawyer's fees. And realize that if you're the higher—or only—wage earner during the marriage, you may be ordered to pay your spouse's lawyer's fees too. If, on the other hand, you've agreed on a plan for dividing your property, congratulate yourselves. Then put your agreement in writing. You will want to use *Divorce and Money* to finalize matters. Below is a sample temporary agreement to begin with.

COOPERATIVE SEPARATION AGREEMENT

Herb and Carol Fitzroy agree as follows:

1. They have decided to separate and no longer plan to live together.

2. Their children, John age 7 and Phillip age 4, will live with Carol; Herb will visit and babysit as much as his job allows—at least two nights and one weekend day per week.

3. Herb will pay child support to Carol. Initially, it will be $400 per month; it will increase yearly by the same percentage that Herb's net salary increases.

4. Neither Herb nor Carol plan to marry again immediately, and they clearly understand and accept that both will have friendships that may involve sexual relationships with people of the same or opposite sex.

5. Herb and Carol will cooperate in getting an amicable divorce, and neither will attempt to influence the court's decision by raising the point that the other is having a sexual relationship, or living, with a person of the same or opposite sex.

Dated: _____   Signature: _____
                                           Carol Fitzroy

Dated: _____   Signature: _____
                                           Herb Fitzroy

This sort of agreement is not enforceable in court, especially as it relates to custody and child support. As we explain below, in making a custody decision, a court must look at all factors and decide what's in the "best interests of the child." Also, child support is set by a state-specific formula, based on parental incomes. Still, an amicable agreement is a valuable reminder that you both want to avoid a court battle. And, if you find yourself in court with your spouse complaining that you are gay or lesbian, a judge might give the agreement considerable weight. She's likely to ask, "If you didn't object to her (or his) sexual orientation the day you signed the agreement, why are you objecting to it now?"

B. Child Custody

Child custody is the issue that presents the biggest problem or potential problem for a lesbian or gay person going through a divorce. If you and your spouse agree on custody, the court will almost certainly accept your arrangement with no questions asked. On the other hand, if you can't agree, and you leave the question to the judge, he must consider all factors and arrive at a decision in the "best interests of the child." This means that anything relating to your life, sexual identity and behavior can be raised in court.

Custody is generally of two types—physical and legal. Physical custody is the right to have the child live with you; legal custody is your right to make the important decisions—such as where to make the home, what school to attend, what doctor to use and what medical treatment to seek. Visitation (discussed later in this chapter) is the right of the parent without physical custody to spend time with the child. Physical and legal custody may be sole or shared (joint).

Joint physical custody works well when the parents get along amicably and are equally dedicated to raising their children. Joint doesn't necessarily mean 50-50; you can divide the time in any percentage that works for you. If you're a mother who doesn't want to share custody with your children's father, bear in mind that studies show that fathers are especially more likely to support and maintain close relationships with their children when they see their children with frequency. A common criticism of joint custody, however, is that arguments between the parents can drag on.

Joint custody isn't for everyone. If you want help in exploring it and other possible custody arrangements, let us suggest mediation. In a number of states, including California, Maryland and Oregon, mediation is mandatory any time the parents can't agree on custody. Even if it's not mandatory in your state, it's an excellent idea. Mediators work with parents to help them come to a mutually agreeable solution. Mediators, unlike judges, don't impose decisions on parents. To locate a mediator, contact your local family or domestic relations court or look in the Yellow Pages under "Mediators."

We don't need to tell you that a lesbian or gay parent faces a difficult struggle trying to gain physical custody in most American courtrooms, especially if that parent lives with a lover. (Many courts won't object to granting joint legal custody so that both parents have a say in how their children are raised.) Indeed, many gay parents have remained in unfulfilling heterosexual marriages, or lived secretive, guarded gay lifestyles after separation, out of fear of losing their children.

But we see progress. A number of courts have held that a parent's sexual orientation cannot, in and of itself, be grounds for automatic denial of custody. For example, in a 1992 Pennsylvania case, a trial court barred a lesbian mother from being with her lover of six years (with whom she lived) while her child was in her custody. Although the trial court found no evidence of detriment to the child, the court limited her custody because of supposed embarrassment, confusion and anger of the child. The appeals court reversed, stating:

The merits of a custody arrangement ought not to depend upon other people's reactions. Would a court restrict a handicapped parent's custody because other people made remarks about the handicapped parent that embarrassed, confused and angered the child? We think not.[9]

But it is fair to say that many judges are ignorant about, prejudiced against, or suspicious of, gay and lesbian parents. Take, for example, a 1993 case. A Georgia court initially granted custody to a gay father, saying that his homosexuality did not disqualify him from having custody. He moved to Alabama, where the mother filed a motion to modify the custody order. The Alabama court granted her request, holding that the father's concealment of his HIV-positive status reflected adversely on his credibility and cast suspicions on the truth of his testimony concerning "his views towards promiscuity, the gay lifestyle and his fears of danger attending each."[10]

Presently, this area of the law is in a tremendous state of flux, with courts falling on both sides of the issue. A clear trend has yet to emerge; recent cases simply emphasize the battle: Since the middle of 1994, we've seen reported cases supporting lesbian and gay parents seeking custody in Alabama, Utah, South Dakota and Tennessee. In particular, the South Dakota Supreme Court refused to hold that awarding custody to a lesbian mother living with her partner would *per se* not be in the best interests of her child—the court found the couple to be "loving and caring parents." Unfortunately, just as many courts are inclined in the opposite direction—lesbian mothers lost custody of their children in Arkansas, Florida, Illinois, Iowa and Wyoming. As

we go to print, the Wyoming case is pending before the state Supreme Court.

So let us reemphasize our earlier point: Only if you and your spouse cannot reach a compromise either working on your own or with a mediator should you bring a contested custody decision to court.

Of course, a case can be brought to court against both parents' wishes. Consider the case of Sharon Bottoms, the lesbian mother from Virginia who lives with her lover. Sharon's own mother sued her for custody of Sharon's son Tyler. Sharon fought it—even her ex-husband testified on her behalf. Nevertheless, in the fall of 1993, the court granted custody of Tyler to his grandmother, holding that a lesbian is presumed to be unfit to have custody of her child if she lives with her lover. National lesbian and gay organizations helped prepare Sharon's appeal, and in June of 1994, she regained custody of her son. Sadly, her victory was short-lived. In April of 1995, the Virginia Supreme Court ruled that "active lesbianism practiced in the home" could stigmatize the child, and returned Sharon's son to the custody of her mother.

 When you first separate, stay with your children if at all possible. If you leave to "get your head together," you risk creating a situation where it's easy for a judge to give custody to the parent who's taking care of the kids. Courts don't like to disrupt the status quo, and often put a high value on keeping kids with whomever they've been living. If you have to get away for a period of time, try to first reach an understanding with your spouse that when you return, the two of you will share custody—and put your agreement in writing.

1. Contested Custody Cases

If you think there's a serious possibility you and your spouse will fight in court over custody, it is imperative that you get a sympathetic at least, knowledgeable if possible, lawyer. Don't be shy about bringing your attorney the list of resources we provide, in Section 5, below. Regarding yourself, the cautious legal advice is not to live with your lover, and to be very discrete, at least until the court has made a decision. Many judges have an easier time giving a lesbian or gay parent custody if she or he lives alone.

And remember, the standard a judge uses is "the best interest of the child." Contested custody cases are full of uncertainties, not just related to sexual orientation. All issues related to what is in a child's best interest can come up. Your spouse may try to raise all kinds of things—your conviction for possession of hashish in the 60s, your religious differences, your sloppy house-keeping and practically anything else he or she can think of.

The judge will view each allegation with his own standards and prejudices. Some judges will frown on drug convictions no matter how old; others won't. Some judges will be concerned if a parent has unusual religious or political leanings. Many are biased against lesbians and gay men. Others are themselves lesbian or gay. Don't over-generalize or jump to conclusions. Each judge is different and each case unique.

During the hearing, the judge may want to talk with the children. Each judge handles this differently. Many talk to children they believe are old enough to have a sensible opinion; others never consult

with kids. Most judges give little weight to the views of children under seven, and give considerable respect to the desires of teenagers. For children between seven and eleven, it usually depends on their maturity. In any event, most judges try to keep brothers and sisters under the same roof unless there's a strong reason not to.

Remember that custody disputes are never truly settled until the child reaches 18. As long as the child is a minor, the court retains power over child custody. Custody decisions can be reopened and changed, if a parent shows "change of circumstances" and that the status quo is not in the child's "best interest." If you hide your sexual orientation during your divorce and your ex-spouse later figures it out, he or she may run back to court claiming a change in circumstance and requesting a change in custody.

2. Gay or Lesbian Parent's Role During the Case

The first step is to get yourself a good support system. Find people or groups concerned with gay or lesbian custody issues. A local lesbian mothers' or gay fathers' group is ideal. You will need a great deal of support if you are going to engage in a court struggle, and no one can give it to you better than folks who have been there. The National Gay and Lesbian Task Force in Washington, D.C., can help you find a local support group. The address and phone number is in Chapter 10, Section E.

Your next step is to get a sympathetic and knowledgeable lawyer—and you do need one. As you have gathered, we favor people doing their own legal work whenever possible, and are convinced that our laws and procedures must be changed to make it easier for people to represent themselves. But a custody battle is not the place to do it. You face an uphill struggle even with a lawyer, and you need someone who knows the local judges and custody laws. It's sad but true— some judges evaluate litigants by the quality of their attorneys.

How do you choose an attorney? If you find a support group, ask around for names of attorneys other gay parents have used. If that doesn't work, we've provided a list of lesbian and gay legal organizations in Chapter 10. Call one for referrals. Get the names of more than one lawyer; call and speak to them before making an appointment. You've got to feel comfortable with the one you hire. If you can't afford an attorney, don't give up. A lawyer might take the case "pro bono"—that is, for free. Also, several lesbian organizations have helped raise funds to pay lawyers representing lesbian mothers and gay fathers in custody battles.

Once you pick a lawyer, work with that person in figuring out exactly what you want, and then to decide what you're willing to settle for. Your strategy is to pursue your wants, and be willing to compromise to obtain what you'll settle for. In court, you'll have to be prepared to persuade a judge why your "wants" are in your children's best interests.

Don't worry about legal technicalities or rules of evidence. That's your lawyer's job. In most custody cases, judges cut through legal b.s. to learn the facts and decide what's in the child's best interest. Most judges flatter themselves that they try to be objective. While convincing a judge that your sexual orientation is irrelevant will be an uphill battle, it's

possible. The most important point you want to make is that you having custody is in your child's best interest. Never, never, never let the judge think you are just trying to punish your spouse.

As your lawyer begins to do work, so must you. Don't give up day-to-day preparation and decision making. Also, by gathering the facts and doing other legwork, you'll be connected to the case and will save some lawyer's fees. Don't pay your lawyer $150 an hour to do background preparation you can do. What follows is a list of some things you can do to help prepare your case. Discuss these with your lawyer before doing any of them.

- Find stable, respectable people (religious officials are always good) who know your situation and will tell the judge why you should have custody.

- Have stable, respectable people send letters to your lawyer stating that you're a good parent. (Your lawyer can try to get these into court.)

- Prepare a list for your attorney of friends, relatives, children's teachers or day care workers, neighbors, clergy and anyone else willing to speak on your behalf. Outline what each is prepared to say and who is likely to impress the judge.

Here is a sample letter. It's included to give you an idea of what is needed, not to copy. The letters you get should be personal, focused on your situation and succinct. Thomas Jefferson once began a long letter by writing "If I had the time, I'd have written you a short letter." Judges have quite a bit of paperwork, and may not give much attention to anything more than a page or two.

SAMPLE LETTER

May 10, 19__

To Whom It May Concern:

I have been a neighbor of Sandra Welch for six years. I know her family intimately, including her children, Joy and Teresa.

Sandra is a warm, sensitive and dependable person and parent. She is wonderfully patient and loving with her children. Her husband, Frank, never seemed very interested in his children and did not spend much time with them.

Sandra has discussed with me the fact that she and Georgia Conrad are lovers. I have visited their home; it is my observation that they are a very stable and caring couple who provide a warm, loving, clean and nurturing home and environment for the children. The children seem comfortable with both women and in a way act as if they have two mothers. Knowing the family background as I do, I am convinced that they are happier with Sandra than they would be living with Frank.

I am a mother and I happen to be heterosexual. Like many others, I had a bit of difficulty accepting that my friend Sandra is a lesbian. It took some getting used to, but I know that it in no way negatively affects her being a good parent. My two children, one boy and one girl, are about the same age as Sandra's. All the kids are in and out of both of our houses all the time and they are very fond of Sandra and Georgia. I have no hesitation about my children being with Sandra and Georgia, and I often leave my children with Sandra when I go out.

After thinking carefully about all the issues involved, I can see no way in which Sandra's sexual identity has adversely affected her children. And I don't see any problem in the future. It's just not related to her being the children's mother.

I would be willing to testify to my observations and beliefs in court if this would be helpful.

Sincerely,

Joyce Johnson

---

3. Making Your Case a "Political" Statement

Some organizations have urged any lesbian or gay man involved in a custody fight to "politicize" it—that is, take a militant gay rights stand, focus media attention on their struggle and use it to advance lesbian and gay causes. This is a decision only you can make. But you're more likely to succeed by down-playing the political concerns of gay custody than by using them as a rallying cry. Winning custody seems enough of a political statement to us. Maybe we're being overly lawyerly, but in most courts, most of the time, you'll do better if your sexual orientation is not made into a political issue.

There are many arenas for fighting for lesbian and gay rights; a child custody case is usually legally difficult and emotionally traumatic enough without adding the risks that politicization brings. If you know your spouse will raise the issue of your sexual orientation, strategically it is wise for you to bring it up first to eliminate any shock value and to present yourself as open and honest. But that's not the same as holding a press conference.

4. Looking for a Non-Homophobic Judge

Parents caught in custody battles often think of moving to a part of the country where judges are likely to have more liberal views. San Francisco can seem like paradise for someone who lives in Oklahoma. Although legally you can take a child to a new state unless a court order prohibits you, a law called the Uniform Child Custody Jurisdiction Act (UCCJA) limits a judge's power to make a custody decision. If you move to San Francisco from Oklahoma and eventually request custody, the San Francisco judge doesn't have the authority (called "jurisdiction") to hear your request, and will send you back to Oklahoma. One purpose of the law is to stop parents from moving about in a search for a court that will grant them custody. The mere presence of a child in a state does not necessarily mean that the state has the power to make a custody ruling. Rather, the law provides that a

court can make a custody ruling if (in this order):

- The state was the child's "home state," generally being the state where the child lived at least six months before the custody case was filed in court.

- It's in the best interests of the child that the court make a decision because the child and at least one parent have a significant connection with the state, and there is available in the state "substantial evidence concerning the child's present or future care, protection, training, and personal relationships."

- The child is physically present in the state and has been abandoned or needs emergency protection from mistreatment or abuse.

- No other state has authority over the case.

The UCCJA disfavors giving custody to a parent who relocates just to create a "home state" or "significant connections." If you've moved, you'd better be able to convince the judge it was for a better job and therefore a better life for your kids, not to find a more "enlightened" court.

If you and your spouse both begin custody proceedings but in different states, the court in the state with lower ranking jurisdiction under the UCCJA must stop all proceedings or dismiss the case. In other words, unless you can show a dire emergency, all you'd get for your trip from Tulsa to San Francisco would be a determination that Oklahoma had jurisdiction. You might even get fined. The act provides that a court can order the parent to pay the other's attorney's fees and travel expenses.

If a court in one state has already issued a child custody order, your chance of persuading a court in another state to modify that order is extremely slim. If you took the child out of state in violation of the order, you may be guilty of kidnapping. The UCCJA provides that a court, in declining to hear a custody case, can notify the prosecuting attorney of the original state that the child has been illegally removed. And a federal law called the Parental Kidnapping Prevention Act can be used to prosecute you for kidnapping.

The UCCJA can work for both parents. Although it greatly limits a gay or lesbian parent's power to move to a more favorable state, it also limits the non-gay parent's power to take a child to a conservative jurisdiction, hoping to get a custody change because the other parent is gay.

Despite our words of caution, in some extreme situations, moving to a new state may be your only hope of gaining custody. Although it doesn't work often, shopping for a better court has been known to work occasionally. If you are contemplating this course of action, see a lawyer familiar with custody law. As we said above, your chances of success are poor and you risk a kidnapping charge if you violate a court order. And think of the effect that running, hiding and living in fear will have on your children.

5. Resources for Lesbian and Gay Parents Seeking Custody

If you're involved in a contested custody case, your lawyer will need help. Chapter 10 includes names and addressees of gay and lesbian legal rights groups; contact any one of them. Below we list resources available through two of those organizations (the National Center for Lesbian Rights and the National Gay and Lesbian Task Force) and elsewhere.

Publications from the National Center for Lesbian Rights (NCLR):

- Achtenberg, *AIDS and Child Custody: A Guide to Advocacy* (1990)

- Achtenberg, *Lesbian and Gay Parenting: A Psychological and Legal Perspective* (1987)

- Hitchens, *Lesbian Mother Litigation Manual* (1990)

- NCLR, *State-By-State Guide to Child Custody* (1996)

- NCLR and the National Lawyers Guild, *A Lesbian and Gay Parents' Legal Guide to Child Custody* (1989).

Publications from the National Gay and Lesbian Task Force (NGLTF):

- *Family Project Bibliography*

- *Twenty Questions About Homosexuality* (a good starting place to gather resources to counter myths and misconceptions)

Other Publications:

- Barret & Robinson, *Gay Fathers* (Free Press, 1990)

- Cramer, *Gay Parents and Their Children: A Review of Research and Practical Implications, Journal of Counseling and Development* (1986)

- Hammer, *Family Law II: The Role of Sexual Preference in Custody Disputes*, 1986 Annual Survey of American Law

- Herek, *Myths About Sexual Orientation: A Lawyer's Guide to Social Science Research*, 1 Law and Sexuality (Summer 1991)

- *Homosexuality and Family Relations* (several articles) (Harrington Park Press, 1990)

- *Homosexuality and the Family* (several articles) (Haworth Press, 1989)

- Kleber, Howell & Tibbits-Kleber, *The Impact of Parental Homosexuality in Child Custody Cases: A Review of the Literature*, 14 Bulletin American Academy of Psychiatry and Law (1986)

- Marcus, *Is It a Choice?* (Harper Collins) (another good place to gather data to counter misconceptions)

- Polikoff, *Educating Judges About Lesbian and Gay Parenting: A Simulation*, 1 Law and Sexuality (Summer 1991).

6.   Using Expert Witnesses

One key to winning your case will be the presentation of expert witnesses. Expert witnesses are psychiatrists, case workers, psychologists and other professionals who testify about an area in which few people have "expert" knowledge. Experts are often used in custody cases, and are a must for a gay parent. An expert can evaluate your home environment, and testify about your fitness as a parent, your child's health, welfare, relationship to you and relationship to the home environment.

But most important, an expert can educate the judge about lesbian and gay parents in general. Attorneys who regularly try custody cases for lesbian and gay parents say that overcoming myths and misconceptions about homosexuality—particularly that gay people are ill, perverted, abnormal and child molesters, and that their children will be harassed at best and become gay at worst—is the biggest obstacle to winning. Here's where the expert comes in.

However you personally feel about psychologists and the like, courts are frequently impressed by credentialed "experts." It takes the wisdom of Solomon to decide many custody cases, and although few judges publicly admit it, most welcome all the help they can get. An expert lets a judge pass the buck to another "professional" when having to make a difficult decision. Ideally, an expert should testify that:

- You are a well-adjusted, stable and fit parent.

- The children are, or will be, well-adjusted, healthy and happy with you.

- It is in the best interests of the children to live with you.

- Gay and lesbian parents are no less likely than heterosexuals to provide loving, stable homes, and that all studies show that children raised by gay or lesbian parents grow up to be happy, healthy and well-adjusted.

- The children won't be molested or seduced by the gay parent or the parent's friends.

- Gays and lesbians are not promiscuous or unstable.

- Gay people are as "adjusted" and happy as heterosexuals.

An expert should also be able to address issues concerning the children's relationships to their peers and anyone significant to you. In other words, the expert should explain away all the fears the judge may have about homosexuality. Your expert will want to review the extensive positive material published regarding gay and lesbian parents and their children. The lists in Section 5, above, is your starting place.

Your expert might be countered by an opposing one. Lawyers know that you can find an expert who will support almost any position, provided you have the money. Cross-examining and discrediting an opposing expert is a job for your lawyer, which is another reason why you'll need someone knowledgeable about lesbian and gay issues.

C. Visitation of Children

Judges have hindered and obstructed gay parents' rights to visit their children with the same coldness and caprice that they have exhibited when denying custody. And hypocrisy? How about the following statement supposedly protecting the constitutional rights of a gay father:

Fundamental rights of parents may not be denied, limited, or restricted on the basis of sexual orientation, per se. The right of a parent, including a homosexual parent, to the companionship and care of his or her child, insofar as it is for the best interest of the child, is a fundamental right protected by the First, Ninth, and Fourteenth Amendments to the United States Constitution. That right may not be restricted without a showing that the parent's activities may tend to impair the emotional and physical health of the child.[11]

Beautiful words, aren't they? Yes, until you realize they were part of a decision in which a father was allowed to see his children as follows:

On alternate Sundays and some holidays and three weeks' visitation during the summer, at some place other than his home, during which he is ordered not to sleep with anyone other than a lawful spouse nor to involve the children in any homosexual-related activities or publicity nor to see his male companion in the presence of his children.

In general, the problems confronting a lesbian or gay parent in a custody proceeding are the same ones to address in a visitation case. But there are significant differences too—legal precedent states that a parent may be denied custody simply when it's not in the child's best interest. To deny visitation, however, the court must find that visitation would be "actually detrimental" to the best interests of the child.

More specifically, before denying (or greatly restricting) a parent's right to see his or her child, the court must find extreme behavior—child abuse, violence, repeated drunkenness or sexual acts in front of the children. Once your spouse learns this, she or he should be much less inclined to fight over visitation; if she or he insists and takes the case to court, you should win.

Our advice to parents worried about visitation is the same that we gave in the custody section—compromise if you can. If you and your spouse agree that you should have visitation, the court will probably give you "reasonable visitation rights" and leave you and your spouse to work out the details. If, however, you're relating so poorly that you cannot agree on when, where and how the visitation will take place, a judge will specifically define visitation rights. For example, a court might make the following order:

Herb Fitzroy is awarded the right to visit with John and Phillip Fitzroy every weekend from 10:00 a.m. Saturday to 8:00 p.m. Sunday, plus six weeks during the school vacations, the weeks to be agreed upon by the parties.

or

Carol Fitzroy is awarded the right to visit with her children on the first and third weekends of each month from 5:00 p.m. Friday to 8:00 p.m. Sunday, and for the children's entire summer vacation, on the condition that she pick up the children from, and deliver them to, the home of Herb Fitzroy.

A judge can impose specific rules on visitation. A noncustodial parent may be required to give the custodial parent 48 hours notice before coming to visit. Or, a court may prohibit the visiting parent from removing the child from the county or the state, or, in rare situations, from the child's own home or the home of a third party. It's common for courts to require that parents with histories of drinking not use alcohol while visiting the children.

But can the court restrain Herb from visiting with his children in the presence of George (the man with whom he lives)? Can the court prohibit the children from spending the night with Herb if George is present? Some courts have said yes; others no.[12] Can a court prohibit a gay father with

AIDS from visiting with his children? Because the children are not at risk of catching AIDS from their father, there's no medical ground for a prohibition. In most cases, visitation has been permitted. But some judges will prohibit visitation, supposedly to "protect the children." In any of these situations, you will want an expert or two to testify on your behalf. If the court rules against you, especially in the case of a gay father with AIDS, consider appealing—but it's rarely wise to violate the court order.

Once a visitation order is entered, it's enforceable just like any other court order. Parents with custody have been known to refuse to comply with visitation orders, to spite their ex-spouse. Whatever the motive, it's not in the best interests of the children, and it's illegal. A parent violating a court order can be held in contempt of court, fined and even jailed.

D. Child Support

In every state, parents are required to support their children. It makes no difference whether the parent has custody or has been denied visitation, or whether the parents were married when the child was born. Although the amount of child support used to be set by the judge, every state has or is in the process of adopting a formula to establish support. You may be able to agree to an amount different from what the formula produces, but only if the judge is convinced your child will be adequately supported.

Only legal parents are obligated to support children. Your lover is welcome to pay the bills, but is not required to. Never-

theless, if your lover pays *your* bills, a court may decide that that frees up your money and you need less child support. Or, if you're the payor, the court might decide that your lover's generosity means you have more money to pay child support.

Here are a few examples showing how child support works.

Example 1: Toni is a bank president and Mort, a bank guard. After a whirlwind courtship behind the vault, they marry. Before long they have twins. Everything is smooth until Toni goes to a series of bankers' conventions and carries on an affair with Keija, who is also in bank management. Toni finally informs Mort that she and Keija plan to live together. Mort, who has some new romantic notions of his own, is not terribly upset and agrees to Toni having custody, but feels he shouldn't have to pay child support because Toni makes more than he does. Too bad. All parents must support their kids. Toni will be fullfilling her obligation to pay support by virtue of having custody. Mort will be ordered to pay support, though less than he'd be required if Toni did not work outside the home.

Example 2: Now Mort has custody. His salary is $20,000 per year and Toni's is $150,000. Toni will be ordered to pay considerable support. She has the ability to do so, and Mort will find it impossible to keep the twins clothed without Toni's help.

Example 3: This time, custody is joint and the kids spend roughly half the year with Toni and half with Mort. Mort will have to pay a small amount of support when the kids are with Toni, and Toni will be required to pay a larger amount when the kids are with Mort.

Example 4: Now Toni has custody. Keija commonly spends large chunks of her salary on the kids. When combined with Toni's income, the twins are lavishly taken care of. Mort wants his support obligation reduced because of Keija's behavior. But her contributions are voluntary—she has no legal obligation to spend as she does. If Mort asked a court to reduce his support obligation, the court won't unless Mort can convince it that because Keija contributes to the household expenses, Toni now has more disposable income to spend on the twins, and he can pay less.

Example 5: Now assume that Mort starts living with Alex and Alex's two kids. Between raising the kids and doing carpentry work, Alex can barely pay for groceries and Mort finds himself chipping in to help support the family. Before long, he's short of money to send Toni. He asks the court to reduce his child support obligation, explaining that he is helping support Alex's kids, who really need it. Will the judge reduce Mort's support obligation? No. Mort has no legal relationship with Alex's kids and no legal duty to support them.

Failure to support is a crime. In all states, it is a crime to fail to support your kids, whether you were ever married or not. It also doesn't matter if you've separated, but not yet divorced.

A parent sometimes tries to avoid paying child support by moving to a different part of the country. Hiding out is hard to do, however, because of laws that connect state and federal governments in their support enforcement efforts. In addition, federal laws make Social Security, IRS and other federal files available to child support enforcement officials. If someone with the ability to work refuses to do so (and therefore claims inability to pay child support), he'll be ordered to pay support anyway. Many judges define "ability to support" to mean "able-bodied," and demand that parents who aren't employed show up in court periodically with lists of potential employers they've contacted.

Must You Pay Child Support When You're Denied Visitation?

Suppose your ex-spouse refuses to comply with court-ordered visitation. Can you retaliate by refusing to pay child support? No. Support and visitation are not intertwined—you must pay support no matter what happens with visitation. A court may grant a reduction, but don't count on it. In addition, you probably can seek reimbursement from the custodial parent for costs incurred in trying to exercise visitation. You must go to court before actually reducing the payments; if you reduce them without court authorization, you may be held in contempt of court under the original support order.

E. After the Divorce

Finally, your marriage is over. You've settled custody, support, visitation and property division. You and your lover are settling down to enjoy your new life. It's nice to be able to forget about courts, lawyers and hassles about who cares for and supports the kids. Sound too good to be true? You're right. It probably is. Questions of custody and child support are never finally settled. Either parent can request the judge to modify custody or child support if the circumstances have significantly changed since the making of the previous order.

Example 1: Remember Mort and Toni? Toni (the banker) has custody and Mort (the guard) was ordered to pay $400 a month in child support. After a year, Toni quit her job to go back to school. Can she ask the court to raise the amount of Mort's support? Of course she can ask. Will the court do so? Maybe. If a judge feels her new education will lead to an even better paying job and lifestyle for her kids, he may increase Mort's support. If her schooling is to learn basket weaving, however, he won't. Had Toni been fired and unable to get another high-paying job, the court would almost surely order Mort to pay more.

Example 2: At the time of the divorce, Mort made $20,000 a year. He later quit his job and went into sales, eventually earning $100,000 a year. Can Toni ask the court to raise the child support? Yes. Does the court have the power to do so? Yes. Will it? Yes.

Example 3: At the time of the divorce, Toni was living with Keija, but the judge never knew this. Later, they moved to a lesbian commune with the kids. Mort asks the court to change custody, claiming that living on the commune is not in the children's best interests. Will he win? Yes, if he can show that the commune is truly detrimental to the children and that he can offer them a good home—or if the judge is biased against lesbian mothers.

There is very little you can do to keep your former spouse from taking you back to court. The best way to avoid or minimize future court hassles is to maintain good communications with your ex. Go more than halfway in the small areas; you'll be in a good position to work out larger ones. If you are unkind and uncooperative, your ex will be too. Be flexible. As incomes go up and down, be ready to adjust, even if it means you pay more or receive less.

If you agree on a change, have the court approve it. It is not difficult to have an agreed-upon child support (or visitation or custody) change entered as part of a court record. It's especially wise to file your papers with the court if your ex has given you trouble or has a history of "forgetting" or ignoring agreements. If you don't have it approved by the court, at least write it down and sign it. This will give you some protection.

SAMPLE SUPPORT CHANGE AGREEMENT

Herb Fitzroy of 27 Apion Way, Spokane, Washington, and Carol Fitzroy of 11 State Street, Yakima, Washington, make the following agreement concerning a change in the amount of child support for their children, John and Phillip:

1. Herb has suffered an attack of hepatitis making it impossible for him to work for nine months; his income has been reduced by 60% because of his inability to work.

2. Herb and Carol want to avoid a court fight and agree to change the amount of support to fit the new circumstances.

3. They agree that commencing July 1, 19__, and continuing until April 1, 19__, the amount of Herb's child support obligation shall be reduced from $600 per month to $240 per month.

4. They further agree that this agreement may be presented to a court with jurisdiction over John and Phillip's child support at any time.

Dated: _____   Signature: _____
                                           Herb Fitzroy

Dated: _____   Signature: _____
                                           Carol Fitzroy

SAMPLE SUPPORT CHANGE AGREEMENT

Veronica Lee of 17 Leafy Lane, Palos Verdes, California, and Robert Lee, of 311 Hennepin Drive, Minneapolis, Minnesota, make the following agreement:

1. Because Veronica has received a promotion to chief buyer at Racafrax Department Store and now earns $3,000 per month, it is fair and equitable that she increase the child support she pays Robert for Ricky and Sharon.

2. Therefore they agree to raise child support from $400 per month to $750 per month to continue at this new rate indefinitely or until they make a subsequent modification.

3. This agreement may be presented by either party to a court having jurisdiction over this case at any time.

Dated: _____   Signature: _____
                                           Robert Lee

Dated: _____   Signature: _____
                                           Veronica Lee

Endnotes

[1] The information and charts on the following few pages are taken from *Nolo's Pocket Guide to Family Law*, by Leonard & Elias (Nolo Press).

[2] Separation-based divorce must also allege incompatibility.

[3] Must allege irretrievable breakdown and separation for no-fault; if both parties consent, two years reduced to six months.

[4] Separation-based divorce allowed only if there are no children.

[5] May be reduced to six months if there are no children.

[6] States not listed have no specific law on the topic.

[7] 5 Family L. Rptr. 2127 (1979).

[8] *Van Dyck v. Van Dyck*, 425 S.E.2d 853 (1993).

[9] *Blew v. Verta*, 617 A.2d 31 (1992).

[10] *H.J.B. v. P.W.*, reported at 19 Family Law Reporter 1482 (1993).

[11] In Re J., S. and C., 129 N.J. Super. Ct. 486, 324 A.2d 90 (1974).

[12] See, for example, *Pennington v. Pennington*, 596 N.E.2d 305 (Indiana 1992), where the court barred a gay father from visiting with his child when his lover was present. The court found that the lover's presence "would be" harmful to the child's emotional development. On the other hand, a recent New York case, *Hart v. Hart* (reported in the New York Law Journal, Feb. 8, 1995, at 31), granted unsupervised visitation to a gay father, finding no evidence that his son would be adversely affected by his father's sexual orientation. The visitation agreement contained no restrictions on whether the father could have male partners over when his son was visiting. ■

CHAPTER 9

Going Separate Ways

Splitting up with a lover is usually a difficult, emotionally traumatic experience. Obviously, no lawyer can assist you with the grief, pain, anger and sense of loss that accompany a separation. Breaking up, especially if you've been together a while, often strikes friends as sad, though it may be (or prove eventually to be) quite healthy for you.

The very language that's used to describe the end of a relationship often gets in the way of reaching a positive understanding of what's happening. Breaking up is often described as a "failure" while a relationship that lasts is called "successful." It seems peculiar that the endurance of a relationship determines its worth. In fact, the very idea that "success" and "failure" can be applied to love strikes us as crazy. We subscribe to the views of E. M. Forster when he discussed a man who sees experience in terms of winning, losing and imposing his will on the world:

> *He fails with a completeness which no artist and no lover can experience, because with them the process of creation is itself an achievement, whereas with him the only possible achievement is success.*[1]

Love is complete in itself; it isn't an effort toward some later result. What matters in a breakup isn't "what do I have to show for my one—five—or fifteen years with you?" but rather the preservation of whatever good remains from living and loving together during those years. Even if in retrospect your time together looks bleak and insincere, you can't salvage anything good from it by being mean or nasty during the separation. We know that it's much easier to say it than live it. Still, it's worth remembering.

Sympathetic people, or organizations, can help a separating couple hold onto their humanity and regard for each other. Call on your friends, family, therapist, pastor or rabbi and others who make up your support system. Don't be afraid to talk about why you originally got together—the positive and creative aspects of your relationship—and why you can no longer live together.

If you and your lover have a child, turn to Chapter 3, where we cover issues relating to parents splitting up.

A. Dividing Your Property

Arguments over who owns what are rarely the real core of separating, although fights over property can become a way for an ex-couple to take out their frustrations against each other. But once started, property disputes often take on a life of their own and degenerate into bitterness that poisons a relationship for years to come, and prevents the ex-couple from maintaining any friendly relationship.

If you and your lover drafted a living together contract or discussed your understandings but never wrote them down, please do yourselves a favor and honor your agreement. If you don't have a contract, you have two choices:

- you can be reasonable and reach a compromise over dividing your property, or

- you can engage in all-out, legal warfare.

A full-scale court battle between former lovers over property will be expensive. Preliminary legal matters and a trial can take months, perhaps years—and all the while the lawyer's meter runs at $100 to $200 or more an hour. To make things worse, you're litigating in a relatively new area of the law; no one can predict results with certainty. Some judges will be hostile to the mere existence of lesbian and gay couples. Others won't be and will find the legal issues of your case interesting.

Whichever, you and your former lover will lose money, time and what remains of your good feelings. Avoid this craziness if at all possible. Of course, in extreme situations, going to court may really be necessary. If your name wasn't put on the deed, but you put up money for it or worked on it, and your former lover refuses to give you any interest in the property or settle the dispute, you might have to sue to get your fair share.

Example 1: Sonia sued Virginia, claiming a partnership interest in Virginia's thriving business. In the carefree days of initial romance, Virginia allowed Sonia to use company credit cards and paid Sonia well for occasional jobs. When they split, Sonia asked a court to restrain Virginia from continuing her own business until Sonia received her claimed half-interest. The

litigation became protracted and nasty. Aside from paying considerable legal fees, Virginia had to stand up to threats of "ruining her image." Finally, after several courtroom defeats, it became apparent to Sonia—and particularly to her lawyer— that no evidence supported the claim of a partnership; the case settled for a minimal amount.

Example 2: Ed bought a house, putting only his money down and took title in his name alone. Ed and Raymond lived in the house for years and acted as if both owned the house in some vague undefined way. Raymond contributed to the monthly mortgage payments and did extensive work on the place. When they separated, after nine years of living in the house, Raymond realized that nothing documented his contributions to the house. And Ed initially denied that Raymond had contributed anything.

But this is a story with a happy ending. After calming down, both men were willing to talk, and Ed soon acknowledged that Raymond had made important contributions. Although the two men couldn't agree how to calculate their respective interests, they agreed to go to mediation to reach a fair settlement. In the process of compromising, they reconciled. But they also had the good sense to change the recorded ownership of the house to reflect their agreement.

The moral of these two tales is that legal disputes over property division don't have to be expensive and destructive, but that they often are. There's a risk you'll end up in a lawsuit if you don't write down your understanding. Remember, nobody anticipates being dragged into court until it's too late.

1. Closing Joint Accounts

When you split up, you must untwine your finances as soon as possible. Creditors need to be notified of your "single" status.

First, close all joint credit accounts. Lots of people get stuck with large bills because their ex-lovers charged a fortune on joint credit card accounts. Notify not only credit card companies, but also any store or business that might extend credit to you jointly—the grocer, the hardware store, the lumberyard and all the rest. Canceling joint credit accounts usually must be done in writing; and keep a copy of the letter you send.

You and your lover are each responsible for all debts you cosigned or otherwise agreed to pay together. On any joint debt, the creditor can come to either of you for payment—even if you agree between yourselves that only one of you will pay the debt. If the creditor comes to you for payment because your ex didn't make the payments as you agreed, make the payments yourself—otherwise, you could get some black marks on your credit file. You can sue her, but that doesn't help much if she's living in the south of France.

2. Separating Your Property

If you don't have a living together agreement, you'll want a separation agreement if you've been together for a long time and have accumulated a lot of property. And even if you have a contract, you can use a separation agreement to pin down details of who gets what and who pays for what. The sooner you make an agreement, the less chance there is for misunderstanding. This doesn't mean that "cooling off" time isn't helpful if pain or anger make communication difficult. And when feelings are raw, a little generosity and a calm attitude often work wonders. As the Bible says, "A soft answer turneth away wrath."

But whatever you do about your property disagreements, don't just hope they'll go away.

If you'd rather continue owning property together—such as a house or business— that's perfectly fine. But now, more than ever, you need to write down a thorough understanding.

So how do you make a separation agreement? Our approach is to list all the property you own. Identify each item as your separate property, your (ex)lover's separate property, your jointly-owned property or property whose ownership you dispute. Make similar lists for your debts. Below are some worksheets.

PROPERTY DIVISION WORKSHEET

Separate property owned by [your name]	Separate property owned by [your lover's name]

Separate debts owed by
[your name]

Separate debts owed by
[your lover's name]

_____

_____

_____

_____

_____

_____

_____

_____

_____

_____

_____

_____

_____

_____

_____

_____

_____

_____

_____

_____

_____

_____

_____

_____

Items we agree we jointly own	Market value	Amount owed	Equity value
_____	_____	_____	_____
_____	_____	_____	_____
_____	_____	_____	_____
_____	_____	_____	_____
_____	_____	_____	_____
_____	_____	_____	_____
_____	_____	_____	_____
_____	_____	_____	_____
_____	_____	_____	_____
_____	_____	_____	_____
_____	_____	_____	_____
_____	_____	_____	_____
_____	_____	_____	_____
_____	_____	_____	_____
_____	_____	_____	_____
_____	_____	_____	_____
_____	_____	_____	_____
_____	_____	_____	_____
_____	_____	_____	_____
_____	_____	_____	_____
_____	_____	_____	_____
_____	_____	_____	_____
_____	_____	_____	_____
_____	_____	_____	_____

TOTAL EQUITY TO BE DIVIDED =========

Debts we agree we jointly owe	Amount	Creditor
_____	_____	_____
_____	_____	_____
_____	_____	_____
_____	_____	_____
_____	_____	_____
_____	_____	_____
_____	_____	_____
_____	_____	_____
_____	_____	_____
_____	_____	_____
_____	_____	_____
_____	_____	_____
_____	_____	_____
_____	_____	_____
_____	_____	_____
_____	_____	_____
_____	_____	_____
_____	_____	_____
_____	_____	_____
_____	_____	_____
_____	_____	_____
_____	_____	_____
_____	_____	_____

TOTAL DEBTS TO BE ALLOCATED =========

Items whose ownership we dispute and reason for dispute	Market value	Amount owed	Equity value
_____	_____	_____	_____
_____	_____	_____	_____
_____	_____	_____	_____
_____	_____	_____	_____
_____	_____	_____	_____
_____	_____	_____	_____
_____	_____	_____	_____
_____	_____	_____	_____
_____	_____	_____	_____
_____	_____	_____	_____

Debts we dispute and the reason for dispute	Amount	Creditor
_____	_____	_____
_____	_____	_____
_____	_____	_____
_____	_____	_____
_____	_____	_____
_____	_____	_____
_____	_____	_____
_____	_____	_____
_____	_____	_____
_____	_____	_____

To best use these worksheets, concentrate on what you agree to, and put off the areas of dispute until later. When you disagree as to who owns or owes something, list it under Disputed Property or Disputed Debts and go on.

Items whose ownership we dispute and reason for dispute	Market value	Amount owed	Equity value
Silverware—Mike says his mother gave it to him and he should have it all. Al says it was a joint gift so he should get half.	$800	$0	$800
Truck—Al says he paid the $400 down payment to buy the truck, so he should get it. Mike says he contributed to half the insurance and half of ten payments, so he wants a two-fifths interest.	$1,400	$400	$1,000
Garbo, the cat—Mike and Al both love her and want her.			

Debts we dispute and reason for dispute	Amount	Creditor	
Vacation to Mexico—Mike says Al paid the entire vacation as a gift to Mike; Al says they agreed to share it.	$1,700	Fiesta Travel Agent	

If you've been able to put all your property and debts in either one of the separate property-debts entries or the shared property-debts category, you are ready for the distribution. Each person keeps his or her separate property and pays his or her debts. Your shared property and debts are divided 50-50, unless you own any items in unequal percentages. Obviously, don't chop your oak table in half. By 50-50, we mean each keeps half the value of all the shared property and pays half of the shared debts. Negotiate and compromise. If disputes remain over how to divide joint property or over whether an item of property or a debt is joint or separate, we urge you to resolve them by mediation. (See Section B, below.)

3. Drafting Your Separation Agreement

Once you've divided your property, it's time to draft a separation agreement. This is no more than putting in writing the division you've reached. Below is a sample that you can use or modify to create your own separation agreement.

SEPARATION AGREEMENT

We, Alice Hobbs and Michele Watson, have agreed to go our separate ways, and to divide our property as specified in this agreement. This is a final division of all our property and can only be changed or amended by both of us, in writing.

Property

We have agreed to divide all of our property as follows:

1. We agreed that the following is the separate property of Alice Hobbs and she has the full right to ownership of each item:

      a. Platform bed

      b. Hockney lithograph

      c. Handblown glass collection

2. We agreed that the following property is the separate property of Michele Watson and she has the full right to ownership of each item:

      a. Fold-out couch

      b. Dresser

      c. Goya print

3. We agreed that we will both retain (share) ownership of the following property:

      a. 1993 Toyota (we will trade off use until one of us buys it from the other or until we sell it)

      b. Paddington, our three-year-old spaniel (we'll alternate months having her)

Debts

We have divided our debts so that each person will be solely responsible for the debts listed below under her name. If the person listed fails to make a payment on a debt, and the other person ends up making the payment, that (other) person may sue the person listed as responsible, for all costs and expenses incurred, including the reasonable legal fees necessary to enforce this agreement.

1. Debts assumed by Alice Hobbs:

      a. Vacation spot—$1,000

      b. Sears—$350

2. Debts assumed by Michele Watson:

      a. Vacation spot—$700

      b. Big Bank Visa—$400

Dated: _____   Signature: _____
                                    Alice Hobbs

Dated: _____   Signature: _____
                                    Michele Watson

You can add as many clauses to your agreement as you need or desire. Our preference is to keep the agreement short and succinct, while covering all financial matters. If you will continue shared ownership in some property, specify the exact terms you've agreed on. If one of you will buy out the other (common in the case of shared real estate), specify all the terms and conditions of the buy-out. (See Chapter 7.)

4. Providing Financial Support

It's conceivable, though not likely, that if one of you sued the other for support, claiming you had an oral agreement for support in the event of separation, a court would award support.

If you had a written agreement explicitly providing for support, however, most courts would enforce it. Without an express provision, if one of you stayed home and did the cooking, cleaning and caring for children, while the other was the sole economic provider, a court might order the partner employed outside the house to pay some support.

If you want to include a support provision in your separation agreement, here's a sample:

SAMPLE SUPPORT AGREEMENT

Alfred Gwynne and Mark Jones have decided to separate and live apart from this time on. For the past seven years, they have lived together; Mark hasn't been employed outside the home during that time and has provided many household services for Alfred.

Alfred and Mark agree that Alfred will pay Mark the sum of $400 a month for one year, commencing December 1, 19__ , with the payments to be made on the first of each month; these payments are to help Mark during his transition following the parties' separation, and to assist him while he seeks gainful employment. In exchange, Mark relinquishes all claims he may have against Alfred for money or support for his services to Alfred during the time they lived together.[2]

Dated: _____   Signature: _____
                                      Alfred Gwynne

Dated: _____   Signature: _____
                                      Mark Jones

Support payments for divorced couples are treated like income—they're deductible for the payor and taxable to the recipient. The tax status of support payments for lesbian and gay couples is uncertain. The payments might be treated as a gift and taxed accordingly (if over $10,000 per year) or regarded as compensation for previous work, treated as income and taxed as income. Talk this over with your tax advisor.

B. Resolving Disputes by Mediation or Arbitration

Separating couples with disputes have alternatives to litigation: mediation and arbitration. These methods of resolving disputes are almost invariably preferable to court battles. Mediation involves a neutral third party assisting the couple in reaching an agreement. In arbitration, the neutral third party issues a binding decision of the disputes submitted to him. Mediation's strength is that neither person feels "I wuz robbed" because the couple discusses, compromises and reaches the agreement. Arbitration's strength is that it's quick and final, as someone else imposes a decision.

In many ways, mediation and arbitration are similar. Both are speedy, informal and economical. Both provide a forum for you to express your views and anger, and be heard by an independent person. In both, the couple voluntarily chooses to participate. If you refuse, you can't be compelled to participate unless you've previously agreed to arbitration or mediation in a living together contract. You select the mediator or arbitrator yourselves. The issues resolved are determined by you; the mediator or arbitrator can't consider an issue you haven't asked them to consider.

Mediation and arbitration can range from costly and formal to inexpensive and down-home. Professional mediators and arbitrators are found in all major cities. The American Arbitration Association (AAA) provides trained, professional arbitrators; we recommend against using them, however. They are costly—often hundreds of dollars per day. Moreover, there's no certainty that an AAA arbitrator would be knowledgeable or sympathetic about lesbian and gay issues. It's wiser and cheaper to select mediators or arbitrators who will understand your situation.

1. Mediation Services for Gay Men and Lesbians

As we've stated throughout this book (and we certainly didn't need to be the ones to tell you), the judicial system is indifferent to, at best, and hostile to, at worst, gay men and lesbians. Relationships are ignored. Judges are bewildered at what gays and lesbians do, with whom and why. Judges cannot believe that gays and lesbians are having and raising kids. Lawyers pit gay men and lesbians against each other, dragging up stereotypes most gays have spent years combating.

So what is the answer when you need help resolving a dispute? Formal gay and lesbian mediation services now exist in Los Angeles (Gay and Lesbian Community Services Mediation Project, 213-993-7675). (There were programs in San Francisco and New York, but they dissolved.) Outside of L.A., you may be able to find lawyers or therapists who do mediation for gay and lesbian couples. Formal programs use professionally trained members of the gay and lesbian community to resolve all kinds of disputes (including roommate conflicts, neighbor disputes, landlord-tenant matters and business conflicts), not just couple break ups.

Mediation is commonly done with one mediator, but more can be used. In arbitration, it's common for each person to select one arbitrator, and then to have the two arbitrators select a third. In addition to selecting the mediator or arbitrator(s), you must decide what issues are to be resolved. You also decide the rules of the proceeding. This is usually done with help from the arbitrator or mediator. Here are a few things to determine:

• When and where is the proceeding to take place?

• Will you limit the number of sessions?

In arbitration, consider these other issues:

• Will you be allowed to submit a written statement?

• Will you represent yourselves, or use attorneys?

• Will you be allowed to cross-examine each other?

• Can the arbitrator(s) order you to produce documents or other evidence?

• Must the decision be explained—that is, how and why the arbitrator(s) reached it?

• Is there a time limit within which the decision must be rendered?

Once you answer these questions, write down your agreement. Below is a sample Agreement to Arbitrate you can use or adapt.

AGREEMENT TO ARBITRATE

1. This agreement is made on April 21, 19__, between Robert Trion and Martin Auberge, of 1 Paris Way, Macon, Georgia.

2. We have chosen to separate, and in order to resolve certain conflicts between us, submit the following issues to arbitration.

a) Who is entitled to remain in the apartment we share at 1 Paris Way?

b) Who is entitled to ownership of the Ford Mustang automobile we own in joint tenancy, and what's fair compensation for the other party?

3. We each will select one arbitrator within 15 days of the date of this agreement. The two arbitrators will jointly agree on a third arbitrator within 15 days. Each party will pay the expenses he incurs, and will bear the expenses, if any, of the arbitrators equally. A decision by a majority of the arbitrators will be binding.

4. The arbitrators will determine the time and place of the arbitration hearing, and the procedures to be followed, except that at least three days' notice shall be required if the arbitrators or either party request to see books, records or other documents.

Dated: _____   Signature: _____
                                                   Robert Trion

Dated: _____   Signature: _____
                                                   Martin Auberge

---

Endnotes

[1] E. M. Forster, "What I Believe," in *Two Cheers for Democracy*.

[2]The contract is phrased in terms of each person relinquishing all claims, not because we're encouraging paranoia about lawsuits, but because of the technical rules of contracts. They're not important to get into, but you need to include the language. ■

CHAPTER 10

Help Beyond the Book

We hope you never need a lawyer. If you follow our urgings and create your own contracts, durable powers of attorney and wills, you may well escape their clutches. Still, there may come a time when you'll need one, especially if you and your lover want to become parents or co-parents, or have valuable assets and need complex estate planning, and so a few words on the subject seem pertinent.

A. Hiring a Lawyer in a Non-Adversarial Situation

There are many reasons you might want a hire a lawyer in a non-adversarial context:

- to review the documents you've pre-pared using this book

- to complete more complex forms than we've provided

- to check your state laws on a particular subject, or

- to assist you in an adoption.

Finding a lawyer isn't a problem; the surplus is huge. But finding the right lawyer can be difficult. Make sure any lawyer you hire is familiar with the issues you bring to her—don't hire a bankruptcy lawyer to review your buying-a-house contract—and sympathetic to lesbians and gay men. In addition, many lawyers—gay or straight—have as their main goal, living well, and you can guess who pays for the Porsches and plumage. So, check fees at the start. The lawyer you hire—female or male; gay, lesbian, or straight; solo practitioner or member of a big firm—must fit your needs.

A lawyer-client relationship should be one of trust and confidence. You should feel comfortable coming out to your attorney, and in fact, should do so. If your attorney doesn't meet your initial expectations, you can fire her. Tell your lawyer you expect to be told of all developments in your legal affairs and expect to make all major decisions, with her advice. The best way to find an attorney is to ask your friends who they used and were pleased with for tasks similar to what you need. If that doesn't work, call a lesbian and gay legal referral (often affiliated with a gay and lesbian community center or with the local legal bar association), or consult the list of national Lesbian and Gay Legal Resources provided in Section E, below.

Hiring a lawyer solely to review your legal documents sounds like a good idea. It shouldn't cost much, and seems to offer a comforting security. Sadly though, it may be difficult, or even impossible, to find a lawyer who will accept the job. While this is unfortunate, we are not willing to excoriate lawyers who won't review a do-it-yourself document. From their point of view, they are being asked to accept what might turn into a significant responsibility for what they regard as inadequate compensation, given their usual fees. Any prudent lawyer sees every client as a potential occasion for a malpractice claim, or at least, serious later hassles—a phone call four years down the line that begins, "We talked to you about our living together contract and now ...." Many experienced lawyers want to avoid this kind of exposure and risk. Also, many lawyers feel they simply don't get deeply enough into a situation to be sure of their opinions if they're only reviewing someone else's work. All you can do here is keep trying to find a sympathetic lawyer—or be prepared to pay more, enough so the lawyer can feel secure that she has been paid adequately to review your documents.

B. Hiring a Lawyer to Help You Bring a Court Case

Judge Learned Hand once said "As a litigant, I should dread a lawsuit beyond almost anything short of sickness and death." Nevertheless, you may someday find yourself in litigation. If you do, no matter what the case is for—suing your lover for breach of your living together contract, defending a suit by a relative of your lover contesting his will, or fighting your spouse for custody of your children—you will need a lawyer. While the saying "a person who represents himself has a fool for a client" has been perpetuated by self-interested lawyers, in court you're on their turf and you need to hire one to play their game.

Hiring a lawyer doesn't mean rolling over and playing dead. You must still retain control over your case. Your lawyer should not decide matters or take steps without consulting you. You can learn to do some legal work yourself, and insist on understanding all of it. If your lawyer can't explain what's going on, you need another lawyer.

Remember what happened to Oscar Wilde in the 1890s when he sought to use the legal system? It led to his physical, economic and professional ruin. Wilde, it seems, was "seeing" Lord Alfred Douglas, son of the Marquis of Queensbury. Queensbury heard rumors of the relationship and chose to fight Wilde. (Queensbury was a celebrated boxer.) He left a visiting card at Wilde's home, adding the words "To Oscar Wilde posing as a sodomite." Wilde, naive, bold or mad, sued for libel.

One defense to libel is truth. After the third day of the trial, Queensbury's lawyers made it clear that they would have witnesses of Wilde's sexual relations with males testify. Wilde dropped his case. Queensbury, however, was far from finished. His lawyers sent their prospective witnesses' statements to the Director of Public Prosecution. Wilde was arrested for and charged with sodomy. While he was awaiting trial, his creditors took his house and possessions, his publisher refused to publish his works, he was socially disgraced and most of friends deserted him. He was tried, found guilty and sentenced to two years of hard labor. He died shortly after he was released. The law of the 1990s isn't as brutal as the law of the 1890s, but the moral hasn't changed: Beware of trying to use the law to your advantage.

C.   Hiring a Lawyer to Bring a Political Case

Whenever a lesbian or gay person is involved in a lawsuit because of her or his sexual orientation, it is possible to make the case a political forum for lesbian and gay legal rights. By treating your case as a "gay rights" case and seeking media coverage, you can turn an ordinary lawsuit into a political cause. This strategy can be seductive to you, and even more so to your attorney who can gain a great deal of publicity and notoriety with little at stake but ego. Consider carefully whether making your case a political one is likely to achieve your goals or help other lesbians and gays. If your attorney raises the possibility, ask yourself if he's putting your interest, or his, first.

But making a discrimination case into a cause for civil rights can work—and the lesbian and gay community owes much of its legal advances to the brave men and women who have come out to fight. One example involves Perry Watkins, who, after being openly gay in the army for 17 years, was discharged for being gay. He fought the Army through the court system, and won on the grounds that the Army knew he was gay when he kept reenlisting and therefore he couldn't be discharged. Watkins's limited success opened the door for many other gay men and lesbians to fight their military discharges. Most likely, the U.S. Supreme Court will someday rule on the constitutionality of the "don't ask, don't tell, don't pursue" policy.

Some cases are effectively battled in the press, as well as in court. A good example was Carl Hill's struggle with the U.S. Immigration and Naturalization Service

(INS). Hill, a British journalist who came to the U.S. for a visit, had gay rights buttons in his suitcase. He was detained upon entering the U.S. because "sexual deviants" were not allowed into the country. He chose to fight the INS, and with the help of his lawyer obtained extensive press coverage. He also challenged the constitutionality of the law in the courts. He won in court and the U.S. has since changed its policy.

In other situations—especially situations involving children—however, publicity and politicizing may be the worst possible strategy. All of the cases granting joint or second-parent adoptions, and most cases where a lesbian or gay parent is awarded custody of or visitation with his or her child, have been done quietly, without stirring things up. This makes sense. To judges, the standard when dealing with kids is what is in their best interest, not what are the civil liberties of their parents specifically or homosexuals in general. If your lawyer suggests turning your petition for a joint adoption into the great gay case of the century, find a new lawyer.

And finally, keep in mind that political cases are often expensive and always exhausting. You run the risk of injuring your personal interests. We admire people who stand and fight injustice, but we urge you to avoid litigation if possible and, if not possible, to carefully consider before you embark on a political case. But if you do— more power to you!

D.   Doing Your Own Research

If you are not involved in contested litigation, you have an alternative to hiring a lawyer: Learn to do your own legal research. This book gives you a good start toward solving most of your legal problems, but many questions, especially peculiarities of state law, may not be answered. Why not research the subject yourself? It'll take time and diligence, and you may conclude it isn't worth the effort, but because lawyers charge $100 to $200 per hour, why not give it a try. Often the work is not difficult.

If you decide to do your own research, you will need a research aid. The best book explaining how to do legal work is *Legal Research: How to Find and Understand the Law,* by Stephen Elias and Susan Levinkind (Nolo Press). This book is available in most public and law libraries.

To do your research, you will need to find a law library or a public library with a good law collection. Many law libraries are housed at county courthouses. These law libraries are supported by tax dollars or fees paid when filing legal papers, and are usually open to the public. The county law librarians are generally helpful and courteous to non-lawyers doing their own legal research. If your county law library is open to lawyers only, too small or nonexistent, contact any large public law school near by. The library there is open to the public.

Once you get to the library, ask a librarian to help locate your state's statutes—called "codes," "laws" or "statutes," depending on the state. You'll want the "annotated version," which contains the statutes, excerpts from relevant cases and cross-references to related articles.

Once you find the statutes, check the index for the subject of your concern. State statutes are usually divided into sections. The major section is the Civil Code, which usually contains laws relating to contracts, living together, divorce, custody, adoption and credit. The Probate Code contains laws relating to wills. There are other codes as well—insurance codes, real property codes, criminal codes and welfare codes. Each code is numbered sequentially, and once you get the code number from the index, it's easy to find the statute you need. If you have trouble, ask the law librarian for help.

Once you look at the statute in the hardcover volume, check the "pocket part" at the back of the book for any amendments. Then skim the summaries of recent court decisions contained in the Annotation section immediately following the statute itself. If the summary looks helpful, you'll want to read the entire case from which the summary was taken.

Judicial cases are printed in books called Reports. In this book, we've included several citations to important legal cases, in the event you want to read the entire text. Interpreting a case citation is easy once you learn the abbreviations. For instance, the citation to the "Gay Olympics" case we mention in the Introduction is *San Francisco Arts and Athletics, Inc. v. United States Olympic Committee,* 483 U.S. 522 (1987). What does this mean?

San Francisco Arts and Athletics, Inc. is the plaintiff—the party that filed the lawsuit—and United States Olympic Committee is the defendant—the party that had to defend the lawsuit. U.S. means the United States Reports, the Report series publishing the case. The volume in which the case appears is the number before the name of the series; here you want Volume 483. The number after the series name is the page on which the case starts: here it's page 522. The last number is the year. This may seem a little confusing (it did to us in law school), but any law librarian can quickly explain it to you.

Another important tool may be a legal encyclopedia. These are indexed by subject (such as custody, insurance, homosexuality, guardianship) and provide a synopsis of your state's law on the subject. Also, ask the law librarian to show you form books. These are collections of sample legal forms lawyers use in dealing with common legal tasks. Finally, ask if your state has any books designed to keep lawyers up-to-date. Most larger states have these "how-to" books for lawyers. These books are fairly easy to use. (They never teach this practical stuff in law school.)

E.   Online Resources

By now you have probably heard of "the Net"—the Internet, the World Wide Web (a user-friendly way to approach the Internet) and online commercial services such as America Online, Prodigy and Compuserve. It is increasingly possible to use these resources to gather information about lesbian and gay legal issues.

For instance, the World Wide Web offers direct access to such important legal resource materials as:

• statutes and regulations

• court case opinions

• pending legislation, and

• federal and state agency rules and regulations.

In addition, you can use the Web to reach many sites specially designed to disseminate information to lesbians and gay men. These sites provide resources such as:

• information on the fight for same-sex marriage, domestic partner benefits and other lesbian and gay rights, along with tips on how to get involved in working toward these goals

• texts of cases, statutes and pending legislation affecting lesbians and gay men

• directions for contacting lesbian and gay elected officials in the U.S., and

• information and announcements from hundreds of lesbian and gay organizations, from the Lesbian Avengers to the Log Cabin Club.

Of course you need the proper equipment to get to these and other valuable online legal resources. This means a computer, a modem, a telephone line and the appropriate software. As a general rule, the computer should be either a Macintosh capable of running System 7 software or a PC with a 486 or better processor and at least 4 megabytes of RAM. The modem should be able to handle transmissions at the speed of at least 14,400 baud. Probably the easiest way to get up and running with maximum access is to subscribe to America Online. Using America Online, you can connect with the World Wide Web resources listed above, plus many others. It's easy to obtain free software for this purpose. Ask your local computer store for details.

You may also wish to purchase a copy of *Law on the Net*, by James Evans (Nolo Press), which can help you locate online legal resources for the lesbian and gay community plus thousands of other resources.

F.   Lesbian and Gay Legal Referrals

Below are lists of national lesbian and gay legal organizations, and local lesbian and gay bar associations that make lawyer referrals. If there's no referral organization near you and you can't find a lawyer to help you with your problem, try calling one of the national organizations, or a local chapter of the American Civil Liberties Union (ACLU) or the National Lawyers Guild. Someone on the other end of the phone may be able to give you the name of a local lawyer, or just offer a sympathetic ear. And if you have a lawyer, your lawyer may want to contact one of the national lesbian and gay legal groups to get some support. Many of the legal problems lesbians and gay men encounter have been faced before—a lawyer who fights for gay and lesbian rights full-time probably has helpful materials or suggestions.

1.   Lesbian and Gay Bar Associations

Gay and Lesbian Community Services Center
    Department of Legal Services
Los Angeles, CA
(213) 993-7400

Tom Homann Law Association
San Diego, CA
(619) 232-8377
(619) 699-3608
(does not operate referral service, but will make informal referrals)

Bay Area Lawyers for Individual Freedom,
    Gay/Lesbian Legal Referral Panel
San Francisco, CA
(415) 621-3900

Gay and Lesbian Legal Association of
    Santa Cruz County
Santa Cruz, CA
(408) 439-8663
(408) 476-2360
(408) 476-2500 (fax)
(does not operate referral service, but will make informal referrals)

Gay and Lesbian Attorneys of Washington
Washington, DC
(202) 842-7723

Gay and Lesbian Law Association of Florida
Miami, FL
(305) 665-3886
(does not operate referral service, but will make informal referrals)

Lesbian and Gay Bar Association of Chicago
Chicago, IL
(312) 404-9574

Massachusetts Lesbian and Gay Bar Association
Boston, MA
(617) 492-5110
(does not operate referral service, but will make informal referrals)

Gay & Lesbian Community Action Council,
    Legal Referrals
Minneapolis, MN
(612) 822-0127

Lesbian & Gay Lawyers Referral Office
New York, NY
(212) 459-4873

Bar Association for Human Rights of Greater
    Houston, Inc.
c/o Mitchell Katine of Williams, Birnberg
    & Anderson, LLP
Houston, TX
(713) 981-9595
(does not operate referral service, but will make informal referrals)

2. National Lesbian and Gay Legal Organizations

American Civil Liberties Union (ACLU)
132 West 43rd Street
New York, NY 10036
(212) 944-9800

American Civil Liberties Union (ACLU)
National Gay Rights Project
1616 Beverly Boulevard
Los Angeles, CA 90026
(213) 977-9500; ext. 237

Custody Action for Lesbian Mothers
P.O. Box 281, Narbeth, PA 19072
(610) 667-7508

Gay & Lesbian Advocates & Defenders
P.O. Box 218, Boston, MA 02112
(617) 426-1350

Lambda Legal Defense & Education Fund
666 Broadway, New York, NY 10012
(212) 995-8585
and
6030 Wilshire Blvd., Suite 200
Los Angeles, CA 90036
(213) 937-2728
(213) 937-0601 (fax)
and
203 N. LaSalle
Chicago, IL 60603
(312) 201-9740

Lavender Resource Fund
P.O. Box 21567, Seattle, WA 98111
(206) 325-2643

National Center for Lesbian Rights
870 Market Street, Suite 570
San Francisco, CA 94102
(415) 392-6257

National Gay & Lesbian Task Force
2320 17th Street NW
Washington, DC 20009
(202) 332-6483

G. AIDS Legal Referrals

Below is a list of organizations that provide legal assistance or legal referrals for people with HIV or AIDS. This list isn't complete. If you need legal assistance and don't know where to turn, check your local telephone directory for a Legal Aid or Legal Services office or your city or county's bar association. Many of those groups do AIDS legal referrals. If you know of an organization that should be included here but isn't, please let us know. A nationwide directory of AIDS legal assistance and referral programs is available for $21.95 from: AIDS Coordination Project, 1800 M St., NW, Washington, DC 20036; (202) 662-1025.

Mobile AIDS Support Services
P.O. Box 40296
Mobile, AL 36640
(334) 471-5277

Alaska AIDS Assistance Association
1057 Firewood, Suite 102
Anchorage, AK 99503
(907) 276-1400
(907) 276-4880

Community Legal Services
Volunteer Lawyers of Maricopa County
305 So. 2nd Ave., P.O. Box 21538
Phoenix, AZ 85036
(602) 258-3434

Berkeley Community Law Center
3130 Shattuck Ave.
Berkeley, CA 94705
(510) 548-4040
(51)) 548-2566 (fax)

Central Valley AIDS Team
625 N. Palm Ave.
Fresno, CA 93744
(209) 264-2127
(209) 268-3541 (fax)

AIDS Service Foundation of Orange County
17982 Sky Park Circle, Suite J
Irvine, CA 92714
(714) 253-1500

AIDS Project of Los Angeles
Dept. of Legal Services
1313 N. Vine St.
Los Angeles, CA 90028
(213) 993-1503
(213) 993-1594 (fax)

AIDS/HIV Discrimination Unit
Los Angeles City Attorney's Office
200 N. Main St., Suite 1600
Los Angeles, CA 90012
(213) 485-4579

Desert AIDS Project
750 S. Vella Rd.
Palm Springs, CA 92264
(619) 323-2118
(619)323-9865 (fax)

Legal Services of Northern California
1370 West St.
Redding, CA 96001
(916) 341-3565
(800) 822-9687
(916) 241-3982 (fax)

AIDS Foundation San Diego
4080 Center St., Suite 101
San Diego, CA 92103
(619) 686-5050
(619) 497-5252 (fax)

AIDS Legal Referral Panel
114 Sansome St., Suite 1129
San Francisco, CA 94104
(415) 291-5454

AIDS Legal Services
111 West St. John, Suite 315
San Jose, CA 95113
(408) 293-3135
(408) 293-0106 (fax)
(408) 294-5667 (TTD)

Santa Cruz AIDS Legal Referral Panel/
    Santa Cruz AIDS Project
P.O. Box 557
Santa Cruz, CA 95061
(408) 427-3900
(408) 458-1878 (fax

San Joaquin AIDS Foundation
4410 N. Pershing, Suite C4
Stockton, CA 95207
(209) 476-8533

Legal Center for Persons with Disabilities
    HIV/AIDS Program
455 Sherman St., Suite 130
Denver, CO 80203
(303) 722-0300
(800) 288-1376

Colorado AIDS Project
P.O. Box 18529
Denver, CO 80218
(303) 830-2437
(800) 333-2437

Bridgeport Women's Program
211 Middle St.
Bridgeport, CT 06604
(203) 333-1822

Hispanos Unidos Contra EL SIDA/AIDS
850 Grand Ave., Suite 202
New Haven, CT 06511
(203) 781-0226

Whitman-Walker Clinic
    Legal Services Project
1407 S St., NW
Washington, DC 20009
(202) 797-3527

AIDS Help, Inc.
P.O. Box 4374
Key West, FL 33041
(305) 296-6196
(800) 640-3867

Escambia AIDS Services & Education
P.O. Box 13584
Pensacola, FL 32591
(904) 456-7079

Florida Bar Individual Rights Committee
AIDS Legal Defense Panel
650 Apalachee Parkway
Tallahassee, FL 32399
(904) 561-5600
(800) 342-8060

AIDS Legal Project
151 Spring St., NW
Atlanta, GA 30303
(404) 614-3969

AIDS Legal Council of Chicago
220 South State St., Suite 1800
Chicago, IL 60604
(312) 427-8990

HIV/AIDS Legal Project
151 N. Delaware, Suite 1800
Indianapolis, IN 46204
(317) 631-9410

University of Iowa College of Law
AIDS Representation Project
Iowa City, IA 52242
(319) 335-9023

AIDSLaw of Louisiana
P.O. Box 30203
New Orleans, LA 70190
(504) 944-5035
(800) 375-5035

University of Maryland Law School
AIDS Legal Clinic
510 West Baltimore St.
Baltimore, MD 21201
(410) 706-3295

AIDS Action Committee
Legal Services Subcommittee
131 Claredon St.
Boston, MA 02116
(617) 437-6200

AIDS Law Clinic
122 Boylston
Jamaica Plain, MA 02130
(617) 522-3003

AIDS Project Worcester
85 Green St.
Worcester, MA 01604
(508) 756-5532

AIDS Legal Referral Service
1234 Porter
Detroit, MI 48226
(313) 964-4188

Minnesota American Indian AIDS TaskForce
1433 E. Franklin
Minneapolis, MN 55404
(612) 870-1723

Minnesota AIDS Project Legal Program
1400 Park Ave. S.
Minneapolis, MN 55404
(612) 341-2060

Good Samaritan Project
3030 Walnut St.
Kansas City, MO 64108
(816) 561-8784

Nevada AIDS Foundation
P.O. Box 478
Reno, NV 89504
(702) 329-2437

Albany Law School, Law Clinic
Albany, NY
(518) 463-8182

Brooklyn AIDS Task Force
465 Dean St.
Brooklyn, NY 11217
(718) 783-0883
and
470 Bergen St.
Brooklyn, NY 11217
(718) 499-0352 (women only)

AIDS Community Services, Legal Services
2269 Sawmill River Rd., Bldg. 1-S
Elmsford, NY 10523
(914) 345-8888

Nassau/Suffolk Law Services
David Project
1 Helen Keller Way
Hempstead, NY 11550
(516) 292-8100

Long Island Association for AIDS Care
Education and Direct Services
P.O. Box 2859
Huntington Station, NY 11746
(516) 385-2437

ACLU Aids Project
132 W. 43rd St.
New York, NY 10036
(212) 944-9800

Gay Men's Health Crises
Department of Legal Services
121A W. 20th St.
New York, NY 10011
(212) 337-3504

Volunteer Lawyers Program
P.O. Drawer 1731
Raleigh, NC 27602
(919) 828-4647

Health Issues Task Force
2728 Euclid Ave.
Cleveland, OH 44115
(216) 621-0766

Columbus AIDS Task Force
1500 West 3rd Ave., Suite 329
Columbus, OH 43212
(614) 488-2437

Cascade AIDS Project
620 SW 5th Ave., Suite 300
Portland, OR 97204
(503) 223-5907

AIDS Law Project of Pennsylvania
1211 Chestnut St., Suite 1200
Philadelphia, PA 19107
(215) 587-9377

Pittsburgh AIDS Task Force
905 West St., 4th Floor
Pittsburgh, PA 15221
(412) 242-2500

Palmetto AIDS Life Support Services
P.O. Box 11705
Columbia, SC 29211
(803) 779-7257
(800) 922-7319

Capital Area AIDS Legal Project
P.O. Box 4874
Austin, TX 78765
(512) 406-6655

AIDS Outreach Center
1125 W. Peter Smith
Ft. Worth, TX 76104
(817) 335-1994

Houston Volunteer Lawyers Program
806 Main, Suite 1600
Houston, TX 77002
(713) 228-0732

Brattleboro AIDS Project
P.O. Box 1486
67 Main St.
Brattleboro, VT 05302
(802) 254-4444

Fan Free Clinic
Richmond AIDS Information Network
1721 Hanover Ave.
Richmond, VA 23220
(804) 358-6343

Volunteer Lawyers for People with AIDS
Bank of California Building, Suite 600
900 4th Ave., Seattle, WA 98164
(206) 624-4772

Center for Public Representation
AIDS Legal Services Project
121 South Pinckney St.
Madison, WI 53703
(608) 251-4008 ■

Appendix

CONTENTS

Durable Power of Attorney for Financial Management

WARNING TO PERSON EXECUTING THIS DOCUMENT

THIS IS AN IMPORTANT LEGAL DOCUMENT. IT CREATES A DURABLE POWER OF ATTORNEY. BEFORE EXECUTING THIS DOCUMENT, YOU SHOULD KNOW THESE IMPORTANT FACTS:

THIS DOCUMENT MAY PROVIDE THE PERSON YOU DESIGNATE AS YOUR ATTORNEY-IN-FACT WITH BROAD POWERS TO MANAGE, DISPOSE, SELL AND CONVEY YOUR REAL AND PERSONAL PROPERTY AND TO BORROW MONEY USING YOUR PROPERTY AS SECURITY FOR THE LOAN.

THESE POWERS WILL EXIST FOR AN INDEFINITE PERIOD OF TIME UNLESS YOU LIMIT THEIR DURATION IN THIS DOCUMENT. THESE POWERS WILL CONTINUE TO EXIST NOTWITHSTANDING YOUR SUBSEQUENT DISABILITY OR INCAPACITY.

THIS DOCUMENT DOES NOT AUTHORIZE ANYONE TO MAKE MEDICAL OR OTHER HEALTH CARE DECISIONS FOR YOU.

YOU HAVE THE RIGHT TO REVOKE OR TERMINATE THIS POWER OF ATTORNEY.

IF THERE IS ANYTHING ABOUT THIS FORM THAT YOU DO NOT UNDERSTAND, YOU SHOULD ASK A LAWYER TO EXPLAIN IT TO YOU.

1. Attorney-in-Fact

I, _____

of _____,

appoint _____ of _____

as my attorney-in-fact to act for me in any lawful way with respect to the powers delegated in Part 6 below. If that person (or all of those persons, if more than one is named) does not serve or ceases to serve as attorney-in-fact, I appoint _____

of _____ to serve as attorney-in-fact.

2. More Than One Attorney-in-Fact

a. Authorization

If more than one attorney-in-fact is designated, they are authorized to act:

☐ jointly. ☐ independently.

b. Resolution of Disputes

☐   If my attorneys-in-fact cannot agree on a decision or action under the authority delegated to them in this durable power of attorney, that dispute shall be resolved by binding arbitration. The arbitration shall be carried out by a single arbitrator, who shall be _____, if available. The arbitration shall begin within five days of written notice by any attorney-in-fact to the arbitrator that a dispute between the attorneys-in-fact has arisen. The details of the arbitration shall be determined by the arbitrator. The written decision of the arbitrator shall be binding on all my attorneys-in-fact.

3. Delegation of Authority

My attorney-in-fact ☐ may ☐ may not delegate, in writing, any authority granted under this durable power of attorney to a person he or she selects. Any such delegation shall state the period during which it is valid and specify the extent of the delegation.

4. Effective Date

This power of attorney is effective:

☐   immediately, and shall continue in effect if I become incapacitated or disabled.

☐   only if I become incapacitated or disabled and unable to manage my financial affairs.

5. Determination of Incapacity

For purposes of this durable power of attorney, my incapacity or disability shall be determined by written declarations by ☐ one ☐ two licensed physician(s). Each declaration shall be made under penalty of perjury and shall state that in the physician's opinion I am substantially unable to manage my financial affairs. If possible, the declaration(s) shall be made by _____ _____. No licensed physician shall be liable to me for any actions taken under this part which are done in good faith.

6. Powers of Attorney-in-Fact

I hereby grant to my attorney-in-fact power to act on my behalf in the following matters, as indicated by my initials by each granted power or on line a, granting all the listed powers.

Powers that are **not** initialed are **not** granted.

INITIALS

_____	a. ALL POWERS (b THROUGH m) LISTED BELOW.
_____	b. Real estate transactions.
_____	c. Tangible personal property transactions.
_____	d. Stock and bond, commodity, option and other securities transactions.
_____	e. Banking and other financial institution transactions.
_____	f. Business operating transactions.
_____	g. Insurance and annuity transactions.
_____	h. Estate, trust, and other beneficiary transactions.
_____	i. Claims and litigation.
_____	j. Personal and family maintenance.
_____	k. Benefits from Social Security, Medicare, Medicaid, or other governmental programs, or civil or military service.
_____	l. Retirement plan transactions.
_____	m. Tax matters.

Note: These powers are defined in Part 17, below.

7. Special Instructions to the Attorney-in-Fact

_____

_____

_____

_____

8. Compensation and Reimbursement of the Attorney-in-Fact

☐ The attorney-in-fact shall not be compensated for services, but shall be entitled to reimbursement, from the principal's assets, for reasonable expenses. Reasonable expenses include reasonable fees for information or advice from accountants, lawyers or investment experts relating to the attorney-in-fact's responsibilities under this power of attorney.

☐ The attorney-in-fact shall be entitled to reimbursement for reasonable expenses and reasonable compensation for his or her services. Reasonable compensation shall be determined exclusively by the attorney-in-fact.

☐ The attorney-in-fact shall be entitled to reimbursement for reasonable expenses and compensation for his or her services of $_____ per _____ .

9. Nomination of Conservator or Guardian

If, in a court proceeding, it is ever resolved that I need a conservator, guardian or other person to administer and supervise my estate or person, I nominate my attorney-in-fact to serve in that capacity. If my attorney-in-fact cannot serve, I nominate the successor attorney-in-fact nominated in Part 1 to serve.

10. Personal Benefit to Attorney-in-Fact

☐   My attorney-in-fact may buy any assets of mine or engage in any transaction he or she deems in good faith to be in my interest, no matter what the interest of or benefit to my attorney-in-fact.

☐   My attorney-in-fact may not be personally involved in or benefit personally from any transaction he or she engages in on my behalf, except _____.

☐   My attorney-in-fact may not be personally involved in or benefit personally from any transaction he or she engages in on my behalf.

11. Commingling by Attorney-in-Fact

My attorney-in-fact ☐ may   ☐ may not   mix (commingle) any of my funds with any funds of his or hers.

12. Bond

The attorney-in-fact shall serve without bond.

13. Liability of Attorney-in-Fact

My attorney-in-fact shall not incur any liability to me, my estate, my heirs, successors or assigns for acting or refraining from acting under this document, except for willful misconduct or gross negligence. My attorney-in-fact is not required to make my assets produce income, increase the value of my estate, diversify my investments or enter into transactions authorized by this document, as long as my attorney-in-fact believes his or her actions are in my best interests or in the best interests of my estate and of those interested in my estate. A successor attorney-in-fact shall not be liable for acts of a prior attorney-in-fact.

14. Gifts by Attorney-in-Fact

My attorney-in-fact may not (i) appoint, assign or designate any of my assets, interests or rights directly or indirectly to himself or herself, or his or her estate or creditors, or the creditors of his or her estate, (ii) disclaim assets to which I would otherwise be entitled if the effect of the disclaimer is to cause such assets to pass directly or indirectly to my attorney-in-fact or his or her estate, or (iii) use my assets to discharge any of his or her legal obligations, including any obligation of support owed to others (excluding me and those whom I am legally obligated to support).

15. Reliance on this Power of Attorney

I agree that any third party who receives a copy of this document may rely on and act under it. Revocation of the power of attorney is not effective as to a third party until the third party has actual knowledge of the revocation. I agree to indemnify the third party for any claims that arise against the third party because of reliance on this power of attorney.

16. Severability

If any provision of this document is ruled unenforceable, the remaining provisions shall stay in effect.

17. Construction of Powers Granted to the Attorney-in-Fact

The powers granted in Part 6 above authorize the attorney-in-fact to do the following:

b. Real estate transactions

Act for the principal in any manner to deal with all or any part of any interest in real property that the principal owns at the time of execution or thereafter acquires, under such terms, conditions and covenants as the attorney-in-fact deems proper. The attorney-in-fact's powers include but are not limited to the power to:

(1) Accept as a gift, or as security for a loan, reject, demand, buy, lease, receive or otherwise acquire ownership of possession of any estate or interest in real property.

(2) Sell, exchange, convey with or without covenants, quitclaim, release, surrender, mortgage, encumber, partition or consent to the partitioning of, grant options concerning, lease, sublet or otherwise dispose of any interest in real property.

(3) Maintain, repair, improve, insure, rent, lease, and pay or contest taxes or assessments on any estate or interest in real property owned, or claimed to be owned, by the principal.

(4) Prosecute, defend, intervene in, submit to arbitration, settle and propose or accept a compromise with respect to any claim in favor of or against the principal based on or involving any real estate transaction.

c. Tangible personal property transactions

Act for the principal in any manner to deal with all or any part of any interest in personal property that the principal owns at the time of execution or thereafter acquires, under such terms as the attorney-in-fact deems proper. The attorney-in-fact's powers include but are not limited to the power to:

Lease, buy, exchange, accept as a gift or as security for a loan, acquire, possess, maintain, repair, improve, insure, rent, lease, sell, convey, mortgage, pledge, and pay or contest taxes and assessments on any tangible personal property.

d. Stock and bond, commodity, option and other securities transactions

Do any act which the principal can do through an agent, with respect to any interest in a bond, share, other instrument of similar character or commodity. The attorney-in-fact's powers include but are not limited to the power to:

(1) Accept as a gift or as security for a loan, reject, demand, buy, receive or otherwise acquire ownership or possession of any bond, share, instrument of similar character, commodity interest or any instrument with respect thereto, together with the interest, dividends, proceeds or other distributions connected with it.

(2) Sell (including short sales), exchange, transfer, release, surrender, pledge, trade in or otherwise dispose of any bond, share, instrument of similar character or commodity interest.

(3) Demand, receive and obtain any money or other thing of value to which the principal is or may become or may claim to be entitled as the proceeds of any interest in a bond, share, other instrument of similar character or commodity interest.

(4) Agree and contract, in any manner, and with any broker or other person and on any terms, for the accomplishment of any purpose listed in this section.

(5) Execute, acknowledge, seal and deliver any instrument the attorney-in-fact thinks useful to accomplish a purpose listed in this section, or any report or certificate required by law or regulation.

e. Banking and other financial institution transactions

Do any act that the principal can do through an agent in connection with any banking transaction that might affect the financial or other interests of the principal. The attorney-in-fact's powers include but are not limited to the power to:

(1) Continue, modify and terminate any deposit account or other banking arrangement, or open either in the name of the agent alone or in the name of the principal alone or in both their names jointly, a deposit account of any type in any financial institution, rent a safe deposit box or vault space, have access to a safe deposit box or vault to which the principal would have access, and make other contracts with the institution.

(2) Make, sign and deliver checks or drafts, withdraw by check, order or otherwise

funds or property of the principal from any financial institution.

(3) Prepare financial statements concerning the assets and liabilities or income and expenses of the principal and deliver them to any financial institution, and receive statements, notices or other documents from any financial institution.

(4) Borrow money from a financial institution on terms the attorney-in-fact deems acceptable, give security out of the assets of the principal, and pay, renew or extend the time of payment of any note given by or on behalf of the principal.

f. Business operating transactions

Do any act that the principal can do through an agent in connection with any business operated by the principal that the attorney-in-fact deems desirable. The attorney-in-fact's powers include but are not limited to the power to:

(1) Perform any duty and exercise any right, privilege or option which the principal has or claims to have under any contract of partnership, enforce the terms of any partnership agreement, and defend, submit to arbitration or settle any legal proceeding to which the principal is a party because of membership in a partnership.

(2) Exercise in person or by proxy and enforce any right, privilege or option which the principal has as the holder of any bond, share or instrument of similar character and defend, submit to arbitration or settle a legal proceeding to which the principal is a party because of any such bond, share or instrument of similar character.

(3) With respect to a business owned solely by the principal, continue, modify, extend or terminate any contract on behalf of the principal, demand and receive all money that is due or claimed by the principal and use such funds in the operation of the business, engage in banking transactions the attorney-in-fact deems desirable, determine the location of the operation, the nature of the business it undertakes, its name, methods of manufacturing, selling, marketing, financing, accounting, form of organization and insurance, and hiring and paying employees and independent contractors.

(4) Execute, acknowledge, seal and deliver any instrument of any kind that the attorney-in-fact thinks useful to accomplish any purpose listed in this section.

(5) Pay, compromise or contest business taxes or assessments.

(6) Demand and receive money or other things of value to which the principal is or claims to be entitled as the proceeds of any business operation, and conserve, invest, disburse or use anything so received for purposes listed in this section.

g. Insurance and annuity transactions

Do any act that the principal can do through an agent, in connection with any insurance or annuity policy, that the attorney-in-fact deems desirable. The attorney-in-fact's powers include but are not limited to the power to:

(1) Continue, pay the premium on, modify, rescind or terminate any policy of life, accident, health, disability or liability insurance procured by or on behalf of the principal before the execution of this power of attorney. The attorney-in-fact cannot name himself or herself as beneficiary of a renewal, extension or substitute for such a policy unless he or she was already the beneficiary before the principal signed the power of attorney.

(2) Procure new, different or additional contracts of health, disability, accident or liability insurance on the life of the principal, modify, rescind or terminate any such contract and designate the beneficiary of any such contract.

(3) Sell, assign, borrow on, pledge, or surrender and receive the cash surrender value of any policy.

h. Estate, trust, and other beneficiary transactions

Act for the principal in all matters that affect a trust, probate estate, guardianship, conservatorship, escrow, custodianship or other fund from which the principal is, may become or claims to be entitled, as a beneficiary, to a share or payment.

i. Claims and litigation

Act for the principal in all matters that affect claims of or against the principal and proceedings in any court or administrative body. The attorney-in-fact's powers include but are not limited to the power to:

(1) Assert any claim or defense before any court, administrative board or other tribunal.

(2) Submit to arbitration or mediation or settle any claim in favor of or against the principal or any litigation to which the principal is a party, pay any judgment or settlement and receive any money or other things of value paid in settlement.

j. Personal and family maintenance

To do all acts necessary to maintain the customary standard of living of the principal, the spouse and children and other persons customarily or legally entitled to be supported by the principal. The attorney-in-fact's powers include but are not limited to the power to:

(1) Pay for medical, dental and surgical care, living quarters, usual vacations and travel expenses, shelter, clothing, food, appropriate education and other living costs.

(2) Continue arrangements with respect to automobiles or other means of transportation, charge accounts, discharge of any services or duties assumed by the principal

to any parent, relative or friend, contributions or payments incidental to membership or affiliation in any church, club, society or other organization.

k. Benefits from Social Security, Medicare, Medicaid, or other governmental programs, or civil or military service

Act for the principal in all matters that affect the principal's right to government benefits. The attorney-in-fact's powers include but are not limited to the power to:

(1) Prepare, execute, file, prosecute, defend, submit to arbitration or settle a claim on behalf of the principal to benefits or assistance, financial or otherwise.

(2) Receive the proceeds of such a claim and conserve, invest, disburse or use them on behalf of the principal.

l. Retirement plan transactions

Act for the principal in all matters that affect the principal's retirement plans. The attorney-in-fact's powers include but are not limited to the power to:

Select payment options under any retirement plan in which the principal participates, make contributions to those plans, exercise investment options, receive payment from a plan, roll over plan benefits into other retirement plans, designate beneficiaries under those plans and change existing designations.

m. Tax matters

Act for the principal in all matters that affect the principal's local, state and federal taxes. The attorney-in-fact's powers include but are not limited to the power to:

(1) Prepare, sign and file federal, state, local and foreign income, gift, payroll, Federal Insurance Contributions Act returns and other tax returns, claims for refunds, requests for extension of time, petitions, any power of attorney required by the Internal Revenue Service or other taxing authority, and other documents.

(2) Pay taxes due, collect refunds, post bonds, receive confidential information, exercise any election available to the principal and contest deficiencies determined by a taxing authority.

I understand the importance of the powers I delegate to my attorney-in-fact in this document. I recognize that the document gives my attorney-in-fact broad powers over my assets, and that these powers will become effective as of the date of my incapacity (or sooner if specified in this document) and continue indefinitely unless I revoke this durable power of attorney.

Signed this _____ day of_____ 19_____.

State of _____ County of _____

_____   _____
Your Signature   Your Social Security Number

Witnesses:

On the date written above, the principal declared to me that this instrument is his or her durable power of attorney for financial management, and that he or she willingly executed it as a free and voluntary act. The principal signed this instrument in my presence.

Name: _____   Name: _____

Address: _____   Address:_____

_____   _____

Certificate of Acknowledgement of Notary Public

State of _____

County of _____ } ss

On _____, 19 _____ , before me,

_____, a notary public, personally appeared

_____,_____ personally known to me or proved to me on the basis of satisfactory evidence to be the person whose name is subscribed to this instrument, and acknowledged that he or she executed it.

_____

Notary Public for the State of _____

(NOTARY SEAL)   My commission expires: _____

California Statutory Durable Power of Attorney (Health Care)

WARNING TO PERSON EXECUTING THIS DOCUMENT

THIS IS AN IMPORTANT LEGAL DOCUMENT. IT CREATES A DURABLE POWER OF ATTORNEY FOR HEALTH CARE. BEFORE EXECUTING THIS DOCUMENT, YOU SHOULD KNOW THESE IMPORTANT FACTS.

THIS DOCUMENT GIVES THE PERSON YOU DESIGNATE AS YOUR AGENT (THE ATTORNEY-IN-FACT) THE POWER TO MAKE HEALTH CARE DECISIONS FOR YOU. YOUR AGENT MUST ACT CONSISTENTLY WITH YOUR DESIRES AS STATED IN THIS DOCUMENT OR OTHERWISE MADE KNOWN.

EXCEPT AS YOU OTHERWISE SPECIFY IN THIS DOCUMENT, THIS DOCUMENT GIVES YOUR AGENT THE POWER TO CONSENT TO YOUR DOCTOR NOT GIVING TREATMENT OR STOPPING TREATMENT NECESSARY TO KEEP YOU ALIVE.

NOTWITHSTANDING THIS DOCUMENT, YOU HAVE THE RIGHT TO MAKE MEDICAL AND OTHER HEALTH CARE DECISIONS FOR YOURSELF SO LONG AS YOU CAN GIVE INFORMED CONSENT WITH RESPECT TO THE PARTICULAR DECISION. IN ADDITION, NO TREATMENT MAY BE GIVEN TO YOU OVER YOUR OBJECTION, AND HEALTH CARE NECESSARY TO KEEP YOU ALIVE MAY NOT BE STOPPED OR WITHHELD IF YOU OBJECT AT THE TIME.

THIS DOCUMENT GIVES YOUR AGENT AUTHORITY TO CONSENT, TO REFUSE TO CONSENT, OR TO WITHDRAW CONSENT TO ANY CARE, TREATMENT, SERVICE, OR PROCEDURE TO MAINTAIN, DIAGNOSE, OR TREAT A PHYSICAL OR MENTAL CONDITION. THIS POWER IS SUBJECT TO ANY STATEMENT OF YOUR DESIRES AND ANY LIMITATIONS THAT YOU INCLUDE IN THIS DOCUMENT. YOU MAY STATE IN THIS DOCUMENT ANY TYPES OF TREATMENT THAT YOU DO NOT DESIRE. IN ADDITION, A COURT CAN TAKE AWAY THE POWER OF YOUR AGENT TO MAKE HEALTH CARE DECISIONS FOR YOU IF YOUR AGENT (1) AUTHORIZES ANYTHING THAT IS ILLEGAL, (2) ACTS CONTRARY TO YOUR KNOWN DESIRES, OR (3) WHERE YOUR DESIRES ARE NOT KNOWN, DOES ANYTHING THAT IS CLEARLY CONTRARY TO YOUR BEST INTERESTS.

THE POWERS GIVEN BY THIS DOCUMENT WILL EXIST FOR AN INDEFINITE PERIOD OF TIME UNLESS YOU LIMIT THEIR DURATION IN THIS DOCUMENT.

YOU HAVE THE RIGHT TO REVOKE THE AUTHORITY OF YOUR AGENT BY NOTIFYING YOUR AGENT OR YOUR TREATING DOCTOR, HOSPITAL, OR OTHER HEALTH CARE PROVIDER ORALLY OR IN WRITING OF THE REVOCATION.

YOUR AGENT HAS THE RIGHT TO EXAMINE YOUR MEDICAL RECORDS AND TO CONSENT TO THEIR DISCLOSURE UNLESS YOU LIMIT THIS RIGHT IN THIS DOCUMENT.

UNLESS YOU OTHERWISE SPECIFY IN THIS DOCUMENT, THIS DOCUMENT GIVES YOUR AGENT THE POWER AFTER YOU DIE TO (1) AUTHORIZE AN AUTOPSY, (2) DONATE YOUR BODY OR PARTS THEREOF FOR TRANSPLANT OR THERAPEUTIC OR EDUCATIONAL OR SCIENTIFIC PURPOSES, AND (3) DIRECT THE DISPOSITION OF YOUR REMAINS.

IF THERE IS ANYTHING IN THIS DOCUMENT THAT YOU DO NOT UNDERSTAND, YOU SHOULD ASK A LAWYER TO EXPLAIN IT TO YOU.

THIS POWER OF ATTORNEY WILL NOT BE VALID FOR MAKING HEALTH CARE DECISIONS UNLESS IT IS EITHER (1) SIGNED BY TWO QUALIFIED ADULT WITNESSES WHO PERSONALLY KNOW YOU AND WHO ARE PRESENT WHEN YOU SIGN OR ACKNOWLEDGE YOUR SIGNATURE OR (2) ACKNOWLEDGED BEFORE A NOTARY PUBLIC IN CALIFORNIA.

Durable Power of Attorney for Health Care

1. Creation of Durable Power of Attorney

To my family, relatives, friends and my physicians, health care providers, community care facilities and any other person who may have an interest or duty in my medical care or treatment: I, _____,
being of sound mind, willfully and voluntarily intend to create by this document a durable power of attorney for my health care by appointing the person designated as my attorney-in-fact to make health care decisions for me in the event I become incapacitated and am unable to make health care decisions for myself. This power of attorney shall not be affected by my subsequent incapacity.

2. Designation of Attorney-in-Fact

The person designated to be my attorney-in-fact for health care in the event I become incapacitated is _____ of _____
_____. If _____
_____ for any reason shall fail to serve or ceases to serve as my attorney-in- fact for health care, _____ of
_____ shall be my attorney-in-fact for health care.

3. Effective on Incapacity

This durable power of attorney shall become effective in the event I become incapacitated and am unable to make health care decisions for myself, in which case it shall become effective as of the date of the written statement by a physician, as provided in Paragraph 4.

4. Determination of Incapacity

The determination that I have become incapacitated and am unable to make health care decisions shall be made in writing by a licensed physician. If possible, the determination shall be made by _____

_____.

5. Authority of My Attorney-in-Fact

My attorney-in-fact shall have all lawful authority permissible to make health care decisions for me, including the authority to consent, or withdraw consent or refuse consent to any care, treatment, service or procedure to maintain, diagnose or treat my physical or mental condition, EXCEPT _____

_____

_____.

6. Inspection and Disclosure of Information Relating to My Physical or Mental Health

Subject to any limitations in this document, my attorney-in-fact has the power and authority to do all of the following:

(a) Request, review, and receive any information, verbal or written, regarding my physical or mental health, including, but not limited to, medical and hospital records.

(b) Execute on my behalf any releases or other documents that may be required in order to obtain this information.

(c) Consent to the disclosure of this information.

7. Signing Documents, Waivers, and Releases

Where necessary to implement the health care decisions that my attorney-in-fact is authorized by this document to make, my attorney-in-fact has the power and authority to execute on my behalf all of the following:

(a) Documents titled or purporting to be a "Refusal to Permit Treatment" and "Leaving Hospital Against Medical Advice."

(b) Any necessary waiver or release from liability required by a hospital or physician.

8. Duration

I intend that this Durable Power of Attorney remain effective until my death, or until revoked by me in writing.

Executed this _____ day of _____,

19___ at _____.

_____
Principal

Statement of Witnesses

(This document must be witnessed by two qualified adult witnesses. None of the following may be used as a witness: (1) a person you designate as your agent or alternate agent, (2) a health care provider, (3) an employee of a health care provider, (4) the operator of a community care facility, (5) an employee of an operator of a community care facility, (6) the operator of a residential care facility for the elderly, (7) an employee of an operator of a residential care facility for the elderly. At least one of the witnesses must make the additional declaration set out following the place where the witnesses sign.)

(READ CAREFULLY BEFORE SIGNING. You can sign as a witness only if you personally know the principal or the identity of the principal is proved to you by convincing evidence.)

(To have convincing evidence of the identity of the principal, you must be presented with and reasonably rely on any one or more of the following:

(1) An identification card or driver's license issued by the California Department of Motor Vehicles that is current or has been issued within five years.

(2) A passport issued by the Department of State of the United States that is current or has been issued within five years.

(3) Any of the following documents if the document is current or has been issued within five years and contains a photograph and description of the person named on it, is signed by the person, and bears a serial or other identifying number:

(a) A passport issued by a foreign government that has been stamped by the United States Immigration and Naturalization Service.

(b) A driver's license issued by a state other than California or by a Canadian or Mexican public agency authorized to issue drivers' licenses.

(c) An identification card issued by a state other than California.

(d) An identification card issued by any branch of the armed forces of the United States.)

(Other kinds of proof of identity are not allowed.)

I declare under penalty of perjury under the laws of California that the person who signed or acknowledged this document is personally known to me (or proved to me on the basis of convincing evidence) to be the principal, that the principal signed or acknowledged this Durable Power of Attorney in my presence, that the principal appears to be of sound mind and under no duress, fraud, or undue influence, that I am not the person appointed as attorney-in-fact by this document, and that I am not a health care provider, an employee of a health care provider, the operator of a community care facility, nor an employee of an operator of a community care facility, an operator of a residential care facility for the elderly, nor an employee of an operator of a residential care facility for the elderly.

Signature: _____ Print Name: _____
Residence Address: _____
Date: _____

Signature: _____ Print Name: _____
Residence Address: _____
Date: _____

(AT LEAST ONE OF THE ABOVE WITNESSES MUST ALSO SIGN THE FOLLOWING DECLARATION.)

I further declare under penalty of perjury under the laws of California that I am not related to the principal by blood, marriage, or adoption, and, to the best of my knowledge, I am not entitled to any part of the estate of the principal upon the death of the principal under a will now existing or by operation of law.

Signature: _____

Signature: _____

Statement of Patient Advocate or Ombudsman

(If you are a patient in a skilled nursing facility, one of the witnesses must be a patient advocate or ombudsman. The following statement is required only if you are a patient in a skilled nursing facility—a health care facility that provides the following basic services: skilled nursing care and supportive care to patients whose primary need is for availability of skilled nursing care on an extended basis. The patient advocate or ombudsman must sign both parts of the "Statement of Witnesses" above AND must also sign the following statement.)

I further declare under penalty of perjury under the laws of California that I am a patient advocate or ombudsman as designated by the State Department of Aging and that I am serving as a witness as required by subdivision (e) of Section 4701 of the Probate Code.

Signature:_____

Notarization

State of California

County of _____ } ss

On this _____ day of _____, in the year 19___, before me, a Notary Public, State of California, duly commissioned and sworn, personally appeared _____, personally known to me (or proved to me on the basis of satisfactory evidence) to be the person whose name is subscribed to this instrument, and acknowledged that _____ executed it. I declare under penalty of perjury that the person whose name is subscribed to this instrument appears to be of sound mind and under no duress, fraud, or undue influence.

_____
Signature of Notary Public

[Notary Seal]   Notary Public for the State of California

My commission expires:_____, 19_____

Florida Designation of Health Care Surrogate

Name:_____ (Last) _____ (First)

_____ (Middle Initial)

In the event that I have been determined to be incapacitated to provide informed consent for medical treatment and surgical and diagnostic procedures, I wish to designate as my surrogate for health care decisions:

Name:_____

Address:_____

_____

Phone: _____

If my surrogate is unwilling or unable to perform his duties, I wish to designate as my alternate surrogate:

Name:_____

Address:_____

_____

Phone: _____

I fully understand that this designation will permit my designee to make health care decisions and to provide, withhold, or withdraw consent on my behalf; to apply for public benefits to defray the cost of health care; and to authorize my admission to or transfer from a health care facility. Additional instructions (optional).

_____

_____

I further affirm that this designation is not being made as a condition of treatment or admission to a health care facility. I will notify and send a copy of this document to the following persons other than my surrogate, so they may know who my surrogate is:

Name: _____

Name: _____

Signed: _____

Date: _____

Witnesses: 1. _____

                    2. _____

Illinois Statutory Short Form
Power of Attorney for Health Care

(NOTICE: THE PURPOSE OF THIS POWER OF ATTORNEY IS TO GIVE THE PERSON YOU DESIGNATE (YOUR "AGENT") BROAD POWERS TO MAKE HEALTH CARE DECISIONS FOR YOU, INCLUDING POWER TO REQUIRE, CONSENT TO OR WITHDRAW ANY TYPE OF PERSONAL CARE OR MEDICAL TREATMENT FOR ANY PHYSICAL OR MENTAL CONDITION AND TO ADMIT YOU TO OR DISCHARGE YOU FROM ANY HOSPITAL, HOME OR OTHER INSTITUTION. THIS FORM DOES NOT IMPOSE A DUTY ON YOUR AGENT TO EXERCISE GRANTED POWERS; BUT WHEN A POWER IS EXERCISED, YOUR AGENT WILL HAVE TO USE DUE CARE TO ACT FOR YOUR BENEFIT AND IN ACCORDANCE WITH THIS FORM. A COURT CAN TAKE AWAY THE POWERS OF YOUR AGENT IF IT FINDS THE AGENT IS NOT ACTING PROPERLY. YOU MAY NAME SUCCESSOR AGENTS UNDER THIS FORM BUT NOT CO-AGENTS, AND NO HEALTH CARE PROVIDER MAY BE NAMED. UNLESS YOU EXPRESSLY LIMIT THE DURATION OF THIS POWER IN THE MANNER PROVIDED BELOW, UNTIL YOU REVOKE THIS POWER OR A COURT ACTING ON YOUR BEHALF TERMINATES IT, YOUR AGENT MAY EXERCISE THE POWERS GIVEN HERE THROUGHOUT YOUR LIFETIME, EVEN AFTER YOU BECOME DISABLED. THE POWERS YOU GIVE YOUR AGENT, YOUR RIGHT TO REVOKE THOSE POWERS AND THE PENALTIES FOR VIOLATING THE LAW ARE EXPLAINED MORE FULLY IN SECTIONS 4-5, 4-6, 4-9 AND 4-10(b) OF THE ILLINOIS "POWERS OF ATTORNEY FOR HEALTH CARE LAW" OF WHICH THIS FORM IS A PART. THAT LAW EXPRESSLY PERMITS THE USE OF ANY DIFFERENT FORM OF POWER OF ATTORNEY YOU MAY DESIRE. IF THERE IS ANYTHING ABOUT THIS FORM THAT YOU DO NOT UNDERSTAND, YOU SHOULD ASK A LAWYER TO EXPLAIN IT TO YOU.)

POWER OF ATTORNEY MADE THIS . . . . DAY OF . . . .
month and year

1. I, _____
insert name and address of principal

_____

hereby appoint: _____
insert name and address of agent

_____

as my attorney-in-fact (my "agent") to act for me and in my name (in any way I could act in person) to make any and all decisions for me concerning my personal care, medical treatment, hospitalization and health care and to require, withhold or withdraw any type of medical treatment or procedure, even though my death may ensue. My agent shall have the same access to my medical records that I have, including the right to disclose the contents to others. My agent shall also have full power to make a disposition of any part or all of my body for medical purposes, authorize an autopsy and direct the disposition of my remains.

(THE ABOVE GRANT OF POWERS IS INTENDED TO BE AS BROAD AS POSSIBLE SO THAT YOUR AGENT WILL HAVE AUTHORITY TO MAKE ANY DECISION YOU COULD MAKE TO OBTAIN OR TERMINATE ANY TYPE OF HEALTH CARE, INCLUDING WITHDRAWAL OF FOOD AND WATER AND OTHER LIFE-SUSTAINING MEASURES, IF YOUR AGENT BELIEVES SUCH ACTION WOULD BE CONSISTENT WITH YOUR INTENT AND DESIRES. IF YOU WISH TO LIMIT THE SCOPE OF YOUR AGENT'S POWERS OR PRESCRIBE SPECIAL RULES OR LIMIT THE POWER TO MAKE AN ANATOMICAL GIFT, AUTHORIZE AUTOPSY OR DISPOSE OF REMAINS, YOU MAY DO SO IN THE FOLLOWING PARAGRAPHS.)

2. The powers granted above shall not include the following powers or shall be subject to the following rules or limitations (here you may include any specific limitations you deem appropriate, such as: your own definition of when life-sustaining measures should be withheld; a direction to continue food and fluids or life-sustaining treatment in all events; or instructions to refuse any specific types of treatment that are inconsistent with your religious beliefs or unacceptable to you for any other reason, such as blood transfusion, electro-convulsive therapy, amputation, psychosurgery, voluntary admission to a mental institution, etc.):

_____

_____

_____

_____

_____

(THE SUBJECT OF LIFE-SUSTAINING TREATMENT IS OF PARTICULAR IMPORTANCE. FOR YOUR CONVENIENCE IN DEALING WITH THAT SUBJECT, SOME GENERAL STATEMENTS CONCERNING THE WITHHOLDING OR REMOVAL OF LIFE-SUSTAINING TREATMENT ARE SET FORTH BELOW. IF YOU AGREE WITH ONE OF THESE STATEMENTS, YOU MAY INITIAL THAT STATEMENT; BUT DO NOT INITIAL MORE THAN ONE):

I do not want my life to be prolonged, nor do I want life-sustaining treatment to be provided or continued if my agent believes the burdens of the treatment outweigh the expected benefits. I want my agent to consider the relief of suffering, the expense involved and the quality as well as the possible extension of my life in making decisions concerning life-sustaining treatment.

Initialed: _____

I want my life to be prolonged and I want life-sustaining treatment to be provided or continued unless I am in a coma which my attending physician believes to be irreversible, in accordance with reasonable medical standards at the time of reference. If and when I have suffered irreversible coma, I want life-sustaining treatment to be withheld or discontinued.

Initialed: _____

I want my life to be prolonged to the greatest extent possible without regard to my condition, the chances I have for recovery or the cost of the procedures.

Initialed:_____

(THIS POWER OF ATTORNEY MAY BE AMENDED OR REVOKED BY YOU AT ANY TIME IN ANY MANNER PROVIDED IN SECTION 4-6 OF THE ILLINOIS "POWERS OF ATTORNEY FOR HEALTH CARE FORM." ABSENT AMENDMENT OR REVOCATION, THE AUTHORITY GRANTED IN THIS POWER OF ATTORNEY WILL BECOME EFFECTIVE AT THE TIME THIS POWER IS SIGNED AND WILL CONTINUE UNTIL YOUR DEATH, AND BEYOND IF ANATOMICAL GIFT, AUTOPSY OR DISPOSITION OF REMAINS IS AUTHORIZED, UNLESS A LIMITATION ON THE BEGINNING DATE OR DURATION IS MADE BY INITIALING AND COMPLETING EITHER OR BOTH OF THE FOLLOWING:)

3. (   ) This power of attorney shall become effective on _____
insert a future date or event during

your lifetime such as court determination of your disability, when you want this power to first take effect

4. (   ) This power of attorney shall terminate on _____
insert a future date or event such as court

determination of your disability, when you want this power to terminate prior to your death

(IF YOU WISH TO NAME SUCCESSOR AGENTS, INSERT THE NAMES AND ADDRESSES OF SUCH SUCCESSORS IN THE FOLLOWING PARAGRAPH.)

5. If any agent named by me shall die, become legally disabled, resign, refuse to act or be unavailable, I name the following (each to act alone and successively, in the order named) as successors to such agent: _____

_____

_____

(IF YOU WISH TO NAME A GUARDIAN OF YOUR PERSON IN THE EVENT A COURT DECIDES THAT ONE SHOULD BE APPOINTED, YOU MAY, BUT ARE NOT REQUIRED TO DO SO, BY INSERTING THE NAME OF SUCH GUARDIAN IN THE FOLLOWING PARAGRAPH. THE COURT WILL APPOINT THE PERSON NOMINATED BY YOU IF THE COURT FINDS THAT SUCH APPOINTMENT WILL SERVE YOUR BEST INTERESTS AND WELFARE. YOU MAY, BUT ARE NOT REQUIRED TO, NOMINATE AS YOUR GUARDIAN THE SAME PERSON NAMED IN THIS FORM AS YOUR AGENT.)

6. If a guardian of my person is to be appointed, I nominate the following to serve as such guardian: _____
insert name and address of nominated guardian of the person

_____

7. I am fully informed as to all the contents of this form and understand the full import of this grant of powers to my agent.

Signed: _____
principal

The principal has had an opportunity to read the above form and has signed the form or acknowledged his or her signature or mark on the form in my presence.

_____ Residing at: _____
witness

(YOU MAY, BUT ARE NOT REQUIRED TO, REQUEST YOUR AGENT AND SUCCESSOR AGENTS TO PROVIDE SPECIMEN SIGNATURES BELOW. IF YOU INCLUDE SPECIMEN SIGNATURES IN THIS POWER OF ATTORNEY, YOU MUST COMPLETE THE CERTIFICATION OPPOSITE THE SIGNATURES OF THE AGENTS.)

Specimen signatures of agent (and successors) | I certify that the signature of my agent (and successors) are correct.

_____   _____
agent   principal

_____   _____
successor agent   principal

_____   _____
successor agent   principal

New York Proxy for Health Care

I, _____, hereby appoint

_____

_____

name, home address and telephone number of agent

as my health care agent to make any and all health care decisions for me, except to the extent that I state otherwise.

This health care proxy shall take effect in the event I become unable to make my own health care decisions.

Note: Although not necessary, and neither encouraged nor discouraged, you may wish to state instructions or wishes, and limit your agent's authority.

Unless your agent knows your wishes about artificial nutrition and hydration [feeding tubes], your agent will not have authority to decide about artificial nutrition and hydration. If you choose to state instructions, wishes or limits, please do so below:

_____

_____

_____

I direct my agent to make health care decisions in accordance with my wishes and instructions as state above or as otherwise known to him or her. I also direct my agent to abide by any limitations on his or her authority as stated above or as otherwise known to him or her.

In the event the person I appoint above is unable, unwilling or unavailable to act as my health care agent, I hereby appoint

_____

_____

name, home address and telephone number

_____

as my health care agent.

I understand that unless I revoke it, this proxy shall remain in effect indefinitely, or until the date or occurrence of the condition I have stated below. (Complete the following if you do NOT want this health care proxy to be in effect indefinitely:)

This proxy shall expire (specify date or condition):

_____

Signature: _____

Address: _____

Date: _____

Statement by Witnesses (must be 18 or older)

I declare that the person who signed or asked another to sign this document is personally known to me and appears to be of sound mind and acting of his or her own free will. He or she signed (or asked another to sign for him or her) this document in my presence, and that person signed in my presence. I am not the person appointed as agent by this document.

Witness 1: _____

Address : _____

Witness 2: _____

Address : _____

Texas Durable Power of Attorney for Health Care

INFORMATION CONCERNING THE DURABLE POWER OF ATTORNEY FOR HEALTH CARE

THIS IS AN IMPORTANT LEGAL DOCUMENT. BEFORE SIGNING THIS DOCUMENT, YOU SHOULD KNOW THESE IMPORTANT FACTS:

EXCEPT TO THE EXTENT YOU STATE OTHERWISE, THIS DOCUMENT GIVES THE PERSON YOU NAME AS YOUR AGENT THE AUTHORITY TO MAKE ANY AND ALL HEALTH CARE DECISIONS FOR YOU IN ACCORDANCE WITH YOUR WISHES, INCLUDING YOUR RELIGIOUS AND MORAL BELIEFS, WHEN YOU ARE NO LONGER CAPABLE OF MAKING THEM YOURSELF. BECAUSE "HEALTH CARE" MEANS ANY TREATMENT, SERVICE, OR PROCEDURE TO MAINTAIN, DIAGNOSE, OR TREAT YOUR PHYSICAL OR MENTAL CONDITION, YOUR AGENT HAS THE POWER TO MAKE A BROAD RANGE OF HEALTH CARE DECISIONS FOR YOU. YOUR AGENT MAY CONSENT, REFUSE TO CONSENT, OR WITHDRAW CONSENT TO MEDICAL TREATMENT AND MAY MAKE DECISIONS ABOUT WITHDRAWING OR WITHHOLDING LIFE-SUSTAINING TREATMENT. YOUR AGENT MAY NOT CONSENT TO VOLUNTARY IN-PATIENT MENTAL HEALTH SERVICES, CONVULSIVE TREATMENT, PSYCHOSURGERY, OR ABORTION. A PHYSICIAN MUST COMPLY WITH YOUR AGENT'S INSTRUCTIONS OR ALLOW YOU TO BE TRANSFERRED TO ANOTHER PHYSICIAN.

YOUR AGENT'S AUTHORITY BEGINS WHEN YOUR DOCTOR CERTIFIES THAT YOU LACK THE CAPACITY TO MAKE HEALTH CARE DECISIONS.

YOUR AGENT IS OBLIGATED TO FOLLOW YOUR INSTRUCTIONS WHEN MAKING DECISIONS ON YOUR BEHALF. UNLESS YOU STATE OTHERWISE, YOUR AGENT HAS THE SAME AUTHORITY TO MAKE DECISIONS ABOUT YOUR HEALTH CARE AS YOU WOULD HAVE HAD.

IT IS IMPORTANT THAT YOU DISCUSS THIS DOCUMENT WITH YOUR PHYSICIAN OR OTHER HEALTH CARE PROVIDER BEFORE YOU SIGN IT TO MAKE SURE THAT YOU UNDERSTAND THE NATURE AND RANGE OF DECISIONS THAT MAY BE MADE ON YOUR BEHALF. IF YOU DO NOT HAVE A PHYSICIAN, YOU SHOULD TALK WITH SOMEONE ELSE WHO IS KNOWLEDGEABLE ABOUT THESE ISSUES AND CAN ANSWER YOUR QUESTIONS. YOU DO NOT NEED A LAWYER'S ASSISTANCE TO COMPLETE THIS DOCUMENT, BUT IF THERE IS ANYTHING IN THIS DOCUMENT THAT YOU DO NOT UNDERSTAND, YOU SHOULD ASK A LAWYER TO EXPLAIN IT TO YOU.

THE PERSON YOU APPOINT AS AGENT SHOULD BE SOMEONE YOU KNOW AND TRUST. THE PERSON MUST BE 18 YEARS OF AGE OR OLDER OR A PERSON UNDER 18 YEARS OF AGE WHO HAS HAD THE DISABILITIES OF MINORITY REMOVED. IF YOU APPOINT YOUR HEALTH OR RESIDENTIAL CARE PROVIDER (E.G., YOUR PHYSICIAN OR AN EMPLOYEE OF A HOME HEALTH AGENCY, HOSPITAL, NURSING HOME, OR RESIDENTIAL CARE HOME, OTHER THAN A RELATIVE), THAT PERSON HAS TO CHOOSE BETWEEN ACTING AS YOUR AGENT OR AS YOUR HEALTH OR RESIDENTIAL CARE PROVIDER; THE LAW DOES NOT PERMIT A PERSON TO DO BOTH AT THE SAME TIME.

YOU SHOULD INFORM THE PERSON YOU APPOINT THAT YOU WANT THE PERSON TO BE YOUR HEALTH CARE AGENT. YOU SHOULD DISCUSS THIS DOCUMENT WITH YOUR AGENT AND YOUR PHYSICIAN AND GIVE EACH A SIGNED COPY. YOU SHOULD INDICATE ON THE DOCUMENT ITSELF THE PEOPLE AND INSTITUTIONS WHO HAVE SIGNED COPIES. YOUR AGENT IS NOT LIABLE FOR HEALTH CARE DECISIONS MADE IN GOOD FAITH ON YOUR BEHALF.

EVEN AFTER YOU HAVE SIGNED THIS DOCUMENT, YOU HAVE THE RIGHT TO MAKE HEALTH CARE DECISIONS FOR YOURSELF AS LONG AS YOU ARE ABLE TO DO SO AND TREATMENT CANNOT BE GIVEN TO YOU OR STOPPED OVER YOUR OBJECTION. YOU HAVE THE RIGHT TO REVOKE THE AUTHORITY GRANTED TO YOUR AGENT BY INFORMING YOUR AGENT OR YOUR HEALTH OR RESIDENTIAL CARE PROVIDER ORALLY OR IN WRITING, OR BY YOUR EXECUTION OF A SUBSEQUENT DURABLE POWER OF ATTORNEY FOR HEALTH CARE. UNLESS YOU STATE OTHERWISE, YOUR APPOINTMENT OF A SPOUSE DISSOLVES ON DIVORCE.

THIS DOCUMENT MAY NOT BE CHANGED OR MODIFIED. IF YOU WANT TO MAKE CHANGES IN THE DOCUMENT, YOU MUST MAKE AN ENTIRELY NEW ONE.

YOU MAY WISH TO DESIGNATE AN ALTERNATE AGENT IN THE EVENT THAT YOUR AGENT IS UNWILLING, UNABLE, OR INELIGIBLE TO ACT AS YOUR AGENT. ANY ALTERNATE AGENT YOU DESIGNATE HAS THE SAME AUTHORITY TO MAKE HEALTH CARE DECISIONS FOR YOU.

THIS POWER OF ATTORNEY IS NOT VALID UNLESS IT IS SIGNED IN THE PRESENCE OF TWO OR MORE QUALIFIED WITNESSES. THE FOLLOWING PERSONS MAY NOT ACT AS WITNESSES:

(1) the person you have designated as your agent;

(2) your health or residential care provider or an employee of your health or residential care provider;

(3) your spouse;

(4) your lawful heirs or beneficiaries named in your will or a deed; or

(5) creditors or persons who have a claim against you.

Designation of Health Care Agent

I, _____ appoint:

Name: _____

Address: _____

_____

Day Phone: _____ Night Phone: _____

as my agent to make any and all health care decisions for me, except to the extent I state otherwise in this document. This durable power of attorney for health care takes effect if I become unable to make my own health care decisions and this fact is certified in writing by my physician.

LIMITATIONS ON THE DECISION-MAKING AUTHORITY OF MY AGENT ARE AS FOLLOWS: _____

Designation of Alternate Agent

(You are not required to designate an alternate agent, but you may do so. An alternate agent may make the same health care decisions as the designated agent if the designated agent is unable or unwilling to act as your agent. If the agent designated is your spouse, the designation is automatically revoked by law if your marriage is dissolved.)

If the person designated as my agent is unable or unwilling to make health care decisions for me, I designate the following persons to serve as my agent to make health care decisions for me as authorized by this document, who serve in the following order:

A. *First Alternate Agent*

Name: _____

Address: _____

_____

Day Phone: _____ Night Phone: _____

B. *Second Alternate Agent*

Name: _____

Address: _____

_____

Day Phone: _____ Night Phone: _____

The original of this document is kept at_____

_____.

The following individuals or institutions have signed copies:

Name: _____

Address: _____

_____

Name: _____

Address: _____

_____

Duration

I understand that this power of attorney exists indefinitely from the date I execute this document unless I establish a shorter time or revoke the power of attorney. If I am unable to make health care decisions for myself when this power of attorney expires, the authority I have granted my agent continues to exist until the time I become able to make health care decisions for myself.

(IF APPLICABLE) This power of attorney ends on the following date:_____ .

Prior Designations Revoked

I revoke any prior durable power of attorney for health care.

Acknowledgement of Disclosure Statement

I have been provided with a disclosure statement explaining the effect of this document. I have read and understand that information contained in the disclosure statement.

(YOU MUST DATE AND SIGN THIS POWER OF ATTORNEY)

I sign my name to this durable power of attorney for health care on _____ day of _____ 19 _____ at _____
city and state

_____
signature

_____
print name

Statement of Witnesses

I declare under penalty of perjury that the principal has identified himself or herself to me, that the principal signed or acknowledged this durable power of attorney in my presence, that I believe the principal to be of sound mind, that the principal has affirmed that the principal is aware of the nature of the document and is signing it voluntarily and free from duress, that the principal requested that I serve as witness to the principal's execution of this document, that I am not the person appointed as agent by this document, and that I am not a provider of health or residential care, an employee of a provider of health or residential care, the operator of a community care facility, or an employee of an operator of a health care facility.

I declare that I am not related to the principal by blood, marriage, or adoption and that to the best of my knowledge I am not entitled to any part of the estate of the principal on the death of the principal under a will or by operation of law.

Witness Signature: _____

Print Name: _____ Date: _____

Address: _____

Witness Signature: _____

Print Name: _____ Date: _____

Address: _____

Durable Power of Attorney for Health Care

To my family, friends, physicians, health care providers, community care facilities and any other person who may have an interest in my medical care:

I, _____, being of sound mind, voluntarily create this Durable Power of Attorney for Health Care.

1. Appointment of Attorney-in-Fact

If I become unable to make health care decisions for myself, I appoint the following person as my attorney-in-fact with authority to make health care decisions for me as I direct in this document:

Name:_____

Address:_____

_____

Day Phone: _____ Evening Phone: _____

2. Appointment of Alternate Attorney-in-Fact

If that person is unable or unwilling to act as my attorney-in-fact for the purpose of making health care decisions, I appoint the following person to serve:

Name: _____

Address:_____

_____

Day Phone: _____ Evening Phone: _____

3. When effective

This durable Power of Attorney for Health Care shall:

- become effective when I sign it
- not be affected by my subsequent disability or incompetence, and
- remain in effect until my death, or until I revoke it.

4. Authority I Grant My Attorney-in-Fact

My attorney-in-fact shall have all lawful authority permissible to make health decisions for me, but must also carry out and enforce any specific directions or limitations I provide in this power of attorney.

5. Specific Directions and Limitations

I specifically direct that _____

_____

_____

_____

_____

_____

_____

Executed this _____ day of _____ at _____

_____.

_____
principal's signature

Declaration of Witnesses

I am at least 18 years old. I declare that the person who signed or asked another to sign this document in my presence is personally known to me, and appears to be of sound mind and acting willingly and free from duress.

I also declare that I do not have a claim against the person, am not the person's heir or beneficiary under his or her will or other document, and am not:

- related to the person by blood, marriage, or adoption
- an employee of a life or health insurance provider for the person
- an employee of a health facility that's treating the person, or
- an employee of a nursing or group home where the person resides.

_____
signature

_____
print name

Residence Address: _____

_____

Date: _____

_____
signature

_____
print name

Residence Address:

_____

_____

Date: _____

Notarization

State of: _____
County of: _____

On this _____ day of _____ in the year _____, before
me, a Notary Public, State of _____, duly commissioned and sworn,
personally appeared _____, proved to me on the basis of
satisfactory evidence to be the person whose name is subscribed to the within instrument,
and acknowleged to me that he or she executed the same.

In witness whereof, I have hereunto set my hand and affixed my official seal in the
State of _____ County of _____ on the date set
forth above in this certificate.

Notary Public
State of _____
My commision expires _____

Will

Will of _____

I, _____, a resident of _____County, _____,

declare that this is my will.

I. Revocation

I revoke all wills and codicils that I have previously made.

II. Prior Marriages

I was married to _____ and am now divorced.

III. Children

A. I have _____ children now living, whose names and dates of birth are:

Name _____

Date of Birth _____

[Repeat as often as needed]

The terms "my children" as used in this will shall include any other children hereafter born to or adopted by me.

B. I have the following children of my deceased child _____.

Name _____

Date of Birth _____

[Repeat as often as needed]

C. If I do not leave property in this will to one or more of my children or my grandchildren named above, my failure to do so is intentional.

D. If at my death any of my children are minors, and a personal guardian is needed, I recommend that _____ be appointed guardian of the persons of my minor children. If _____ cannot or refuses to serve, I nominate _____ as guardian of the persons of my minor children.

E. If at my death any of my children are minors and a property guardian is needed, I name _____ to be appointed guardian of the property of my minor children. If _____ cannot or refuses to serve, I name _____ to be appointed guardian of the property of my minor children.

IV. Gifts

A. I make the following gifts of money or personal property:

1. I give every child or grandchild listed in Clause III $1.00 (one dollar) in addition to any other property I may give them elsewhere in this will, or otherwise.

2. I give the sum of $ _____ to _____ if he/she/it survives me by 60 days; if he/she/it doesn't, this gift shall be made to

_____.

[Repeat as often as needed]

B. I make the following gifts of real estate:

1. I give my interest in the real estate in _____, commonly known as _____, to _____ if he/she/it survives me for 60 days. If he/she/it doesn't survive me for 60 days, that property shall be given to _____.

[Repeat as often as needed]

V. Residue

I give the residue of my property subject to this will as follows:

A. To _____, if he/she/it survives me by 60 days.

B. If not, to _____ if he/she/it survives me by 60 days.

C. If neither _____ nor _____ survives me by 60 days, then to _____.

VI. Executor

A. I nominate _____ as executor of this will, to serve without bond.
If _____ shall for any reason fail to qualify or cease to act as executor, I nominate _____ to serve without bond.

B. I grant to my executor the right to place my obituary of her/his choosing in the papers she/he thinks appropriate.

VI. No Contest

If any person or persons named to receive any of my property under my will, in any manner contests or attacks this will or any of its provisions, that person or persons shall be disinherited and shall receive none of my property, and my property shall be disposed of as if that contesting beneficiary had died before me leaving no children.

VIII. Simultaneous Death

If _____ and I should die simultaneously, or under such circumstances as to render it difficult or impossible to determine who predeceased the other, I shall be conclusively presumed to have survived _____ for purposes of this will.

I subscribe my name to this will this [day] of [month], [year], at [city, county], [state].

_____
your full name

IX. Signature and Witnessing

On this [day] of [month], [year], [your full name] declared to us, the undersigned, that this instrument was [his/her] will, and requested us to act as witnesses to it. [He/she] thereupon signed this will in our presence, all of us being present at the time. We now, at [his/her] request, in [his/her] presence, and in the presence of each other, subscribe our names as witnesses and declare we understand this to be [his/her] will, and that to the best of our knowledge the testator is competent to make a will, and under no constraint or undue influence.

We declare under penalty of perjury that the foregoing is true and correct.

Witness's Signature:_____

Address:_____

Witness's Signature: _____

Address: _____

Witness's Signature:_____

Address:_____

Codicil

_____ **Codicil to the Will of** _____ **dated** _____

I, _____, a resident of _____ County, _____, declare this to be the _____ codicil to my will dated _____.

First. I revoke Item _____ of Clause _____, and substitute the following:

_____

_____

_____.

Second. I add the following new Item _____ to Clause _____: (**Add whatever is desired.**)

Third. In all other respects I confirm and republish my will dated _____, this _____ day of _____, at _____.

_____

signature

On the date written below, _____ declared to us, the undersigned, that this instrument, consisting of _____ pages, including this page signed by us as witnesses, was the _____ codicil to [his/her] will and requested us to act as witnesses to it. [He/she] thereupon signed this codicil in our presence, all of us being present at the same time. We now, at [his/her] request, in [his/her] presence, and in the presence of each other, subscribe our names as witnesses, and declare we understand this to be [his/her] will, and that to the best of our knowledge the testator is competent to make a will, and under no constraint or undue influence. Executed on _____, at _____, _____. We declare under penalty of perjury that the foregoing is true and correct.

Witness's Signature:_____
Address:_____
Witness's Signature:_____
Address:_____
Witness's Signature:_____
Address:_____

Living Together Agreement—
Keeping Things Separate

We, _____ and _____, agree as follows:

1. This contract sets forth our rights and obligations toward each other, which we intend to abide by in the spirit of joy, cooperation and good faith.

2. We agree that all property owned by either one of us as of the date of this agreement shall remain separate property and cannot be transferred to the other unless done by writing. We have attached a list of our major items of separate property.

3. The income of each person, as well as any accumulations of property from that income, belongs absolutely to the person who earns the money.

4. We shall keep our own bank accounts, credit accounts, etc., and neither is in any way responsible for the debts of the other.

5. Living expenses, which include groceries, utilities, rent, and day-to-day expenses, shall be equally divided.

6. We may from time to time decide to keep a joint checking or savings account for some specific purpose, or to own some property jointly. Any joint ownership shall be reflected in writing or shall be reflected on the ownership document of the property. If we fail to otherwise provide in writing for the disposition of our jointly owned property, should we separate, we agree to divide the jointly held property equally. Such agreements aren't to be interpreted as creating an implication that other property is jointly owned.

7. Should either of us receive real or personal property by gift or inheritance, the property belongs absolutely to the person receiving the gift or inheritance and cannot be transferred to the other except by writing.

8. We agree that neither of us shall have any rights to, or financial interest in, any separate real property of the other, whether obtained before or after the date of this contract, unless that right or interest is in writing.

9. Either one of us may terminate this contract by giving the other a one-week written notice. In the event either of us is seriously considering leaving or ending the relationship, that person shall take at least a three-day vacation from the relationship. We also agree to at least one counseling session if either one of us requests it.

10. In the event that we separate, all jointly owned property shall be divided equally, and neither of us shall have any claim for support or for any other money or property from the other.

11. We agree that any dispute arising out of this contract shall be mediated by a third person mutually acceptable to both of us. The mediator's role shall be to help us arrive at our solution, not to impose one on us. If good-faith efforts to arrive at our own solution to all issues in dispute with the help of a mediation prove to be fruitless, either of us may:

(a) Initiate arbitration by making a written demand for arbitration, defining the dispute and naming one arbitrator;

(b) Within five days from receipt of this notice, the other shall name the second arbitrator;

(c) The two named arbitrators shall within ten days name a third arbitrator;

(d) Within seven days an arbitration meeting will be held. Each of us may have counsel if we choose, and may present evidence and witnesses pertinent;

(e) The arbitrators shall make their decision within five days after the hearing. Their decision shall be in writing and shall be binding upon us;

(f) If the person to whom the demand for arbitration is directed fails to respond within five days, the other must give an additional five days' written notice of his or her intent to proceed. If there's no response, the person initiating the arbitration may proceed with the arbitration before the arbitrator he or she has designated, and his/her award shall have the same force as if it had been settled by all three arbitrators.

12. This agreement represents our complete understanding regarding our living together and replaces any and all prior agreements, written or oral. It can be amended, but only in writing, and must be signed by both of us.

13. We agree that if a court finds any portion of this contract to be illegal or otherwise unenforceable, the remainder of the contract is still in full force and effect.

Signed this _____ day of _____ at _____.

_____   _____
signature   signature

Exhibit A

Separate personal property of _____:

Exhibit B

Separate personal property of _____:

Living Together Agreement—
Sharing Most Property

We, _____ and _____, agree as follows:

1. This contract sets forth our rights and obligations toward each other, which we intend to abide by in a spirit of joy, cooperation, and good faith.

2. All property earned or accumulated prior to this date belongs absolutely to the person who earned or accumulated it and cannot be transferred to the other except in writing. Attached is a list of the major items of property we own separately.

3. All income earned by either of us while we are living together and all property accumulated from that income belongs in equal shares to both of us, and should we separate, all accumulated property shall be divided equally.

4. Should either of us receive real or personal property by gift or inheritance, the property belongs absolutely to the person receiving the gift or inheritance and cannot be transferred to the other except by writing.

5. We agree that neither of us has any rights to, or financial interest in, any separate real property of the other, whether obtained before or after the date of this contract, unless that right or interest is in writing.

6. Either one of us may terminate this contract by giving the other a one-week written notice. In the event either of us is seriously considering leaving or ending the relationship, that person shall take at least a three-day vacation from the relationship. We also agree to at least one counseling session if either one of us requests it.

7. In the event we separate, all jointly-owned property shall be divided equally, and neither of us shall have any claim for support or for any other money or property from the other.

8. We agree that any dispute arising out of this contract shall be arbitrated under the terms of this clause. If we both choose, we shall first try to resolve the dispute with the help of mutually agreeable mediator(s). Otherwise, either one of us may:

   (a) Initiate arbitration by making a written demand for arbitration, defining the dispute and naming one arbitrator;

   (b) Within five days from receipt of this notice, the other shall name the second arbitrator;

(c) The two named arbitrators shall within ten days name a third arbitrator;

(d) Within seven days an arbitration meeting will be held. Each of us may have counsel if we choose, and may present evidence and witnesses pertinent;

(e) The arbitrators shall make their decision within five days after the hearing. Their decision shall be in writing and shall be binding upon us;

(f) If the person to whom the demand for arbitration is directed fails to respond within five days, the other must give an additional five days' written notice of his or her intent to proceed. If there's no response, the person initiating the arbitration may proceed with the arbitration before the arbitrator he or she has designated, and his/her award shall have the same force as if it had been settled by all three arbitrators.

9. This agreement represents our complete understanding regarding our living together and replaces any and all prior agreements, written or oral. It can be amended, but only in writing, and must be signed by both of us.

10. We agree that if the court finds any portion of this contract to be illegal or otherwise unenforceable, that the remainder of the contract is still in full force and effect.

Signed this _____ day of _____ at _____.

_____   _____
signature   signature

Exhibit A

Separate personal property of _____:

Exhibit B

Separate personal property of _____:

Exhibit C

Jointly-owned property:

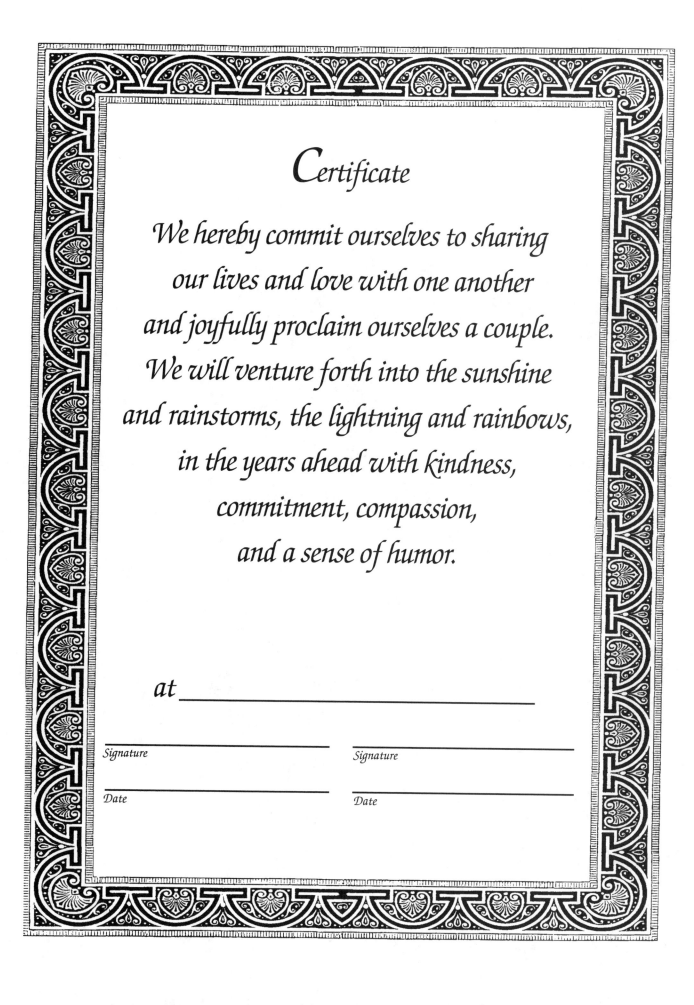

Certificate

We hereby commit ourselves to sharing
our lives and love with one another
and joyfully proclaim ourselves a couple.
We will venture forth into the sunshine
and rainstorms, the lightning and rainbows,
in the years ahead with kindness,
commitment, compassion,
and a sense of humor.

at _____

_____   _____
Signature   Signature

_____   _____
Date   Date

This is to Certify

That we,_____

and _____

do hereby commit ourselves each to the other.

> *Intreat me not to leave you*
> *Or to return from following after you—*
> *For whither you go, I will go,*
> *And where you lodge, I will lodge.*
> *Your people will be my people*
> *And your life my life—*
> *Where you die, I will die,*
> *And there will be buried*
> *May only death part us.*

> > *from Ruth 1:16*

On this day of_____

in the company of _____

> *signed* _____

> _____

CATALOG
...more from Nolo Press

		EDITION	PRICE	CODE

BUSINESS

		EDITION	PRICE	CODE
	Business Plans to Game Plans	1st	$29.95	GAME
	Helping Employees Achieve Retirement Security	1st	$16.95	HEAR
▫	Hiring Indepedent Contractors: The Employer's Legal Guide	1st	$29.95	HICI
	How to Finance a Growing Business	4th	$24.95	GROW
▫	How to Form a CA Nonprofit Corp.—w/Corp. Records Binder & PC Disk	1st	$49.95	CNP
▫	How to Form a Nonprofit Corp., Book w/Disk (PC)—National Edition	3rd	$39.95	NNP
▫	How to Form Your Own Calif. Corp.—w/Corp. Records Binder & Disk—PC	1st	$39.95	CACI
	How to Form Your Own California Corporation	8th	$29.95	CCOR
▫	How to Form Your Own Florida Corporation, (Book w/Disk—PC)	3rd	$39.95	FLCO
▫	How to Form Your Own New York Corporation, (Book w/Disk—PC)	3rd	$39.95	NYCO
▫	How to Form Your Own Texas Corporation, (Book w/Disk—PC)	4th	$39.95	TCI
	How to Handle Your Workers' Compensation Claim (California Edition)	1st	$29.95	WORK
	How to Market a Product for Under $500	1st	$29.95	UN500
	How to Write a Business Plan	4th	$21.95	SBS
	Make Up Your Mind: Entrepreneurs Talk About Decision Making	1st	$19.95	MIND
	Managing Generation X: How to Bring Out the Best in Young Talent	1st	$19.95	MANX
	Marketing Without Advertising	1st	$14.00	MWAD
	Mastering Diversity: Managing for Success Under ADA and Other Anti-Discrimination Laws	1st	$29.95	MAST
▫	OSHA in the Real World: (Book w/Disk—PC)	1st	$29.95	OSHA
▫	Taking Care of Your Corporation, Vol. 1, (Book w/Disk—PC)	1st	$26.95	CORK
▫	Taking Care of Your Corporation, Vol. 2, (Book w/Disk—PC)	1st	$39.95	CORK2
	Tax Savvy for Small Business	1st	$26.95	SAVVY
	The California Nonprofit Corporation Handbook	7th	$29.95	NON
	The California Professional Corporation Handbook	5th	$34.95	PROF
	The Employer's Legal Handbook	1st	$29.95	EMPL
	The Independent Paralegal's Handbook	3rd	$29.95	PARA
	The Legal Guide for Starting & Running a Small Business	2nd	$24.95	RUNS
	The Partnership Book: How to Write a Partnership Agreement	4th	$24.95	PART
	Rightful Termination	1st	$29.95	RITE
	Sexual Harassment on the Job	2nd	$18.95	HARS
	Trademark: How to Name Your Business & Product	2nd	$29.95	TRD
	Workers' Comp for Employers	2nd	$29.95	CNTRL
	Your Rights in the Workplace	2nd	$15.95	YRW

CONSUMER

		EDITION	PRICE	CODE
	Fed Up With the Legal System: What's Wrong & How to Fix It	2nd	$9.95	LEG
	Glossary of Insurance Terms	5th	$14.95	GLINT
	How to Insure Your Car	1st	$12.95	INCAR
	How to Win Your Personal Injury Claim	1st	$24.95	PICL
	Nolo's Pocket Guide to California Law	4th	$10.95	CLAW
	Nolo's Pocket Guide to Consumer Rights	2nd	$12.95	CAG
	The Over 50 Insurance Survival Guide	1st	$16.95	OVER50
	True Odds: How Risk Affects Your Everyday Life	1st	$19.95	TROD
	What Do You Mean It's Not Covered?	1st	$19.95	COVER

ESTATE PLANNING & PROBATE

		EDITION	PRICE	CODE
	How to Probate an Estate (California Edition)	8th	$34.95	PAE
	Make Your Own Living Trust	2nd	$19.95	LITR
	Nolo's Simple Will Book	2nd	$17.95	SWIL
	Plan Your Estate	3rd	$24.95	NEST
	The Quick and Legal Will Book	1st	$15.95	QUIC
	Nolo's Law Form Kit: Wills	1st	$14.95	KWL

FAMILY MATTERS

		EDITION	PRICE	CODE
	A Legal Guide for Lesbian and Gay Couples	8th	$24.95	LG
	Child Custody: Building Agreements That Work	1st	$24.95	CUST
	Divorce & Money: How to Make the Best Financial Decisions During Divorce	2nd	$21.95	DIMO
	How to Adopt Your Stepchild in California	4th	$22.95	ADOP
	How to Do Your Own Divorce in California	21st	$21.95	CDIV
	How to Do Your Own Divorce in Texas	6th	$19.95	TDIV
	How to Raise or Lower Child Support in California	3rd	$18.95	CHLD
	Nolo's Pocket Guide to Family Law	4th	$14.95	FLD
	Practical Divorce Solutions	1st	$14.95	PDS
	The Guardianship Book (California Edition)	2nd	$24.95	GB
	The Living Together Kit	7th	$24.95	LTK

▫ Book with disk

	EDITION	PRICE	CODE

GOING TO COURT

Title	Edition	Price	Code
Collect Your Court Judgment (California Edition	2nd	$19.95	JUDG
Everybody's Guide to Municipal Court (California Edition)	1st	$29.95	MUNI
Everybody's Guide to Small Claims Court (California Edition)	12th	$18.95	CSCC
Everybody's Guide to Small Claims Court (National Edition)	6th	$18.95	NSCC
Fight Your Ticket ... and Win! (California Edition)	6th	$19.95	FYT
How to Change Your Name (California Edition)	6th	$24.95	NAME
Represent Yourself in Court: How to Prepare & Try a Winning Case	1st	$29.95	RYC
The Criminal Records Book (California Edition)	5th	$21.95	CRIM

HOMEOWNERS, LANDLORDS & TENANTS

Title	Edition	Price	Code
Dog Law	2nd	$12.95	DOG
Every Landlord's Legal Guide (National Edition)	1st	$29.95	ELLI
For Sale by Owner (California Edition)	2nd	$24.95	FSBO
Homestead Your House (California Edition)	8th	$9.95	HOME
How to Buy a House in California	3rd	$24.95	BHCA
Neighbor Law: Fences, Trees, Boundaries & Noise	2nd	$16.95	NEI
Safe Homes, Safe Neighborhoods: Stopping Crime Where You Live	1st	$14.95	SAFE
Tenants' Rights (California Edition)	12th	$18.95	CTEN
The Deeds Book (California Edition)	3rd	$16.95	DEED
The Landlord's Law Book, Vol. 1: Rights & Responsibilities (California Edition)	5th	$34.95	LBRT
The Landlord's Law Book, Vol. 2: Evictions (California Edition)	5th	$34.95	LBEV

HUMOR

Title	Edition	Price	Code
29 Reasons Not to Go to Law School	1st	$9.95	29R
Poetic Justice	1st	$9.95	PJ

IMMIGRATION

Title	Edition	Price	Code
How to Become a United States Citizen	5th	$14.95	CIT
How to Get a Green Card: Legal Ways to Stay in the U.S.A.	2nd	$24.95	GRN
U.S. Immigration Made Easy	5th	$39.95	IMEZ

MONEY MATTERS

Title	Edition	Price	Code
Building Your Nest Egg With Your 401(k)	1st	$16.95	EGG
Chapter 13 Bankruptcy: Repay Your Debts	1st	$29.95	CH13
How to File for Bankruptcy	5th	$25.95	HFB
Money Troubles: Legal Strategies to Cope With Your Debts	3rd	$18.95	MT
Nolo's Law Form Kit: Personal Bankruptcy	1st	$14.95	KBNK
Nolo's Law Form Kit: Rebuild Your Credit	1st	$14.95	KCRD
Simple Contracts for Personal Use	2nd	$16.95	CONT
Smart Ways to Save Money During and After Divorce	1st	$14.95	SAVMO
Stand Up to the IRS	2nd	$21.95	SIRS

PATENTS AND COPYRIGHTS

Title	Edition	Price	Code
Copyright Your Software	1st	$39.95	CYS
Patent, Copyright & Trademark: A Desk Reference to Intellectual Property Law	1st	$24.95	PCTM
Patent It Yourself	4th	$39.95	PAT
Software Development: A Legal Guide (Book with disk—PC)	1st	$44.95	SFT
The Copyright Handbook: How to Protect and Use Written Works	2nd	$24.95	COHA
The Inventor's Notebook	1st	$19.95	INOT

RESEARCH & REFERENCE

Title	Edition	Price	Code
Law on the Net	1st	$39.95	LAWN
Legal Research: How to Find & Understand the Law	4th	$19.95	LRES
Legal Research Made Easy (Video)	1st	$89.95	LRME

SENIORS

Title	Edition	Price	Code
Beat the Nursing Home Trap: A Consumer's Guide	2nd	$18.95	ELD
Social Security, Medicare & Pensions	6th	$19.95	SOA
The Conservatorship Book (California Edition)	2nd	$29.95	CNSV

SOFTWARE

Title	Edition	Price	Code
California Incorporator 2.0—DOS	2.0	$47.97	INCI2
Living Trust Maker 2.0—Macintosh	2.0	$47.97	LTM2
Living Trust Maker 2.0—Windows	2.0	$47.97	LTWI2
Small Business Legal Pro—Macintosh	2.0	$39.95	SBM2
Small Business Legal Pro—Windows	2.0	$39.95	SBW2
Nolo's Partnership Maker 1.0—DOS	1.0	$47.97	PAGI1
Nolo's Personal RecordKeeper 3.0—Macintosh	3.0	$29.97	FRM3
Patent It Yourself 1.0—Windows	1.0	$149.97	PYW1
WillMaker 6.0—Macintosh	6.0	$41.97	WM6
WillMaker 6.0—Windows	6.0	$41.97	WIW6

SPECIAL UPGRADE OFFER

Get 25% off the latest edition of your Nolo book

It's important to have the most current legal information. Because laws and legal procedures change often, we update our books and kits regularly. To help keep you up-to-date we are extending this special upgrade offer. Cut out and mail the title portion of the cover of your old Nolo book and we'll give you 25% off the retail price of the NEW EDITION or latest kit when you purchase directly from us. For more information call us at 1-800-992-6656. This offer is to individuals only.

ORDER FORM

Code	Quantity	Title	Unit price	Total
		Subtotal		
		California residents add Sales Tax		
		Basic Shipping ($5 for 1 item; $6 for 2-3 items, $7 for 4 or more)		
		UPS RUSH delivery $7–any size order*		
		TOTAL		

Name

Address

(UPS to street address, Priority Mail to P.O. boxes)

* Delivered in 3 business days from receipt of order. S.F. Bay area use regular shipping.

FOR FASTER SERVICE, USE YOUR CREDIT CARD AND OUR TOLL-FREE NUMBERS

Order 24 hours a day	1-800-992-6656
Fax your order	1-800-645-0895
e-mail	NoloInfo@nolopress.com
General Information	1-510-549-1976
Customer Service	1-800-728-3555, Mon.-Sat. 9am-5pm, PST

METHOD OF PAYMENT

☐ Check enclosed

☐ VISA ☐ MasterCard ☐ Discover Card ☐ American Express

Account #   Expiration Date

Authorizing Signature

Daytime Phone

Prices subject to change.

Visit our store

If you live in the Bay Area, be sure to visit the Nolo Press Bookstore on the corner of 9th and Parker Streets in West Berkeley. You'll find our complete line of books and software, all at a discount. We also have t-shirts, posters and a selection of business and legal self-help books from other publishers. Open every day.

NOLO PRESS 950 PARKER ST., BERKELEY, CA 94710